July 29, 94

LIVING THE PROMISES OF GOD

LIVING THE PROMISES OF GOD

365 Readings for Recovery from Grief or Loss

PAUL F. KELLER

AUGSBURG Publishing House • Minneapolis

LIVING THE PROMISES OF GOD
365 Readings for Recovery from Grief or Loss

Library of Congress Cataloging-in-Publication Data

Keller, Paul F., 1922–
LIVING THE PROMISES OF GOD.

1. Consolation. 2. Devotional exercises. I. Title.
BV4905.2.K44 1988 242'.4 88-7405
ISBN 0-8066-2368-3

Manufactured in the U.S.A. APH 10-4031

3 4 5 6 7 8 9 0 1 2 3 4 5 6 7 8 9

To all who suffer
loss, sorrow, grief:
to our humanity.

PFK

Introduction

This book is a ministry for one-day-at-a-time recovery from loss, sorrow, and grief and for the renewal of faith, hope, and love.

Recovery is spiritual, before it is emotional or physical.

Recovery is learning new ways of dealing with ourselves.

Recovery is uncovering the healing grace of God.

Recovery is believing and living the promises of God.

We are spiritual beings, states the premise of this book, who are spiritually connected to God, the universe, ourselves, and others. In order to recover from loss, sorrow, and grief, we must work with these connections. Provided in these pages are time-tested principles for health and healing.

How to use the daily exercises toward recovery

Find a quiet place where you can be alone. Do not hurry. Do not rush. Relax yourself in the presence of God. Be quiet before the Lord.

Read the scripture. (Pause and reflect.) What, if anything, does this mean to me in my condition?

Read the meditation. (Pause and reflect.) How does this apply to me or not apply to me?

Read the stated wish for the day: "May I . . ." (Pause and reflect.) "Is this what I want for myself? If not, then what?"

Read the three intentional sentences, one at a time: "I will . . . I will . . . I will . . ." (Pause and reflect.) "Are these intentions what I want to be doing with my life today? For my recovery? If not, then what?"

Read the two brief prayer starters, turning them into prayers of your own making. (Pause and reflect.) "Is this what I want my prayers to be? If not, then what?"

Read the two reflective questions. (Pause and reflect.) "What am I doing with my life?"

As we use these daily exercises to make the promises of God our own, we are on our way to saying yes to life. May we live the promises of God.

God grant me the serenity
to accept the things I cannot change,
the courage to change the things I can,
and the wisdom to know the difference.

Being Willing to Pray

When famine or plague comes to the land . . . when enemies besiege . . . whatever disaster or disease may come, and when a prayer or plea is made by any of your people . . . each one aware of his [or her] afflictions and pains . . . then hear [O Lord] from heaven.

—2 Chronicles 6:28-30

Grief is intense suffering caused by severe and deeply felt loss.

Grief is acute sorrow, deep distress, and profound sadness.

Grieving is our attempt to recover from our suffered loss.

The way of Christ is the way through grief, into recovery.

The way of Christ is the way of the embrace—the way for us to say yes to life, in the midst of our loss, sorrow, and grief.

The way of Christ is the way of prayer: "Ask and it will be given to you; seek and you will find; knock and the door will be opened to you."

Prayer is the way into the divine embrace, by which we are healed. Prayer is the beginning of our recovery from loss, sorrow, and grief.

May I pray God to help me.

I will believe God's promise to heal. I will start to pray. I will pray for God to help me.

Prayer: *May I be open to prayer. May I ask God to help me.*

Am I willing to pray? Am I ready to turn my will and my life over to the care and keeping of God?

Being Willing to Believe

Therefore once more I will astound these people with wonder upon wonder.

—Isaiah 29:14

In the midst of our deepest woe the process of our healing begins, slowly but surely.

Slowly but surely God's grace comes into focus.

Slowly but surely we sense that God is at work in our lives to bring about our recovery from loss, sorrow, and grief.

Slowly but surely we come to trust the faithfulness of the Lord to be with us always.

Slowly but surely
the helplessness of our sorrow lessens;
the deep shadows lighten;
lost energy is regained;
and hope is restored.

Slowly but surely we become astounded by the healing wonders of God at work in our lives.

May I believe the Lord will bring me into recovery from my loss, sorrow, and grief.

I will believe that with God all things are possible. I will believe God can heal my broken heart. I will trust God to work wonders in my life.

Prayer: *May I believe the promises of God to heal. May I be open to the healing hand of the Lord.*

Am I ready to believe the promises of God? Am I willing to entrust myself into the care and keeping of God?

Seeking God's Good Counsel

The Lord Almighty [is] wonderful in counsel and magnificent in wisdom.

—Isaiah 28:29

In the depths of our sorrow it can be very difficult knowing what to do with ourselves.

We may feel like turning to anyone who is willing to listen and do whatever they say. Or, we may want no advice, no interference, no help from anyone: "Just leave me alone."

There is a time for everything, including wanting to be left alone for awhile. However, it always is helpful to seek the good counsel and wisdom of the Lord, in prayer.

Our task is to be receptive to the Lord's good counsel.

We can do this by remaining spiritually open and ready to be led through the deep valleys and dark shadows. The "good counsel" and the "wisdom" of the Lord lightens our way.

Those who learn to wait for the wonderful counsel and wisdom of the Lord are never disappointed.

The counsel and wisdom of the Lord always satisfy, always bring healing to the broken.

May I seek God's good counsel and wisdom.

I will believe God is going to do what is best for me. I will seek the good counsel and wisdom of the Lord through prayer and meditation. I will trust God with my life and my recovery from sorrow.

Prayer: *May I believe God. May I seek God's good counsel and wisdom for my life.*

Am I looking to the wisdom of the Lord to lead me? Am I seeking the good counsel of the Lord for my recovery?

Yearning for God

My soul yearns for you in the night; in the morning my spirit longs for you.

—Isaiah 26:9

With bereavement there is a deep sense of yearning for replacement . . . wishing . . . wanting.

We may want the loved one returned, if only just long enough to make amends: to say once more, or for the first time, "I love you." Or, "I have treated you shabbily." Or, "There are so many things I should have done that I didn't; and so much I shouldn't have done that I did."

There is another kind of yearning that is deeper and stronger: our yearning for God.

Whether we know it consciously or not, all of us are seeking, are yearning, to find our rest in God.

It is helpful to recognize this yearning and to affirm it; to say, "This is what my soul yearns for. This is what I really want for myself. I want to be with my Lord God."

Once we affirm this yearning for God, we are better prepared to move on with our recovery.

May I understand that I am yearning for God.

I will be aware of my yearning for God. I will affirm that my deepest desire is to be with God. I will entrust myself to the Lord's care and keeping.

Prayer: *May I seek God. May I place my confidence in the Lord.*

Do I believe that my deepest yearning is for God? Am I willing to open myself to God's leading in the midst of my sorrow and grief?

Affirming Life

You restored me to health and let me live.

—Isaiah 38:16

When it comes to having down and out feelings there is nothing like the experience of bereavement.

With bereavement our energy dwindles.

We feel as though we are hardly alive.

We feel as though we are being overcome by the stress of the suffered loss that engulfs us.

"My bones have become as dust. There is nothing left of me," says one writer.

It is "normal" to feel devastated when we are bereft; to feel that there is not much left of us.

So let us not be surprised if we find ourselves being drained, emotionally, spiritually, and physically.

But, let us also pray the words of our scripture for today: Lord, restore me to health and make me live.

In so doing we will be affirming life over death, and the Lord will minister to us.

May I trust God to restore me to health and make me alive.

I will affirm life. I will seek health. I will recover from my sorrow and I will live.

Prayer: *May I affirm life and live it fully. May I recover from my sorrow and grow.*

Am I affirming life and wanting to live it? Am I willing to recover from my sorrow and grow in the Lord?

Trusting God with Our Lives

Trust in the LORD forever, for the LORD, the LORD, is the Rock eternal.

—Isaiah 26:4

In our recovery from loss, sorrow, and grief we must establish an attitude of trust, must come into a state of trustfulness.

Life simply cannot go on productively if we are not living in an attitude of trust.

Without trust in God our grief grows deeper, rather than diminishing. Without trust in God the pain of our separation intensifies.

Once we decide to trust the Lord, with no qualifications (and, as our scripture says, "forever") we begin to come into a place of peacefulness, of calm.

Of course, this isn't easy. Not when we are experiencing loss, sorrow, and grief. An attitude of trust can be very difficult to come by. It is only accomplished through prayer.

The confession of trust is in our scripture for today: The Lord is the rock eternal. The Lord will not be washed away, like sand. Or blown away like straw. And neither will we.

The Lord is a firm foundation upon whom we can build with confidence, without ever having to be disappointed.

May I trust the Lord with my life.

I will place my trust in the Lord. I will believe that the Lord is like an everlasting rock, the stability and hope of my life. I will give over my life to the Lord.

Prayer: *May I trust the Lord forever. May I believe that the Lord is my everlasting rock.*

Am I ready to trust God for my recovery from sorrow? Am I believing that God is going to bring about my healing?

Returning and Resting

In repentance and rest is your salvation.

—Isaiah 30:15

Part of bereavement can be the feeling of being scattered—as though we are going to pieces, as though we are "outside" of ourselves, away from home base where nothing seems to fit.

We also may find ourselves being tired and in need of more sleep. Or in some cases, we are not able to sleep well at all.

Also, there can be agitation—nervousness—when we can't get ourselves settled down.

Behind this upset there is fear, the feeling we might not be able to make it through the pain of our loss, sorrow, and grief.

We must be reminded, again and again, that the promises of God are true: if we continue to repent, continue to return to God the Source of our strength, we find salvation from fear, anger, and resentment.

We come to rest in God. We find rest for our souls. We begin to heal, as sorrow makes way for joy.

May I find strength for my soul in the presence of God.

I will believe my strength is not in myself but in God. I will seek the presence of God through prayer and meditation. I will trust the power of God to bring me through these darkened days.

Prayer: *May I believe my strength is in the Lord. May I rest myself in the presence of the Lord.*

Do I believe God is the strength of my life? Am I returning to the Lord to find rest for my soul?

Waiting for God to Work

In quietness and trust is your strength.

—Isaiah 30:15

It is important to wait for God to move, to wait with quietness and trust.

The key to quietness is trust, believing that God is ready and eager to go to work on our broken hearts to heal our wounded spirits, to bring us through the dark places of suffered loss, to put us together again.

Quietness, trusting the Lord, becoming still before the Lord—these are steps toward recovery. Being certain that God knows what is best, being convinced that God is worthy of our trust, being ready to invest our wills and our lives into the care and keeping of God, being able to do this one day at a time—these are keys to recovery.

Waiting for God to work, waiting for God to do what we cannot do for ourselves, waiting on the Lord because we believe the Lord knows best—these are the open doors to new life.

Let us be quiet before the Lord. Let us trust God with our whole heart. For, "in quietness and trust is your strength."

May I find my strength in the Lord.

I will believe that in quietness and trust I will find strength for my life. I will take time to be quiet before God. I will trust God to be with me, in my sorrow.

Prayer: *May I be quiet before God. May I trust God to heal my broken heart.*

Am I willing to be quiet before God? Am I willing to trust God to do for me what I cannot do for myself?

• DAY 9 •

Accepting God's Mercy

The Lord longs to be gracious to you.

—Isaiah 30:18

In our sorrow we discover that we need something more than another person can give. Our hurt is that deep and that painful. Because of this we can feel very isolated.

We may long to hear the voice of the missing loved one, feeling deeply the pain of our loss, the void, the vacuum, the emptiness.

At such times it can be helpful to visualize God's grace filling the void like water filling an empty glass.

When we accept the mercy of God into our life, the pain of separation begins to heal. Slowly, but surely.

The Lord is ready and eager to help: "How often I have longed to gather [you.]"

The Lord offers an open invitation: "Come to me, all you who are weary and burdened and I will give you rest."

Remember this promise: "The Lord longs to be gracious to you." The gift is ours when we are ready to receive it.

May I accept the mercies of God into my life.

I will believe the Lord is eager to help me heal. I will accept the mercies of God into my life. I will allow God to do for me what I cannot do for myself.

Prayer: *May I accept the grace of God offered to me for my healing. May I be healed by God's mercy.*

Am I accepting the grace of God into my life? Am I allowing myself to be healed by the mercies of God?

Being Unashamed of Tears

You will weep no more. How gracious [the Lord] will be when you cry for help.

—Isaiah 30:19

Weeping can be a helpful part of our recovery process. Tears are healing gifts from God, washing away sorrow and pain, clearing our souls. It is important not to hold back tears when they want to come.

Yes, there are those who regard tears as weakness, who believe that one's faith in God is lacking if one weeps.

Let us remember that at the tomb of Lazarus our Lord also wept.

The pain of a loss remains for a time, but the promise is that God will pay heed to us, will hear the pain of our sorrow.

Finally, the deep pain will be washed away through the graciousness of our Lord.

You will weep no more. How gracious the Lord is when we cry for help.

May I not be ashamed of tears.

I will believe God has power to heal my broken heart. I will not be ashamed of my tears. I will believe the Lord hears my cries.

Prayer: *May I believe God hears my cries. May I place my trust in the faithfulness of God.*

Am I trusting the promises of God? Am I believing God will mend my broken heart?

Seeing through Adversity

Although the Lord gives you the bread of adversity and the water of affliction, your teachers will be hidden no more; with your own eyes you will see them.

—Isaiah 30:20

Is it true the Lord gives us the bread of adversity to eat, and affliction we must bear?

In the deepest pits of his suffering, Job came to the conclusion he didn't know the answer to this pressing question.

But of one thing Job was firmly convinced: "I know that my Redeemer lives!"

Many, who have gone through the darkest experiences of loss, sorrow, and grief, have looked back to see that something of great importance spiritually was gained as the result of their experience. It's as though everything had been planned: the adversity, the affliction, and God's grace to heal.

The Lord promises we shall see the goodness of God, in the midst of our adversity and afflictions.

The Lord does not hide from us in our adversity and affliction, although many times over it may seem so.

Through prayer and meditation we begin to see the healing hand of God at work, in and through our adversities.

May I believe that in my adversity I will see God at work.

I will wait on the Lord to show me the light of love in adversity. I will trust there is something in my sorrow that is going to be helpful for my spiritual growth. I will wait on the Lord.

Prayer: *May I see the hand of the Lord at work in my life. May I believe that my sorrow will be turned into joy.*

Am I willing to believe something good can come out of my adversity? Am I expecting to see the hand of the Lord at work in my life?

Walking God's Way

Your ears will hear a voice behind you, saying, "This is the way; walk in it."

—Isaiah 30:21

Sometimes it is difficult to hear what others are saying to us. Our minds simply turn off what cannot be dealt with.

However, the time comes when we want to hear a new voice.

We may implore the Lord to give us a sign, to say something we can understand, something to help us along the way.

And often, there will be silence; the healing silence of God.

We can't hear in the midst of noise and confusion. There must be silence before we can hear God.

When we are ready to listen carefully, eventually we hear the voice saying, "This is the way. Walk in it."

And we begin to see our healing coming into view.

May I be ready to walk in the way of the Lord.

I will take my steps one at a time. I will listen carefully for the word of the Lord to come to me. I will be ready to walk in the way of the Lord as it is given to me.

Prayer: *May I be ready to hear the word of the Lord however it comes to me. May I be ready to walk in the way of the Lord.*

Am I open to hear the word of the Lord? Am I ready to walk the way of the Lord?

Being Open to Receive and to Grow

He will also send you rain for the seed you sow in the ground, and the food that comes from the land will be rich and plentiful.
—Isaiah 30:23

When we are deep in sorrow it is very difficult to have voices speaking "at" us, telling us how everything is going to work out the way it should, for our own best interests. And yet, that essentially is what we find in the word and promises of God: the assurance that everything is going to come out as it should, and that we are going to be all right.

We will receive the good rain in due time; and the seeds of faith, hope, and love which we now sow will come into fruition.

And, we need the rain of God's grace to fall on us. Also, we need to be open, to receive the goodness of God in order to recover from our loss, sorrow, and grief.

The seeds of faith we now sow will bear fruit, as we are fed by God's grace.

The spiritual harvest will be plenteous, far more abundant than we ever could have imagined possible.

May I accept the rain and harvest of God's grace.

I will make myself available to the goodness of God. I will be open to receive whatever God provides for my healing. I will come to believe that the harvest of God is going to be plentiful in my life.

Prayer: *May I be receptive soil for the rain and seed of God's love to be experienced in my life. May I believe that my life is going to be spiritually rich and plenteous.*

Am I trying to be positive about my life and my future? Am I ready to receive the goodness of God and to give thanks?

Hearing a Song in the Night

You shall have a song as in the night, and gladness of heart; as one who sets out to the sound of the flute, to go to the mountain of the Lord.

—Isaiah 30:29

Nights can be difficult and frightening.

The empty bed can make us wonder how we ever are going to come through our ordeal.

We may dread the darkness of night with its isolation, its loneliness.

Can there actually be a song in the night with eagerness to worship the Lord?

God's promise is that there can be "gladness of heart," even in the dead of night.

But, when we are able to openly speak our fears to the Lord, the dread of night begins to lessen.

The time comes when we begin to hear the healing sound of the Good Shepherd leading his flock to pasture, beside the still waters.

The time comes when we are joyfully able to "go to the mountain of the Lord."

The time comes when we are able to praise God, with peace of mind and heart.

May I be able to hear a song in the night.

I will hear a song in the night. I will experience gladness of heart. I will go to the mountain of the Lord with my prayers of praise and thanksgiving.

Prayer: *May I experience gladness of heart. May I be filled with praise and thanksgiving.*

Do I believe that I can have gladness of heart? Am I ready to receive the goodness of God?

Believing God's Miracles

The desert becomes a fertile field.

—Isaiah 32:15

Bereavement is like being thrown out into a barren desert; like being desolated, abandoned, isolated, forsaken.

In his bereavement Jesus felt the desolation of isolation, the terror of forsakenness.

In agony he cried out on the cross, "My God, why have you forsaken me?" Truly, at that moment his soul was like a desert.

In the desolation of our isolation we also are like a desert where nothing seems able to grow.

No life.

No hope.

No zest.

But God promises that the desert of our bereavement can become a fertile field.

By believing and living the promises of God we will recover from our loss, sorrow, and grief.

By believing and living the promises of God we will bear new spiritual fruit like a desert becoming a fertile field of faith, hope, and love.

May I believe I will be made new.

I will believe my desolation is going to be turned into joy. I will trust God is able to make the desert of my spirit spring forth with new life. I will not be anxious about how or when God is going to do this miracle with my life.

Prayer: *May I believe my desolation can be turned into hope and joy. May I trust God to give me new life.*

Am I believing God can work miracles in my life? Am I ready to trust God to give me new life in abundance?

Finding Our Resting Place in God

My people will live in peaceful dwelling places, in secure homes, in undisturbed places of rest.

—Isaiah 32:18

Everyone, including warriors, is looking for a peaceful life, a quiet resting place. We deeply long for peace with ourselves, with others, and with God. However, this is not always apparent; not with all of the strife, conflict, and war.

Especially do we long for undisturbed places of rest when we are suffering loss, sorrow, and grief. We may feel ourselves cracking emotionally, spiritually, and sometimes, physically.

We desire secure homes where we can feel protected; out of the danger zones of life—peaceful dwelling places.

There is deep anxiousness within our souls, as though there is no quiet resting place. And we can't "think" our way out of the desolation. Rather, we must "feel" our way through it.

Recovery begins when we believe and live the promise: "My people will live in peaceful dwelling places, in secure homes, in undisturbed places of rest."

That place of rest is with God.

May I find my quiet resting place in God.

I am ready to believe God has a peaceful dwelling place for my broken heart. I will trust God to take me to an undisturbed place of rest for my troubled spirit. I will surrender my will and my life into the care and keeping of God.

Prayer: *May I find my resting place in God. May I trust God to take me to a secure place.*

Am I ready to find my resting place in God? Am I ready to be secure in God's care and keeping?

• DAY 17 •

Focusing on God

You will keep in perfect peace him whose mind is steadfast because he trusts in you.

—Isaiah 26:3

Everyone is looking for peace that passes human understanding. However, such a blessing can seem distant in time of loss, sorrow, and grief.

Nevertheless, there is the gift of peace.

Once we fix our minds and hearts on the Lord, with all of the goodness that awaits us there, we begin to experience the peace for which our hearts long.

Just as it is promised.

The problem, of course, is to keep our hearts and minds focused on the Lord, "Whose mind is steadfast."

Recovery is focusing on the Lord.

Recovery is getting ourselves located again.

Recovery is feeling "centered," and at home with ourselves, with others, and with God.

When we turn ourselves over to the care and keeping of God we begin to find peace for our souls.

May I focus myself on God's gift of peace.

I will believe the peace of God is mine to have. I will ask God for the gift of peace. I will trust God to bless me with the offering of peace.

Prayer: *May I focus my attention on God. May I believe the Lord brings peace to my broken heart.*

Do I believe God's peace is available to me? Am I ready to accept the gift of a peaceful heart?

✓

Accepting Forgiveness

In your love you kept me from the pit of destruction; you have put all my sins behind your back.

—Isaiah 38:17

Bereavement can leave us feeling as though we are being destroyed because of something we may have done or left undone.

We may remember sins of omission and commission, things we did and didn't do that we wish we could change, but can't.

With this there also can be hidden or conscious sensations of shame and guilt.

If so, it is timely to turn to the Lord with our burdens, accepting the forgiveness that God provides.

The Lord offers release from all sin, guilt, and shame. Speaking out of personal experience Isaiah says to the Lord, "You have cast my sins behind your back."

No longer is there need for guilt and shame because you, Lord, have cast our sins behind your back.

Let us believe God's promised forgiveness and make the most of it.

By accepting the truth of God's forgiveness, we are able to release ourselves from guilt and shame because God already has released us.

Now, we may only need to release ourselves.

May I accept the forgiveness of the Lord.

I will remember the Lord forgives. I will accept the forgiveness of the Lord. I will release myself of guilt and shame.

Prayer: *May I believe the Lord forgives. May I forgive myself as the Lord forgives me.*

Am I accepting the forgiveness of the Lord? Am I forgiving myself as the Lord forgives me?

Trusting God's Salvation

The Lord will save me, and we will sing . . . all the days of our lives. . . .

—Isaiah 38:20

When we finally get to the very bottom of the barrel, we begin to see new life.

It often isn't until we have hit our rock bottom, emotionally and spiritually, that the Lord is able to give us a new song to sing. In our own time and place we come to see that only the Lord can bear us up.

Only the Lord can restore us to faith, hope, and love.

Only the Lord is able to take us through fear and dread.

Only the Lord is able to save.

At the bottom of the pit it is difficult to imagine joy, singing, and thanksgiving. However, a new song is promised for our broken hearts: "And we will sing . . ." with our voices joined.

This is the promised vision to post in our hearts, minds, and spirits. This is the assurance of our recovery from loss, sorrow, and grief.

The day comes when we, together with the whole creation, will break out of sorrow into singing.

May I see the Lord's salvation and sing for joy.

I will believe the Lord is saving me. I will trust the salvation of the Lord. I will believe there is a song for me to sing.

Prayer: *May I trust the salvation of the Lord. May I find my song to sing.*

Am I trusting the salvation of the Lord? Am I looking for a song to sing?

Clearing the Way for the Lord

In the desert prepare the way for the Lord; make straight in the wilderness a highway for our God.

—Isaiah 40:3

In bereavement we have entered a wilderness with no immediate landmarks that we are able to see, no visible signs telling us which direction to go, which course of action to take.

Nevertheless, it is in this wilderness of our sorrow that we must find out what to do with our lives.

It is in this very painful wilderness that we must build new roads, in order to have a new life for ourselves.

The message is to "make straight in the wilderness a highway for our God," to make room for the spirit of the Lord to minister to us in our loss, sorrow, and grief.

In the wilderness of our bereavement let us prepare the way for the Lord to come to us.

In the wilderness of our sorrow let us believe God's promise to minister to us.

In the wilderness of our fear let us surrender our will and our lives into the care and keeping of the Lord, making straight a highway for God's grace to come and to heal.

May I clear the path for God's grace to come to me.

I will open myself to the coming of God into my sorrow and pain. I will build a straight highway for God's grace to come to me. I will get myself out of the way so God is able to come in, to heal my broken heart.

Prayer: *May I be open to God. May I get myself out of the way for God to come to me.*

Am I opening myself to God? Am I getting myself out of the way for God to come to me?

Getting through the Rugged Places

The rough ground shall become level, the rugged places a plain.
—Isaiah 40:4

Bereavement is like standing on uneven ground, like being in very rough places, like being out of level, like being tilted.

Life can be like that at times—very rugged—sometimes so rugged we don't know how we will find our way through.

In near despair we may cry, "This is too rough for me! I can't go on with my life this way! I want to die!"

The rugged places simply seem like too much.

But, experience tells us we can count on the promises of God, the rugged places are going to be leveled.

One day we will see the rugged places being ironed out in our hearts and souls.

One day we will see recovery is a day-by-day process.

One day we will accept the fact that recovery goes through the rugged places, never around them.

One day we will surrender to the reality that recovery always is painful, but also that it can be highly rewarding and strengthening to our spirits.

One day, we will be healed of our loss, sorrow, and grief.

May I go through the rugged places trusting the Lord.

I will not attempt to avoid the pain of my loss. I will make room for God to enter my life, and lead me. I will go through the dark, rugged places, believing God is with me.

Prayer: *May I have the courage to deal with the pain of my loss. May I believe that one day I will be healed.*

Am I accepting the pain of my loss and working with it? Am I trusting that God is going to help me?

Becoming Aware of God's Glory

And the glory of the LORD will be revealed, and all . . . will see it.

—Isaiah 40:5

With bereavement comes the sensation of darkness, depression of spirit, inability to see clearly.

And yet, in the depths of our sorrow and suffering, the work of God is in process; whether we see it right away or not, the glory of the Lord is being revealed.

If we continue in our recovery program, if we do not run from the pain, but work with it, eventually we begin to experience the glory of the Lord in our lives.

At first we are unaware of what is going on. Then, one day, we begin to see things in a different light; not as in darkness, but as in light. Shadows give way to the sunlight of God's Spirit.

We begin to feel better, becoming more conscious of the work of God in our lives.

People see something good is at work in us. Eventually, we are able to see the glory of the Lord through the darkness of our sorrow.

We are on the road to recovery.

May I see the glory of the Lord at work in my life.

I will become aware of God's work being done in my life. I will see what God is doing for me in the pain of my sorrow. I will be healed by the Lord.

Prayer: *May I be aware of God's work in my life. May I see the glory of the Lord in the midst of my pain.*

Am I aware of God's work in my life? Am I coming to see the glory of the Lord in the midst of my pain?

Trusting the Word of God

The grass withers and the flowers fall, but the word of our God stands forever.

—Isaiah 40:8

In times of deep suffering we need something more lasting than material substance, something more enduring than our physical bodies, or the bodies of our loved ones.

During bereavement we can become acutely aware of the truth that we are like grass that withers, like flowers that fade.

Indeed, "we are like yesterday when it is past . . . like a watch in the night."

However, the Word and promises of God tell us that even though there is the withering and dying, there also is the reality of eternal life in God.

While we must accept and affirm our walk through the dark valleys of life and death, affirm that we are like grass that withers and flowers that fall, we also can and should affirm eternal life in the Word and promises of God.

The promises in the Word of God are that life is eternal, that life never really ends.

May I believe the Word and promises of God.

I will believe God's Word and promises are forever. I will place my trust and confidence in them. I will live this day in the Word and promises of God.

Prayer: *May I believe and live the Word and promises of God.*

Am I believing the Word and promises of God? Am I living the Word and promises of God?

Seeing God at Work

Here is your God.

—Isaiah 40:9

The reality of God often grows stronger when we are in severe circumstances, even though our vision is shadowed.

When we come to the end of our rope, when we don't know where to turn next, when everything is going nowhere like a blind alley, we need a vision of God simply in order to go on with our lives.

It is in times of deep distress that we need to hear someone saying to us, "Here is your God."

Right where we are.

In the midst of our suffering and pain.

If we look closely it is our opportunity and privilege to see the hand of God moving in our lives to help and to heal.

To be sure, God often works quietly, in ways we cannot know right away.

And often we have to look backwards in order to see the hand of God active in our lives.

Let us behold the healing hand of God at work in our loss, sorrow, and grief.

May I see the hand of God at work in my life.

I will look for God at work in my life and recovery. I will believe God is active, even when I am unable to see. I will trust God to bring healing.

Prayer: *May I see the hand of God in my recovery. May I believe God is active in my life.*

Am I seeing God at work in my recovery? Do I believe God is active in my life?

Trusting God's Power

See, the Sovereign LORD comes with power.

—Isaiah 40:10

There is something that really doesn't work to bring about a good recovery from loss, sorrow, and grief: trying to be a hero of faith, pretending we aren't hurting, pretending we have everything under control.

The truth is God is the hero, not we ourselves.

It is God who comes with the might and power to heal our broken hearts, to mend our broken lives.

Neither we ourselves nor other people have this kind of power. Trying to pretend otherwise is a waste of time and energy.

As children of God we can expect the power of God to work in our lives when we need it.

It is then that we discover the truth of the promise, "See, the Sovereign LORD comes with power."

Let us not try to be heroes in these painful times.

Let us wait for the Lord to move with power in our lives, bringing us into the sunshine of a new day.

May I see the might and power of God in my life.

I will not try to be a hero in these days of my sorrow. I will turn to the Lord for help. I will entrust myself completely to the Lord's care and keeping.

Prayer: *May I see the power of God at work in my life. May I believe that God's power is sufficient for all my needs.*

Am I turning to God for the power I need to heal? Am I believing the power of God is sufficient to supply my needs?

Seeing the Gentleness of God

He tends his flock like a shepherd: He gathers the lambs in his arms and carries them close to his heart; he gently leads those that have young.

—Isaiah 40:11

What is important, in this promise, is that the Lord is not going to lose sight of us.

In these times of severe distress, the Lord is watching out for us, as a shepherd taking care of his sheep, protecting them from predators.

The promise is that we are going to be dealt with gently, even though it may not seem so at times.

For, there are times when life is far more rough than gentle.

However, there is God's profound gentleness leading us out of our suffering.

If we look closely, we are going to see this gentleness of God at work in our lives.

If we look closely, we are going to see how deeply we are being cared for.

If we look closely, we are going to see how we are being carried in the bosom of the Lord.

May I see the gentleness of God in my life.

I will believe the Lord is being gentle with me. I will trust that God knows best. I will rest myself in God's gentle care and keeping.

Prayer: *May I be aware of God's gentle hand in my life. May I trust God completely with my life.*

Am I believing God? Am I trusting God with my life?

Having Confidence in God

Do you not know? Have you not heard? Has it not been told you from the beginning? . . . [The LORD] sits enthroned above the circle of the earth.

—Isaiah 40:21-22

In the presidential campaigns of the 1950s, Adlai Stevenson said something very pertinent. "What we want to know," he said, "is who's running the store?"

This question always is being asked, not only in politics, but also in religion and faith.

Our scripture addresses that question and answers it: God is in charge. God is running the store.

What is more, the one who is in charge has complete capacity to be in charge. This means that everything is going to be all right.

This means that when everything is said and done we also are going to be all right. Because God is in control.

When we place our confidence in God, for our recovery from sorrow, we become settled on a sure foundation and cannot possibly go wrong.

God has the creative power to give new life and new hope in abundance. God is in charge. God is running the store.

May I place my confidence in the Lord.

I will believe God has the power to heal my broken heart. I will trust God to heal me in God's good time. I will be grateful for the presence of God in my life.

Prayer: *May I trust the strength of the Lord. May I live one day at a time in the power of God.*

Am I placing my confidence in the Lord? Am I trusting God one day at a time?

Knowing God as Everlasting Friend

The LORD is the everlasting God, the Creator of the ends of the earth.

—Isaiah 40:28

Our God is not just of the heavens, but also of the earth, where we are born into our bodies. Where we live and die.

The Lord is not distant from us. The Creator of all that is, the giver of life, is with us.

As we suffer the pain of separation from ourselves, from others, and from God, it is helpful to be recalled to the eternal closeness of the Lord, even though, in times of sorrow, the Lord may sometimes seem far removed from us.

We are in the care and keeping of God.

The Lord is everlasting and the Lord will not forsake us.

The Lord is the Creator of all that is, and has power to free us from the pain of our sorrow.

Let us place our trust in the Lord because the Lord is our everlasting friend.

May I know the Lord as my everlasting friend.

I will remember the Lord. I will not forget who has created me. I will believe God will be with me through this time of sorrow.

Prayer: *May I remember my Creator. May I believe the Lord cares for me in my sorrow.*

Am I remembering my Creator in my time of sorrow? Do I know the Lord as my everlasting friend?

Believing God and Letting Go

He will not grow tired or weary, and his understanding no one can fathom.

—Isaiah 40:28

Those close to us may want us to be finished with our grief and grieving sooner than we probably are able.

Not everyone will understand us as we would like to be understood.

But God understands us completely, and God does not grow weary of our need to recover slowly.

The Lord does not grow weary of our need to be understood from the deepest reaches of our souls.

The Lord understands the unsearchable.

The Lord knows us completely.

The Lord sees what we cannot see.

The Lord is able to do for us what we cannot do for ourselves.

The Lord leads us through the dark valleys and restores us, once again, to life.

May I trust the Lord to stay with me.

I will believe the Lord does not grow weary of me. I will trust God to understand me completely. I will let go and let God.

Prayer: *May I believe God understands me completely. May I turn to God with my deepest needs.*

Am I trusting the faithfulness of the Lord? Am I letting go and letting God?

Hoping in the Lord

Those who hope in the Lord will renew their strength.
—Isaiah 40:31

Bereavement brings an amount of fatigue, and sometimes a sense of deep weariness. This is part of the depression that comes when we suffer severe loss and separation.

At times we feel there is no hope for our recovery from sorrow. We feel strength will never return to our soul.

However, the promise is that "those who hope in the Lord shall renew their strength."

This promise is given to us in the deserts and prisons of our lives.

The Lord is able to fulfill this promise for renewal on a day to day basis, step by step, one step after the other—provided we are ready to be renewed.

The secret, as always, is to place our hope in the Lord, to wait on the Lord.

We must wait patiently and trust the Lord to move in our lives.

If we wait for the Lord he will give us the hope and strength we need to accomplish what has been given us to do.

"Those who hope in the Lord will renew their strength."

May I place my hope in the Lord to be strengthened.

I will be patient and trusting. I will hope for the Lord to move in my life. I will believe the Lord will give me the strength I need to recover.

Prayer: *May I be patient and trusting. May I hope for the Lord to give me strength.*

Do I live in hope that God will give me strength to go on? Am I willing to let the Lord remove my sorrow?

Soaring on Wings like Eagles

You] will soar on wings like eagles.

—Isaiah 40:31

Bereavement uses us up in many ways: physically, emotionally, spiritually.

And as we said yesterday, sometimes we can feel drained of energy.

Therefore, the thought of soaring on wings like eagles can seem farfetched.

Sometimes we doubt we can do anything more than stay stuck in one place with our grief.

However, God's promises are about strength.

Strength not only to endure our sorrow, but to live beyond it, to rise above it, and eventually, to leave it behind.

Believing these promises of God, we come to experience the inner strength that enables us to "soar" from the pits of sorrow into the sunlight of God's eternal light and love.

Making a decision to believe the promises of God is a strong step into recovery and new life.

Living the promises is the next step, as are all the steps that follow.

May I rise up from my sorrow.

I will believe the promises of God. I will believe I can grow beyond my sorrow. I will believe God gives me the strength I need to rise up from my sorrow, to heal.

Prayer: *May I believe I can grow beyond my sorrow. May I rise from sorrow into the sunlight of God's love.*

Am I willing to believe there is new life waiting for me? Am I ready to rise above my sorrow?

Walking without Fainting

You] will run and not grow weary, [you] will walk and not be faint.

—Isaiah 40:31

Getting from one place of spiritual growth to another can be difficult at times, especially when we are bogged down with loss, sorrow, and grief.

As we have been saying, the energy simply isn't always there—neither is the desire to go on.

However, one day we start moving on with our lives.

We take one step at a time.

We live one day at a time.

We walk slowly, step by step, without fainting.

We discover we are able to move on with our lives, that we are capable of growth.

We experience a bit of zest, a little healthy excitement. Not a lot, but some; enough to get our attention, to perk us up a bit.

We are beginning to heal.

May I run and not grow weary, walk and not be faint.

I will expect to be healed of my sorrow. I will be ready to move along slowly with my recovery. I will trust God to give me new strength and new life.

Prayer: *I pray for new strength and new life. I pray for God's strength to grow in my life.*

Am I believing I will receive new strength and new life from God? Am I expecting God's strength to grow in my life?

Listening in Silence

Be silent before me you islands.

—Isaiah 41:1

Silence can be a powerful tool for healing.

Simply having nothing to say—about ourselves, what we think has really happened to us, what is happening right now, or what might happen and not happen in the future—can be healing.

Listening for the Lord's leading can be very relaxing, very peaceful.

When we decide to let God lead us, things begin to change.

We have no need for an agenda about what is going to happen, how things are going to work out for us.

While this may sound passive, actually it is anything but.

Listening to the Lord in silence is a deep investment of ourselves.

Listening to the Lord in silence is an act of faith.

Listening to the Lord in silence takes courage, which the Lord provides.

Silent meditation, at least once or twice a day, is the time-tested way to bring healing.

May I be ready to listen to the Lord in silence.

I will take time to be silent before the Lord. I will relax myself in the presence of God. I will wait for the Lord to lead me.

Prayer: *May I be silent before the Lord. May I trust the Lord to help and to heal.*

Am I taking time to be silent before the Lord? Am I believing the Lord will heal me?

Believing God's Faithfulness

I have chosen you and have not rejected you.

—Isaiah 41:9

Bereavement can leave us feeling like outcasts. This is not true for all who grieve, but it is true for many—sometimes pitifully true.

Even those who were close to us may not come around as often as they once did.

We may ask ourselves, "Where did everyone go?"

It is not a good feeling to be deserted.

And yet, sometimes, this is what happens. People become frightened, and people desert.

But God does not desert.

Nor does God reject us. "I have chosen you and have not rejected you," says the Lord.

We have been chosen to be God's children.

In no way is God going to reject us.

God is faithful.

God is worthy of our trust.

May I trust God never to reject me.

I will believe God has chosen me. I will believe the Lord never rejects me. I will trust the love of the Lord forever.

Prayer: *May I believe God truly loves me. May I trust the Lord never to reject me.*

Am I believing God loves me? Am I trusting the Lord never to reject me?

✓

Living beyond Dismay

Do not be dismayed, for I am your God.

—Isaiah 41:10

In bereavement there are times when we feel we are breaking down. We become *dis*-heartened. We feel frightened about not being able to cope. We feel shattered and unable to put the pieces of our life back together. We become dismayed.

These are "normal" grief experiences.

But the Lord says, "Do not be dismayed, for I am your God."

In the early stages of bereavement this may or may not have meaning for us.

However, the deeper we go into our pain, the more we come to see we need outside help, the more these words come into focus. We are helped with our dismay and given the power to live beyond it.

We are being watched over.

This means help is available.

This means we need not be isolated, alone, forsaken, disheartened, and shattered.

"Do not be dismayed, for I am your God."

This means we can live beyond dismay.

May I live beyond dismay.

I will believe God is with me. I will not be dismayed and disheartened. I will live the promises of God.

Prayer: *May I not be dismayed and disheartened. May I believe the Lord is with me.*

Am I disheartened and dismayed? Am I believing the Lord is with me?

Accepting God's Strength

I will strengthen you.

—Isaiah 41:10

Sometimes getting enough strength to live one day at a time can be a real problem.

Our systems—emotional, physical, and spiritual—simply crack.

Sometimes we break down, due to the stress of suffered loss.

What is needed is new strength.

But we soon find out the strength we need can't come only from ourselves; and sometimes not at all from ourselves. In and of ourselves we are too weak, too insufficient.

So, we must turn elsewhere for strength.

But where?

We need the strength that only God is able to give. Strength to go on with our lives purposefully, and hopefully, with joy.

Let us receive the strength that comes from God.

Let us live the promises of God.

Let us find rest for our souls.

The Lord is able to give us strength when we are ready to receive it.

"I will strengthen you," says the Lord.

May I accept the strength that comes from the Lord.

I will believe my strength comes from the Lord. I will trust God to provide me with the strength I need. I will be thankful for the gifts of God.

Prayer: *May I accept the strength of the Lord. May I rest myself in God's power for new life.*

Am I turning to God for strength? Am I trusting God to give me the strength I need to recover and heal?

• DAY 37 •

Believing God's Help

I will . . . help you.

—Isaiah 41:10

"Help me!" The cry. The wish. The prayer.

In grief we all need help.

And somehow we know that by ourselves we are not able to do what must be done in order to heal.

Even when we bravely say, "I'll make it. I'll get through this. I can do it," our words lack conviction.

However, if we are very quiet, and if we listen carefully, we begin to hear quiet assurance from the Lord.

"I will help you."

This is the assurance we need to hear day by day, because recovery is a day by day program and process.

What we came to know and believe yesterday we easily forget today.

That is why the promises of God must be repeated day after day, as we are doing in these meditations.

Let us believe this promise with all our heart.

Let us live its truth one day at a time.

"I will help you," says the Lord.

May I believe the Lord will help me.

I will believe the Lord will help me. I will let the Lord help me. I will give thanks to the Lord for helping me along the way.

Prayer: *May I trust God to help me along the way. May I accept the help that is offered.*

Am I willing to believe God is able and willing to help me? Am I ready to have God do this work in me right now?

Being Upheld by God's Power

I will uphold you.

—Isaiah 41:10

Yesterday the promise was, "I will help you."

Today the promise is, "I will uphold you. I will support you. I will protect you."

For all of us there come those let-down feelings, especially when we are suffering from loss, sorrow, and grief.

At such times we are like little children needing to be held, and we may feel embarrassed because of our helpless feelings. We may even be afraid of them—afraid of admitting them to ourselves, afraid of sharing them with others.

It's as though we will fall apart completely if someone else comes to know the "secret" of our wanting to be held.

But then, everyone has a need to be held from time to time.

In and of ourselves we have no lasting capacity to hold ourselves up, not with our limited amount of strength and endurance.

The story of salvation, from beginning to end, is summed up in the promise, "I will uphold you," which means, "I will walk with you. And when you are unable to carry yourself, I will carry you."

May I trust the Lord to uphold me.

I will believe the Lord upholds me. I will trust the Lord to keep me from falling. I will give thanks to the Lord for supporting me.

Prayer: *May I permit God's power to support me. May I be upheld by the power of God.*

Am I ready to let God uphold me? Am I willing to accept the help that is offered?

Surrendering Fear

I am the Lord, your God, who . . . says to you, "Do not fear."
—Isaiah 41:13

Too often, the last thing we will admit to is our fear, because we are afraid of fear.

Hidden fear builds stress and results in breakdowns.

The time comes when we simply must say, "I am afraid." We need to find someone to talk to.

Then things begin to get better as we are able to do something with our pain.

However, left to ourselves there is more fear than we can productively handle.

All of us need a voice of authority saying, "Do not fear." A voice we can trust. A voice of power.

We have this voice of authority from one who has overcome the world of darkness, fear, and death. He is saying to us, "Take heart! I have overcome the world."

"Do not let your hearts be troubled. Trust in God; trust also in me. In my Father's house are many rooms. . . . I am going there to prepare a place for you. . . . that you also may be where I am."

May I surrender my fear to the Lord.

I will listen to Jesus saying, "Do not fear." I will seek professional help if necessary. I will ask God that I be released from my fears.

Prayer: *May I surrender my fear(s) to the Lord. May I do this day after day.*

Am I surrendering my fear(s) to the Lord? Am I doing this one day at a time?

Trusting God's Restoration

See, I will make you into a threshing sledge, new and sharp, with many teeth.

—Isaiah 41:15

There is this promise of restoration, when we regain the strength of our true self, when we are useful again. New and sharp, with many teeth.

We are destined to be restored.

But for this to happen we must believe it possible.

Without faith there is no hope, no possibility for newness.

Therefore, it is essential to believe God, to live the promise that we will be made new and sharp, that we are going to be restored to spiritual health.

The most important restoration is spiritual, when we are brought into contact with our true inner self which is the "Imago Dei," the image of God in which we have been created.

"See, I will make you into a threshing sledge, new and sharp, with many teeth," says the Lord. This means we are in the process of being reborn, new and vitally; we are being restored to health, in the Lord.

May I believe God is restoring me to health.

I will believe the Lord is in the process of restoring my life. I will trust the Lord to give me a measure of living hope. I will give thanks to the Lord for all these mercies.

Prayer: *May I believe God will restore me to health during bereavement. May I trust God to give me new life.*

Am I trusting God to restore my life? Am I ready to receive the gift of new life being offered to me by the Lord?

Threshing and Purifying

You will thresh the mountains and crush them.
—Isaiah 41:15

There are the mountains of fear.

Also, there are mountains of hopelessness, faithlessness, ingratitude, and separation—all part of the human menu.

It takes God's power to overcome such obstacles.

There also are things that can't be treated with kid gloves, which we ask God to crush: resentment, self-centeredness, and exaggerated self-pity. God provides the power to thresh such mountains and crush them.

However, such radical treatment of our character defects is very frightening.

But, as the prophets taught, gold must be refined by fire in order to be purified and made useful. And this is painful.

However, there always is pain involved with healing. And one of the greatest pains is the threshing out, the crushing of our false pride that keeps us from asking God to help us; false pride that prevents our healing.

May I be ready to let God crush everything that prevents me from healing.

I will ask God to do what is necessary to bring about my healing. I will believe God will do with me what is best. I will give thanks to God.

Prayer: *May I be healed by the purifying power of God. May my character defects be threshed and crushed.*

Am I willing to be purified by the mighty hand of God? Am I ready to give up all that prevents me from healing?

Do What Must Be Done

The poor and needy search for water, but there is none; their tongues are parched with thirst. But I the Lord will answer them; I, the God of Israel, will not forsake them.

—Isaiah 41:17

Sometimes life gets so painful that we, like bodies parched with thirst with no water in sight, can see no possibility for release.

But then, we are told, when "the poor and needy search for water" (*search for* with emphasis on *search*), the Lord is able to answer. And the Lord does. The Lord does not forsake those who search.

But, recovery only comes to those who are willing to ask, to seek, and to knock as Jesus said.

This means we have to make decisions.

This means we must *do* something.

This means that while there is a time for waiting, there also is a time for seeking, a time to look for ways to help ourselves into health and healing. But to do this we need help.

And, there is a promise: "When you are poor and needy, and your tongue is parched with thirst, I, the Lord, will answer you. I will not forsake you."

May I do what must be done to heal.

I will take responsibility for my health and healing. I will make moves to bring about my recovery. I will ask God for help.

Prayer: *May I take the necessary steps to bring about my recovery. May I ask God for the help I need in order to heal.*

Am I willing to make moves to help my recovery? Am I ready to believe the Lord will never forsake me?

Remembering God's Care

I will make rivers flow on barren heights, and springs within the valleys.

—Isaiah 41:18

Day by day it's important to concentrate attention on the promises of God.

For as surely as the day passes, so does our memory of God's care and God's grace which provides what we need for recovery and growth.

We may feel like parched land, with no water in sight.

Sometimes, we may feel without hope.

But, the Lord promises to bring new life into the picture, to open rivers of grace into the barenness of our souls.

The Lord promises to provide fountains of freshness in the midst of dry valleys.

The Lord promises new rivers of water on the bare heights where nothing seems able to grow.

The Lord waits to do this for us, in us, and through us.

The Lord promises to give us new life in abundance.

But first God's promises have to be taken seriously.

We must place our trust in God's capacity to do this wonderful work of healing in us.

May I believe the Lord is giving me new life.

I will trust the Lord to open the springs of grace to fill my soul. I will believe the Lord is going to restore my life. I will trust the Lord to do mighty works in me.

Prayer: *May I trust God to open the springs of grace to fill my soul. May I believe I am going to be restored.*

Am I open to the gifts of God being freely offered for my healing? Am I allowing the Lord to restore my soul?

Seeing God's Keeping

I will take hold of your hand. I will keep you. . . .

—Isaiah 42:6

God is our keeper.

Even when God seems far from us in our bereavement, God keeps us.

When we look deeply into our lives we see the hand of the Lord at work, reaching for us.

The Lord is holding us.

The Lord is keeping us in God's care.

Remembering God's care and keeping is our recovery from sorrow and grief.

Without knowledge of God's presence in our lives, recovery is needlessly painful and even impossible.

The Lord says, "I will take hold of your hand. I will keep you."

Let us see how this is happening to us right now.

Let us see how the Lord is taking us by the hand.

Let us see how the Lord is keeping us, in the midst of our sorrow and pain.

May I see how God is caring for me right now.

I will believe God has taken me by the hand. I will trust God to keep me in God's loving care. I will recover from my sorrow with the Lord leading me.

Prayer: *May I believe God is caring for me. May I surrender to the care and keeping of the Lord.*

Am I believing God cares for me? Am I trusting the Lord to lead me through my recovery from sorrow?

Ready for New Life

See, the former things have taken place, and new things I declare; before they spring into being I announce them to you.
—Isaiah 42:9

Recovery from loss, sorrow, and grief is part of the "new things" which God has in store for us.

However, looking for something new to happen is not always easy. Sometimes, in fact, it is virtually impossible to feel upbeat, expectant, hopeful, and joyous.

Nevertheless, the new things to come do, in fact, include our recovery.

But it is first necessary for us to become open and receptive to inheriting the promise.

When we do this our outlook begins to change for the better.

Can we actually believe we are going to be healed?

If we look back over the promises of God, we find they always are in the process of being fulfilled.

We see fulfillment in the history of God's people, even in the most horrendous times of persecution and death.

The mercy of God continues to "spring into being" in ways we never imagined possible.

May I be ready for new life to spring forth in me.

I will believe God has bountiful goodness and mercy in store for me. I will trust God to give me what I need to recover from my sorrow. I will be grateful for the goodness of God in my life.

Prayer: *May I turn to God for goodness and mercy. May I trust God to give me what I need to heal.*

Am I grateful for the goodness of God in my life? Am I ready to receive God's love and mercy into my life?

Finding a New Song to Sing

Sing to the Lord a new song.

—Isaiah 42:10

One of the problems in recovery is to get ourselves deprogrammed, since suffered loss of any consequence leaves deep and painful impressions in our hearts and souls. And, there is no quick or immediate healing for this.

What we have to do, like it or not and painful as it may be, is to find a new song to sing: to sing praise to the Lord rather than lamentations.

Easier said than done.

And never done until we are ready.

But, stopping short of finding a new song is stopping short of recovery. It simply is not enough to quit our lamentations if we want a strong recovery. We must actually find a new song of praise to the Lord.

While this sounds difficult, if not impossible, it is the real need for healing a broken heart.

And, the new song can be sung in the midst of our tears, because God will provide the song.

May I find a new song to sing to the Lord.

I will ask God to provide me with a new song to sing. I will believe the Lord gives a new song. I will be ready to sing praise to the Lord.

Prayer: *May I find a song of joy to sing to the Lord. May I sing the song of joy to the Lord.*

Am I asking for a new song of joy to sing to the Lord? Am I ready to sing the song when it is given to me?

Believing God's Redemption

Fear not, for I have redeemed you.

—Isaiah 43:1

Is the Lord actually interested in us? Is there help for our troubled souls? Can we recover from our sorrow?

"Will I ever be a whole human being again?"

The truth is in our scripture for today.

Already we have been redeemed and restored, even if it doesn't feel that way, even if we don't know this to be true right now for ourselves.

We may be afraid that everything is hopeless, that there is no restoration, no recovery, no redemption for us. But the promises of God are positive.

Our redemption is always in process, and, in a sense, already has taken place.

We already have been redeemed from sin and death.

Already we are on our way to being restored and healed. We are on our way to freedom from grief and all its pain.

We might not see it now, but our recovery is in process because we are redeemed children of God.

May I see that God has redeemed me.

I will believe God has redeemed me from sin and death. I will trust God's love to save me from falling into despair. I will accept the goodness of God into my life.

Prayer: *May I believe God has redeemed my life from destruction. May I trust God to care for me.*

Am I trusting God with my life? Do I believe God has redeemed my life from destruction?

• DAY 48 •

Belonging to the Lord

I have summoned you by name; you are mine.

—Isaiah 43:1

In our grief it is not difficult to lose sight of the Lord's determination to keep us in God's everlasting love.

Sometimes it seems the Lord not only is far away, but even that we have been abandoned by God.

However, the Lord is close, even intimate. We are known in detail and above all, we are claimed by God.

There is a passion about this divine claim on our lives. It isn't like a little passing fancy on the part of the Lord: here today, gone tomorrow.

Rather God's established claim on our lives is filled with an energy that cannot be turned aside.

The Lord seeks us out no matter what, just as the good shepherd goes looking for one lost sheep.

We are precious to the Lord because we belong to God.

The Lord is not going to let go of us.

Hopefully we will be able to see through the fog of our sorrow, and realize we are deeply loved by God.

May I believe I am deeply loved and wanted by God.

I will listen carefully to the promises of God. I will believe I am known and loved by God. I will give thanks to God.

Prayer: *May I believe God has claimed me. May I believe God will not let go of me.*

Am I trusting God not to let go of me? Am I believing God has laid hold of my life to claim it?

Being Brought Through

When you pass through the waters, I will be with you; and when you pass through the rivers, they will not sweep over you.
—Isaiah 43:2

Recovery is a series of steps, none of which can be avoided if we want to find lasting relief, hope, and joy.

The first step is to face the reality of the loss, with its pain.

There are those, of course, who choose to do otherwise, who decide not to deal with the pain. Sometimes this is done with the help of alcohol or other drugs, many of which are prescribed by well-meaning physicians.

Most medication, however, does not promote recovery, but may even forestall it; it may put some of the pain to sleep, but only for a while.

Yes, the way to recovery is painful, but we also have the promises of God that the deep waters of sorrow will not overwhelm, and the current of the rivers will not be too strong.

The promise is that we will not be given more than we are able to bear. The Lord is with us all the way, through the deep waters of our grief.

May I believe God will bring me through.

I will believe the Lord is with me. I will believe I am not going to be overwhelmed by the pain of my grief. I will be grateful for the Lord's help.

Prayer: *May I be confident the Lord is with me. May I trust the Lord to bring me through this sorrow.*

Am I believing I will not be overwhelmed by my sorrow? Am I trusting God to bring me through the deep waters of my sorrow and grief?

Being Led through the Fire

When you walk through the fire, you will not be burned; the flames will not set you ablaze.

—Isaiah 43:2

With bereavement there can be increased anxiousness, even anxiety attacks.

We may experience restlessness, nervousness, confusion, and fear.

We may feel jumpy, out of control, antsy, and not able to get a grip on things.

We may be afraid of losing the control we imagined we had.

We may be ashamed of our fears and try to hide them.

When asked how we are doing, we may not be able to tell the truth, afraid of being consumed by the agony of our loss.

It is as though we are being consumed by our loss, sorrow, and grief, that we are being burned by fire.

These are normal feelings. We should not discredit ourselves or our faith for having them.

Let us believe that our Lord will lead us through the fire, and that we will not be consumed by the pain of our loss.

May I believe I will be led through.

I will have confidence in the promises of God. I will believe my sorrow is not going to consume my life. I will give thanks for the faithfulness of God.

Prayer: *May I have confidence in God's power to save me. May I not be afraid of what is to come.*

Am I placing my confidence in God's power to save me? Am I willing to turn my fears over to God?

Believing the Lord's Presence

Do not be afraid, for I am with you.

—Isaiah 43:5

So many of God's dealings with us have to do with fear, and the admonition, "Don't be afraid."

Recovery from sorrow is helped along as we remember and believe, "Do not be afraid, for I am with you."

Some of us are ashamed of our fear; we ask ourselves, "If I am a believer in God, why am I afraid?"

Or, we may simply deny fear: "I am not afraid."

However, fear is part of our being human. And with bereavement, fear sensations often increase in intensity.

Let us remember that we have honest reasons for being afraid. We live in a dangerous world and, as we already know, there are many dangers over which we have no control, just as we had no control over the loss of our loved one.

However, we can hear and believe the promise, "Do not be afraid, for I am with you," says the Lord.

May I believe the Lord is with me and I need not be afraid.

I will believe the Lord is with me. I will not allow myself to be afraid today. I will give thanks to God for being with me in my sorrow.

Prayer: *May I not be afraid. May I trust the Lord to be with me all the way.*

Am I ready to believe the Lord is with me? Am I turning my fears over to the Lord?

Turning to the Lord for Help

I, even I, am the Lord, and apart from me there is no savior.
—Isaiah 43:11

The way of the Lord is the way to recovery and health.

The way of the Lord is the way of faith, hope, and love; the opposite of despair, hopelessness, and fear.

We can know this way of love by knowing the Lord, who is our Savior from fear, hopelessness, and despair.

By ourselves we can go only so far toward healing and health.

Without the Lord becoming active in our lives, we are left with an emotional and spiritual void that neither ourselves nor others can fill.

This is why it is essential to entrust our recovery to God, turning over our hurt, sorrow, and grief to the Lord to heal.

When we turn to the Lord for help, we are set on the healing path.

May I turn to the Lord to be my Savior, to help me.

I will turn to the Lord as my Savior. I will believe the Lord is able to redeem me from the pits of my sorrow. I will give thanks to the Lord for the gift of new life.

Prayer: *May I believe the Lord is able to lift me up. May I trust the Lord to save me.*

Am I turning my life over to the Lord? Am I trusting the Lord to be my Savior?

Being Firmly Held by the Lord

No one can deliver [you] out of my hand.

—Isaiah 43:13

Once we have found a sense of security in the Lord there still are days when we feel that the bottom is going to fall out of our lives.

And so it may.

However, the promise is that we cannot be snatched out of the loving arms of God.

Even though we may have to face additional pain and suffering, the Lord will still be holding us with love and care.

We need not fear what is to come. Nothing can snatch us from the Lord's protection and care.

Whatever we are called to do, the Lord always is with us. We are secured by the mighty hand of God.

Our task is to live one day at a time, trusting the Lord to stay with us; believing that the Lord has a firm hold on us, and that we cannot slip away.

May I believe the Lord has a firm hold on me.

I will trust the Lord to hold me. I will believe the Lord will not let go of me. I will give thanks to the Lord for staying with me.

Prayer: *May I trust the Lord to hold me. May I believe the Lord will never let go of me.*

Am I trusting the Lord to hold me? Do I believe the Lord will never let go of me?

Seeing God at Work

When I act, who can reverse it?

—Isaiah 43:13

God is active in the world and in our lives.

God doesn't sit in a far-off place paying little or no attention to us in our sorrow and grief.

When we are in doubt about our lives, whether life has meaning and value anymore, it is good to remember that God is at work in us—whether we know it or not.

There is no burden too heavy for the Lord to help us lift.

With God's help there are no circumstances we are unable to handle.

The Lord is working in and through us, toward our health and healing.

Even while we are sleeping, the Lord is working for us and with us.

Believing God is present in our lives is essential for a healthy recovery from loss, sorrow, and grief.

The Lord is at work, whether we know it or not. The blessings increase as we are able to see God at work in our lives.

May I see God active in my life.

I will believe God is working in my life. I will trust God never to give up on me. I will give thanks to the Lord.

Prayer: *May I believe the Lord is active in my life. May I trust God never to give up on me.*

Am I believing the Lord is active in my life? Am I trusting God never to give up on me?

Dealing with Feelings

Forget the former things; do not dwell on the past.

—Isaiah 43:18

A danger of bereavement can be that of selective forgetting—deciding not to remember what has been painful, rather than reflecting on the circumstances and working them through.

With bereavement there also can be anger and resentment, coupled with guilt feelings and shame.

There may be anger at ourselves or toward the lost loved one for having left us, or anger because of something we or they did that hurt, that was not worked through satisfactorily.

And, we can't really walk away from the way we feel about it all.

We must face up to what has been and what is in order to be ready for what is to come.

If there are feelings of anger, resentment, guilt, and shame, we must be ready to deal with them constructively by facing our feelings and acknowledging them. We must finally release ourselves from them by accepting the forgiveness of the Lord.

Then we are ready to "forget the former things."

Then we are able to move on with our lives.

May I face what has been and then move on.

I will deal with my feelings. I will ask God to remove anger, resentment, guilt, and shame. I will be released from all that is negative and move on.

Prayer: *May I deal with all of my feelings. May I be released of all negative feelings and move on.*

Am I dealing with my feelings? Am I accepting release for everything that is over and done with?

Seeing Something New

See, I am doing a new thing.

—Isaiah 43:19

"I am doing a new thing."

But how can this be when we don't feel at all "new," and when we have little or no faith that things can ever change for the better?

Believing that the Lord actually is "doing a *new thing*" in us is a firm step toward recovery.

While we may not be able to see how this can be, it is important to be reminded that things are never going to be as they once were.

In this sense, everything that happens to us is going to be new.

The "new thing" the Lord is doing in our lives, right now, will not be quickly recognized.

Others may see the newness before we do.

Or, we might know it before anyone else can see it.

The "new thing" is renewed faith, hope, and love.

It is God's intention for us to experience an abundance of these gifts. The promise is given: "See, I am doing a new thing."

May I see that the Lord is doing something new in me.

I will believe the Lord is reshaping my life. I will trust God to quietly lead me where I am to be going. I will thank God for the many gifts of grace given to me.

Prayer: *May I trust God to remake my life day by day. May I let God lead me where I am to be going.*

Am I trusting God to remake my life daily and richly? Am I seeing that God is leading me where I am to be going?

Looking in Hidden Places

Now it springs up; do you not perceive it?

—Isaiah 43:19

When is something different going to happen? When am I going to feel better? When is the pain going to stop? Will I ever experience hope, love, joy, and a sense of belonging?

The answer is that all of this is in process because God is working actively for us and in us.

However, the only way we can perceive and see the newness is to look in the hidden places; that is, where God works.

However, seeing the hand of God at work in our lives is not always that easy.

Often we may look and not see, or hardly see—like "through a glass darkly"—because we are in the shadows of our sorrow and bereavement.

Things simply are not clear, including the promises and work of God.

Yet God's promise is that something new is springing up in our lives.

It is time to look closely, to see newness of life eager to bloom, eager to bear the fruit of love, hope, and joy.

May I look for God in the hidden places of my life.

I will believe God is making all things new. I will trust the Lord is leading me into a new life of hope. I will give thanks to the Lord for every gift received.

Prayer: *May I see that God is reshaping my life. May I trust God to lead me into new life and hope.*

Am I looking for God in the hidden places of my life? Am I trusting God to lead me into new life, hope, and joy?

Deciding to Walk the Way of the Lord

I am making a way in the desert and streams in the wasteland.
—Isaiah 43:19

Finding our way through the sorrow and the grief, into newness of life, is the problem and the challenge.

While the Lord makes a way for us in the desert, we must make a decision to walk in that way.

While the Lord will provide streams in the wasteland of our sorrow, we must come to the streams to quench our thirst.

Recovery calls for commitment, the willingness to heal, the desire to regain ourselves emotionally and spiritually.

Sometimes it may be that we have little or nothing to regain, but a great deal to acquire as far as our spiritual growth is concerned.

We have the promise that the Lord will make a way for us to travel in and through the desert of our sorrow.

But it is left up to us whether we are ready to follow the path and come to the streams of life.

It is up to us.

We can begin this trip and continue on the path through prayer.

May I walk the way which the Lord has prepared.

I will walk on the prepared way of the Lord through the desert of my sorrow. I will trust the path of the Lord to lead me to streams of new life. I will thank God for every grace and benefit given to me.

Prayer: *May I see the path laid out before me by the Lord. May I permit the Lord to lead me to the streams of life.*

Am I willing to seek the path of the Lord in the desert of my sorrow? Am I ready to let the Lord lead me into newness of life?

Seeking God's Refreshment

I provide water . . . to give drink to my people, my chosen, the people I formed for myself.

—Isaiah 43:20-21

In the midst of trials, suffering, and sorrow, we can easily forget who we are.

We can forget that we have been formed and chosen by God, made in the image of God, made in the likeness of God.

This makes us special in the eyes of the Lord.

However, the truth is we don't always remember who we are. Nor do we always allow ourselves to be refreshed by the Lord, who offers us new waters of life.

If we don't expect God to refresh us, there is no way to inherit what is being offered.

The refreshment of the Lord comes to those who wait on the Lord.

Refreshment comes to those who believe and live the promises of God.

In trying times there is deep need for refreshment that comes from the Lord.

We will find that refreshment as we seek the Lord in prayer.

May I seek the refreshment God is offering me.

I will look to the Lord in prayer and meditation to find refreshment for my soul. I will believe the Lord has formed and chosen me. I will believe I belong to the Lord.

Prayer: *May I be refreshed by the Lord to newness of life. May I let God do for me what I cannot do for myself.*

Am I seeking the refreshment God offers? Am I trusting God to do for me what I cannot do for myself?

Believing and Accepting Forgiveness

I have swept away your offenses like a cloud, your sins like a morning mist.

—Isaiah 44:22

God promises that he will not remember our sins. This is important because the deeper we go into our recovery from sorrow and grief, the more we may become aware of our sins.

Perhaps, as we have said before, we remember some unfinished business we had with the lost loved one or sad feelings about unresolved conflicts, when we or they may not have fought fair, when things were said which we now regret.

Whatever the regrets, there is nothing we can do about them that will change things now, nothing that will give us another opportunity to turn a wrong into a right.

And that is the pain of it all, that we are unable to undo or redo what we or they have done. This is when the promise of the Lord has its deepest meaning, when there is nothing we can do to change what has happened.

Then we need to hear the promise of our Lord, "I have swept away your transgression(s) like a cloud, and your sins like mist."

We must forgive ourselves as God has forgiven us.

May I believe my sins are swept away.

I will believe the Lord has swept away my sins like a cloud. I will trust the Lord's forgiveness. I will give thanks to the Lord for blessing me with the gift of forgiveness

Prayer: *May I believe God forgives all my sins. May I forgive myself as God forgives me.*

Do I believe that my sins are swept away like a cloud? Am I forgiving myself as God forgives me?

Returning to the Lord

Return to me, for I have redeemed you.

—Isaiah 44:22

Sometimes, during times of loss, sorrow, and grief, there is a sensation of wandering, of being disconnected and far away, and, especially, far away from God.

Also, we may feel that we have no right to approach God because of some particular sin or sins.

If so, it is good to remember that the Lord always invites us back: "Come to me. Return to me."

"I have redeemed you."

"I have called you by name."

"You are mine!"

God has gone to every length to open the invitation for us to return, to be restored and strengthened, to be given new hope and joy.

That invitation always is open.

There is no reason for us to avoid the Lord, to stay away from the goodness of God.

The Lord always wants us back where we belong.

And, we belong to God.

May I always return to the Lord.

I will return to the Lord in prayer and thanksgiving. I will believe the Lord has redeemed me from sin and death. I will give thanks to the Lord for the Lord is good.

Prayer: *May I believe the Lord has redeemed me from sin and death. May I return to the Lord and be healed.*

Am I believing the Lord has redeemed my life from sin and death? Am I giving thanks to the Lord?

Opening Our Hearts in Praise

Sing for joy, O heavens, for the LORD has done this.
—Isaiah 44:23

We are invited to see beyond ourselves, to look up, to see what the Lord has done and is doing to help and to heal.

We are invited to sing praises to the Lord.

But, we may not feel like singing.

Our hearts may be too heavy with loss, sorrow, and grief. Nevertheless, we are urged to remember what the Lord has done, and to sing for joy.

There's no doubt that the more we praise God, the better we feel.

A grateful heart is a hopeful and healing heart. So, let us open our hearts and give thanks to the Lord.

"Sing for joy, O heavens, for the Lord has done this"; the Lord has washed away all our transgressions.

The Lord calls us into fellowship.

The Lord offers us healing and eternal life.

The Lord promises to be with us now and forever.

"Sing for joy, O creation, for the Lord has done this."

The Lord reaches out to save.

May I open my heart and give praise to the Lord.

I will open my heart and give praise to the Lord. I will give praise where praise is due, praising the Lord! I will sing to the Lord a new song of hope and joy.

Prayer: *May I open my heart in praise to the Lord. May I sing praises to the Lord.*

Am I opening my heart to the Lord? Am I giving praise to God?

Following the Leading of the Lord

I will go before you and will level the mountains.

—Isaiah 45:2

Some things simply are bigger than we, beyond our capacity to handle.

Emotionally and spiritually we may find ourselves quite depressed and frightened at times.

Sometimes we may wonder how we can endure another day, because the mountains before us are uncrossable.

It is time, once again, to turn to the promises of the Lord: "I will go before you. I will take care of those frightening mountains. I will give you a place to walk, with no monstrous peaks or deep valleys so that you are unable to move on."

Is this true? Is this how the Lord actually works?

The way to find out is to talk to someone who knows.

Or to remember from our own experiences how the Lord has gone before us, how the Lord has leveled uncrossable mountains to provide us with safe passage.

Let us follow the leading of the Lord.

May I follow the leading of the Lord.

I will believe that the Lord goes before me into unknown and frightening places. I will trust the Lord to level the uncrossable mountains. I will follow the leading of the Lord.

Prayer: *May I trust God to lead me. May I believe the Lord will give me a level place on which to walk.*

Am I ready to trust the Lord with my life? Am I willing to follow the leading of the Lord?

Allowing Barriers to be Broken

I will break down gates of bronze and cut through bars of iron.
—Isaiah 45:2

In bereavement there is a tendency to withdraw into ourselves emotionally and spiritually for fear of getting hurt some more.

Then too, we don't always know where we are with ourselves, with others, or with God.

At times, we may become quite immobilized by our loss, sorrow, and grief.

It isn't good to stay in a bound-up position too long. If we do, our grief may become deeply set, even permanent.

If we find ourselves being bound up emotionally and spiritually, we must try to remember that the Lord is able to open us up when we aren't able to open ourselves.

The Lord is able to open us to the promises of God and to hope.

The Lord is able to unlock us emotionally, spiritually, and physically.

The Lord is able to "cut through bars of iron," to break the barriers of separation, isolation, and loneliness.

May I allow the Lord to break every barrier within me.

I will trust the Lord with my life. I will allow the Lord to break up my defensive barriers. I will not hide.

Prayer: *May I allow God to open my heart. May I not be locked up within myself.*

Am I allowing God to break the barriers within me? Am I trusting God's love to heal my broken spirit?

Being Strengthened by the Lord

I am the LORD, and there is no other; apart from me there is no God. I will strengthen you.

—Isaiah 45:5

There are times when we simply feel that we don't know God, or that we are known by God, much less that God is going to do anything for or with us. This is particularly true during times of bereavement, when sorrow and grief would consume us.

But, the Lord remains faithful, even when we are out of touch with God.

Yes, sometimes it is difficult to hear, much less believe, the promise of God's wraparound love. Perhaps this is because we are not ready to release ourselves from our sorrow and grief, for reasons of our own.

However, when we are ready to heal and move on with our lives, we become aware of God's strengthening love.

"I will strengthen you," is the promise given us this day.

God is eager for us to respond, by placing our trust and confidence with the Lord, where it really makes a difference.

May I be strengthened by the Lord.

I will believe God's love for me. I will accept God's care and keeping. I will give thanks for the love of God that surrounds me.

Prayer: *May I affirm God's love for me. May I believe God takes care of me.*

Do I believe I am surrounded by God's love? Am I trusting God's love to heal?

Allowing New Life to Come Forth

Let the earth open wide, let salvation spring up.

—Isaiah 45:8

For something to grow, something must open. The shell on the seed must be split by life's energy.

The ground must give way, just as a heart that is closed by grief must become open to love, if it is to live.

But sometimes we harden ourselves without knowing that we are doing so.

We are not necessarily doing this intentionally. It just happens.

Eventually, however, if the desire to heal is real, the hardness must be cracked, the defenses brought down, the heart opened.

It is like the growth process, like a seed sprouting, like the earth giving way to a new plant.

It is life being born again.

If we feel that we may be cutting ourselves off from the healing power of God, it is helpful to ask the Lord for an open heart, allowing God's new life to spring up.

May I allow God's new life to spring up in me.

I will open myself to God. I will trust the Lord to bring forth new life in me. I will accept the new life offered to me by the Lord.

Prayer: *May I open myself to the love of God. May I allow God to bring forth new life in me.*

Am I willing to open myself to God? Am I accepting the new life God is offering me?

Finding Our Location with God

It is I who made the earth and created mankind upon it.
—Isaiah 45:12

Who am I?

Where do I belong?

Who's in charge?

These are questions that often come with loss, sorrow, and grief.

To have a sense of location is important for our emotional and spiritual stability.

It's important to know and believe that God has made us in God's own image, "in the image of God."

This means we are a someone.

This means we belong to someone.

This means we are important to God.

To recover from loss, sorrow, and grief, we need a sense of self-worth. Our worth is with God.

It is God who also has created the earth.

It is God who has made us.

It is God who gives us our sense of belonging.

May I find the location of my life with God.

I will believe God has made me. I will believe I belong to God. I will believe I am important to God.

Prayer: *May I find the location of my life with God. May I believe I am important to God.*

Do I believe I am God's child? Do I believe I am important to God?

Hearing the Voice of the Lord

I have not spoken in secrets from somewhere in a land of darkness.

—Isaiah 45:19

When the children of Israel were slaves, the Lord did not remain hidden. The Lord came in the person of Moses to deliver them from the land of darkness, from bondage.

Not all of them appreciated their deliverance. Many complained. Some said they were better off in Egypt. But it's the human condition to at times feel cheated and deserted and to resent it.

There also are those who do not want to recover from the bondage of disappointment and bereavement, who want to live in their grief. As long as this is the case, there can be no healing, no recovery.

But when we are ready to hear the Lord's voice in and through the darkness of our sorrow, we are ready to be healed.

There are going to be times when we feel we have been led into darker places than before, even deserted by the Lord.

But if we listen carefully, we will hear God speak to us: "I do not stay silent in your darkness. I come to you. I reveal myself to you in and through your sorrow. I heal you."

May I hear the voice of the Lord speaking to me.

I will believe the Lord is speaking to me. I will be quiet and listen for the voice of the Lord in the darkened places of my life. I will wait patiently for the Lord to lead me through the darkness of my sorrow.

Prayer: *May I listen for the voice of the Lord. May I trust God to lead me out of the wilderness of my sorrow.*

Am I expecting to see and hear God working in my life? Am I ready to be led through the darkness of my grief?

Being Relieved of Negatives

You will never be put to shame or disgraced, to ages everlasting.
—Isaiah 45:17

Feelings of shame and confusion can be painful parts of bereavement.

We may feel that something is wrong with us:

That we are unclean, so to speak.

That we are different than other people.

That we have a kind of disease.

That we are tainted.

We may feel as though we are being put to shame and disgraced; that we are mixture of elements that cannot connect with one another; that we are fractured and cannot heal.

We may also feel that, before the Lord, we should be filled with shame because of our past behavior.

But the Lord will never shame us.

Nor will the Lord attempt to confound us, to mix us up, or put us down.

If we are having negative feelings, they do not come from the Lord.

"You will never be put to shame or disgraced," says the Lord.

May I be relieved of all negative feelings about myself.

I will turn my negative feelings over to the Lord. I will trust the Lord to put me together again. I will believe the Lord is able to heal me.

Prayer: *May I not live in shame and guilt. May I be relieved of negative feelings about myself.*

Am I willing to turn myself over to the Lord? Am I ready to let go of my shame, guilt, and confusion?

Being Gathered by the Lord

Gather together and come; assemble, you fugitives from the nations.

—Isaiah 45:20

By and large we human beings are survivors. God has built that energy into our systems.

But, we do not "survive" all by ourselves.

We need to be reassembled emotionally and, especially, spiritually.

We need to draw ourselves together in prayer and meditation, thanksgiving, and praise.

We need new confidence, the belief that we are going to see our way through the turmoil, confusion, and loss.

It's important to hear the Lord's invitation, even command: "Gather together, and come [to me]."

It is important to answer this call. In our sorrow we can be as fugitives, as lost souls—scattered—without a home of our own.

It is important for us to reassemble ourselves before the Lord, trusting the Lord to help and to heal.

May I go to the Lord for help and healing.

I will believe the Lord is putting me back together again. I will believe I am a survivor. I will believe I am going to heal.

Prayer: *May I be brought into the presence of the Lord. May I be helped and healed.*

Am I going to the Lord with my sorrow? Am I trusting the Lord to help and to heal?

Asking for Help

Declare what is to be, present it. . . .

—Isaiah 45:21

Sometimes we can feel as though we have no rights, particularly no rights to stand up for ourselves.

It's a feeling that often comes along with guilt and shame, about which we have talked before.

The Lord, however, asks us to be open about what we want and need, to present our case, to ask for help.

Perhaps we need to ask help for something specific we need done, which we cannot do by ourselves. And maybe we feel unworthy, afraid we will be rejected. But then, everyone fears rejection. And none of us handles rejection very well.

There come times, however, when we simply must make our case known—must ask for what we need and want.

Asking for help is a vital part of our recovery from loss, sorrow, and grief.

May I ask for help when I need it.

I will declare my case. I will ask for what I need and want. I will trust God and others to hear me.

Prayer: *May I be ready to declare my wants and needs. May I ask for the help I need and want.*

Am I making my wants and wishes known to God and to others? Am I asking for the help that I need?

Turning Away from Hopelessness

Turn to me and be saved.

—Isaiah 45:22

Hopelessness is the most destructive force of all.

Hopelessness kills.

We have our days of hopelessness.

We have those times when nothing seems worth the effort any longer, when we don't feel like getting out of bed, or going on with our life.

However, we need not be without hope.

God is ready to provide us with the gift of hope, when we are ready to receive it.

The eternal invitation is "turn to me and be saved."

We are being invited to be saved from hopelessness.

The old hymn is true: "Hope of the hopeless."

And the prayer of that old hymn is as it should be: "Lord, abide with me."

Hopelessness is destructive, but we don't have to be overcome by it. The Lord always is making the invitation, even the admonition: "Turn to me and be saved—from your hopelessness."

May I turn to the Lord.

I will believe the Lord wants to save me from hopelessness. I will trust the Lord to give me new hope. I will give thanks for the gift of hope.

Prayer: *May I believe the Lord will give me hope. May I call upon the name of the Lord to help me.*

Am I turning my hopelessness over to the Lord? Am I allowing myself to be given hope?

Letting God in to Help

I have made you and I will carry you; I will sustain you and I will rescue you.

—Isaiah 46:4

Sometimes we need to be carried, when we are weak and incapable of going it alone, when in deep need of help.

Like a child looking to a parent, we may look for someone to carry us.

The secret is to turn in the right direction—to turn to the Lord for help.

When we need to be carried for a time, we can ask God to carry us, and to help us walk again.

As we are being carried by the Lord we find sensations of fear and hopelessness retreating.

We also discover that we are not so much being carried, as a child being carried by a parent, but rather that God is walking with us, hand in hand.

We find that God is attending to us with loving care.

We discover that God is helping us do for ourselves what needs to be done for our healing.

God carries us.

But even more so, God walks with us.

God helps us along the way into healing and health.

May I let God help me along the way to healing and health.

I will allow God into my life, to help me along. I will let God lift me out of my distress. I will trust God to give me new life and new hope.

Prayer: *I will trust God to stay with me. I will trust God to help me along the way.*

Am I trusting God to be with me? Am I permitting the Lord to save me from needless distress?

Believing God's Deliverance

I am bringing my righteousness near, it is not far away.
—Isaiah 46:13

Someone says, "This too shall pass." But how does that make us feel?

Relieved or upset?

Better or bitter?

Satisfied or angry?

Regardless of how it may make us feel, it is true: "This too shall pass" because God's deliverance is near—because God never is far off.

However, recovery is a process in which there are dark valleys that cannot be avoided if we are to heal, and there is pain that must be felt and lived through, for us to heal.

Bereavement does not end with the flick of a switch, nor is sorrow turned into joy overnight.

Nevertheless the Lord will make things right, and the Lord is not far away.

We are told that God's righteousness is near, which is another way of saying that everything is going to come out (right) in the wash, that we are in the process of being healed.

It is true, then, that our bereavement will pass because the healing of God is not far away.

May I believe God is bringing healing.

I will believe I am going to be delivered from my sorrow. I will trust the Lord is not far from me. I will believe I am going to recover from loss, sorrow, and grief.

Prayer: *May I believe God is not far from me. May I trust God to deliver me from my sorrow.*

Am I trusting God to stay near me? Am I being delivered from my sorrow?

Believing God's Salvation

My salvation will not be delayed.

—Isaiah 46:13

Salvation is the act of God coming to us where we are, in the depth of our loss, sorrow, and grief.

The promise is that God continues to move toward us, without hesitation, with no holding back.

But how do we know this is true? Doesn't it actually sometimes seem to be just the opposite, as though God is not only delaying, but staying far removed from us?

This can be a deceptive impression, especially if we are expecting God to come to us in specific ways, according to our wishes and desires.

If so, we will be disappointed.

We may even give up.

When, however, we look closely into the hidden places of our lives, where we generally would not expect God to be moving, more than likely we will be surprised by joy.

Let us expect the unexpected and we will see the salvation of God moving in our lives for our recovery.

May I believe God's salvation is moving in my life.

I will believe God is active in my life. I will trust God's help will not be held back. I will open my heart and be receptive to the help of the Lord.

Prayer: *May I trust God to help me through my sorrow. May I believe God does not hesitate to help me.*

Am I trusting God's salvation to help and to heal? Am I open and receptive to the help of the Lord?

Hearing and Learning New Things of God

From now on I will tell you of new things, of hidden things unknown to you.

—Isaiah 48:6

With loss, sorrow, and grief, there is the certainty that things are never going to be the same again.

And there is not any use trying to pretend otherwise.

We cannot return to yesterday, cannot fill yesterday's empty spaces.

Realizing this to be true, it is good to hear the promise: "From now on I will tell you of new things, of hidden things unknown to you."

This means we are in for new experiences.

This means life is going to be different for us from now on.

This means we will see and learn things we never knew before.

Recovery is not replacing what has been.

Recovery is learning new ways of dealing with ourselves.

Recovery is uncovering the hidden things of God, which we have not previously known.

Recovery is seeing and living a new way of life.

May I see and hear the new things of God.

I will believe the Lord has new things in store for me. I will let God lead me into new experiences of life and living. I will trust God to help me build a new life for myself.

Prayer: *May I be open to the leading of God. May I be ready to hear and learn a new way of life.*

Am I ready for God to show me something new? Am I ready to do something new with my life?

Growing through Affliction

I have tested you in the furnace of affliction.

—Isaiah 48:10

When we are seriously afflicted the question arises, Did God do this to me?

And if so, why?

We may believe God does this to people, particularly to those who are especially loved.

We may even believe we are being punished by God.

Regardless of what we believe about this, the truth is that the "furnace of affliction" always is present, always is painful, always is bringing out the best and the worst in us.

We find ourselves agreeing with those who say our most productive growth takes place as the result of affliction.

Why this is so, we don't really know.

However, during times of affliction we are able to discover more about life: Who we are. Who God is. What God can do.

It is in the furnace of affliction that the gifts of patience, faith, hope, and love are built.

The Lord is not afflicting or punishing us. The Lord is offering us the opportunity to grow.

May I grow in and through my afflictions.

I will believe the Lord is with me, not against me. I will trust God to take me through my affliction. I will thank God for being with me.

Prayer: *May I trust the Lord to be with me in my affliction. May I believe the Lord is going to see me through.*

Am I trusting God to be with me in my affliction? Am I believing the Lord is going to see me through my bereavement?

Drawing Near to God

Come near me and listen to this.

—Isaiah 48:16

We don't necessarily do what is best for ourselves.

For one thing, we may distance ourselves from God, closing ourselves off from the Word of God.

We also may refuse to listen, to hear what God is trying to say to us.

Recovery demands that we listen, that we make decisions and follow through.

While we can't do this in the early stages of our recovery, the time comes when we have to make some moves—that is, if we want to recover from our loss, sorrow, and grief.

The question is what to do.

And the answer is in our scripture for today. "Come near me and listen to this," says the Lord.

The Lord says: "Hear me and what I am trying to tell you. You are going to be all right. Because I am with you. Because I never will leave or forsake you."

When we draw near to the Lord and believe the promises, we are well on our way to being healed.

May I draw near to the Lord.

I will draw near to the Lord through prayer and meditation. I will listen for what God has to say to me. I will do what I am given to do.

Prayer: *May I draw near to the Lord. May I do what I am given to do.*

Am I drawing near to the Lord? Am I doing what God gives me to do?

Being Led by the Lord

I am the LORD your God . . . who directs you in the way you should go.

—Isaiah 48:17

When the children of Israel came out of Egypt they were led by God through Moses; they had no real idea where they were going.

Out of slavery into what?

Many complained because they couldn't see where they were being led.

Some even wanted to return to Egypt, saying that it was better for them back there, as slaves.

The way out of grief, into recovery, is to let God lead us through the darkened valleys and desolate places.

As with the children of Israel, we need someone to lead us.

The promise is that the Lord will lead us in the way we are to be going, which is the "best way" for us to be going with our lives.

At times this may be difficult to grasp, but we eventually can come to see that the way of the Lord is the better way for us; it is the way of healing and health.

Let us ask God to lead us.

May I ask the Lord to lead me.

I will ask the Lord to lead me. I ask the Lord to show me the way I am to be going. I will trust the Lord with my life.

Prayer: *May I trust the Lord with my life. May I let the Lord lead me.*

Am I asking the Lord to lead me through my afflictions? Am I allowing the Lord to show me the way through?

Being Sustained by the Lord

They did not thirst when he led them through the deserts.
—Isaiah 48:21

The ancient story about the children of Israel being given water from a rock in the wilderness is told over and over again.

It is told in order to remind each new generation that the Lord can be trusted to deliver new life.

This kind of reminder, this belief and faith, helps us through our difficult times.

We benefit greatly by remembering what the Lord has done in times past: how the Lord always has led people through desert places; how the Lord always has met our needs in the wildernesses of life.

The Lord is faithful and is able to quench our spiritual thirst for the "living water" of faith, hope, and love.

Jesus promises: "Whoever drinks the water I give him will never thirst."

Jesus is that "living water."

Jesus can minister to our deepest needs.

Jesus can help us along the way.

Jesus brings us into recovery from sorrow and grief.

May I believe the Lord will save me.

I will trust the Lord to quench the thirst of my loneliness. I will trust the Lord to lead me through my desert places. I will believe the Lord meets all my needs.

Prayer: *May I be led through the desert of my sorrow. May my thirst be quenched.*

Am I trusting God to quench my loneliness? Am I letting God lead me through this desert of my sorrow?

Using the Strength of God

My God has been my strength.

—Isaiah 49:5

Bereavement absorbs a lot of energy, sometimes leaving us in a weakened condition, feeling listless.

There can be a draining of physical, emotional, and spiritual energy.

During such times it can be difficult to think about recovery. Even "thinking" about recovery becomes painful.

We finally discover that strength has to come from the Lord, that we have little or none of our own.

We learn to put our trust in the Lord to give us strength, to help us bear our grief and surpass it, to regain our energy.

Understanding where strength comes from is important for our recovery.

Going to that source of strength is our daily privilege and task in recovery.

May we go to the Lord in prayer. May we ask God to restore us to life. May we believe that God will supply us with the strength that we need.

May I go to the Lord to find strength for my life.

I will go to the Lord for strength. I will trust the Lord to give me what I need to recover from my sorrow. I will renew my energy in the strength of the Lord.

Prayer: *May I have my energy renewed. May I find new strength in the Lord.*

Am I going to the Lord for strength? Am I allowing God to give me the strength I need to recover?

Trusting God's Faithfulness

The LORD, who is faithful, . . . has chosen you.
—Isaiah 49:7

There are gloomy times on the road to recovery, when we feel that we have been forgotten.

After the funeral or memorial service, when we try to get ourselves together to go on with our lives, there comes that sense of emptiness, of being in a void.

At such times it's helpful to affirm the promise: "The Lord who is faithful has chosen you."

"The Lord who is faithful" singles each one of us out.

"The Lord who is faithful" does not lose sight of us as individuals, with our own particular and personal needs.

Regardless of where we are, what we have done, or what has happened to us, the words of Jesus are true: "You did not choose me, but I chose you."

To know and believe that the Lord is faithful, that the Lord has chosen us, is to be strengthened in faith, hope, and love.

Let us trust the Lord.

For, "The Lord has chosen you."

May I trust the faithfulness of the Lord to be with me.

I will believe the Lord is faithful. I will believe the Lord has chosen me to be his own. I will trust the Lord to heal me.

Prayer: *May I believe the Lord has chosen me. May I trust the Lord to be faithful to me.*

Am I believing the Lord is faithful? Am I trusting the Lord to be with me?

Remembering What God Has Done for Us

In the day of salvation I will help you.

—Isaiah 49:8

Sometimes it is difficult to remember what the Lord has done for us.

We ask: "But what have you done for me lately?"

Looking back to our rough experiences we can see—if we really look—the salvation of the Lord helping and healing.

Eventually, in our recovery from loss, sorrow, and grief, we are able to see how God has reached into our lives in ways we never could have imagined possible.

Looking back we also note that there was a turning point, like a "day of salvation." Our eyes were opened to the mercies of God at work in our lives.

When we began to see things differently.

When we began to look at life more positively.

When our feelings began to change for the better.

When we began to take steps to move beyond loss, sorrow, and grief.

When we became alert to God's work in our lives.

When we saw how God had been helping us along the way.

May I be alert to God's helping hand.

I will be alert to the presence of God in my life. I will see how God has led me. I will thank God for helping me along the way.

Prayer: *May I be alert to God's salvation in my life. May I give thanks for the blessings of God.*

Am I seeing God's salvation for me and my life? Am I giving thanks for God's help and healing?

Being Led and Fed by the Lord

They will feed beside the roads and find pasture on every barren hill.

—Isaiah 49:9

There's something to be gained in every experience.

There's something upon which our souls can feed, and from which we can learn, even in times of loss, sorrow, and grief.

We can discover that in the most barren parts of our lives, where seemingly there is no food, no support, no life, God provides sustenance.

We begin to see that within these barren places there is food for our souls, for the uplifting of our spirits.

We begin to take an inventory of our lives and recovery, seeing little hints of progress, of getting better, of healing.

We begin to see that the Lord is leading and feeding us along the way.

Where everything was so heavy and hopelessly barren, we see how the Lord has reached out to us, with the promise of new life.

We begin to get a new taste of faith, hope, and love.

We begin to give thanks to the Lord for feeding us along the way.

May I see how the Lord is feeding me along the way.

I will trust the Lord to feed me along the way. I will believe the Lord is leading me. I will give thanks, for the Lord is good.

Prayer: *May I allow the Lord to lead me through my pain. May I allow the Lord to feed my spirit along the way.*

Am I allowing the Lord to lead me through my pain? Am I allowing the Lord to feed my hungry spirit?

Singing for Joy

Shout for joy, O heavens; rejoice, O earth; burst into song, O mountains.

—Isaiah 49:13

Have we permitted ourselves the healing that comes through music? Perhaps there are some favorite hymns we have laid aside?

It is good to sing. Even if we don't do it well. Even if we do it just for ourselves. The whole creation is urged to rejoice and be glad. "Shout for joy, O heavens; rejoice, O earth!"

There is something in each of us that is bigger than words can express. There is an urging to release ourselves from bondage, to turn our spirits loose, to open up, to ventilate our grief.

One might do this by singing, by shouting, or by exercising any spiritual gift. In all of us there is a song to be sung, even if we don't have adequate notes or musical talent to do it well.

How well we do it is of no consequence.

What's important is to find a way to open our hearts and spirits to the Lord in praise and thanksgiving.

Sing and shout for joy because the Lord is near. For the Lord heals our brokenness.

May I joyously open my heart to the Lord.

I will open my heart to the Lord. I will remember the mercies of the Lord given to me. I will sing for the joy of God's blessings.

Prayer: *May I open my heart to the blessings of God. May I sing for joy for the mercies of God.*

Am I opening my heart to the blessings of God? Am I ready to sing my praises with joy?

Receiving Comfort

The Lord comforts his people.

—Isaiah 49:13

Comfort is restful.

Comfort begins to come as we surrender our wills and our lives into the care and keeping of God.

Comfort comes quietly.

One day, in our recovery, there is a taste of comfort; and we begin to feel better.

With feelings of comfort there may also come a bit of guilt for feeling better.

As though we are forgetting the lost loved one.

"How can you feel better at a time like this?" we may ask ourselves.

And so, there may be a tendency to push comfort feelings aside, as being selfishly irreverent.

No matter.

The Lord fulfills the promise not to leave us comfortless.

However, it is up to us to recognize this gift of God and receive it with gratitude and thanksgiving.

May I gratefully accept the comfort of the Lord.

I will receive the comfort of the Lord. I will permit God to comfort me. I will give thanks to the Lord.

Prayer: *May I receive the comfort of the Lord. May I permit the Lord to bring comfort into my sadness.*

Am I willing to be comforted? Am I ready to receive the comfort of the Lord?

Living the Promise

I will not forget you.

—Isaiah 49:15

There's nothing quite like the feeling of being left out or left behind. And during times of bereavement it can feel just that way.

We may feel frightened and abandoned, as though even God has forgotten who we are.

As though God is gone.

In some cases friends may desert because of their own fears of death and dying.

The phone may not ring as often. And people don't drop in as once they may have done.

The one we can count on completely is the Lord who promises, "I will not forget you."

Repeating the promises of God to ourselves and others is a good way to start living them.

And living the promises, with trust in the Lord, is the way to healing and health.

Let us believe that the Lord is not going to forget us.

Let us believe that we will not be left behind and abandoned.

May I believe God is not ever going to forget me.

I will believe God is never going to forget me. I will trust God to stay with me. I will live my life on the promises of God.

Prayer: *May I trust God never to forget me. May I live my life on the promises of God.*

Am I believing God is never going to forget me? Am I living my life on the promises of the Lord?

Being Assured of God's Care

See, I have engraved you on the palms of my hands.
—Isaiah 49:16

"Does God really know where I am or care who I am?" Asked or unasked, these are questions that lurk in the recesses of our souls, especially when we experience loss and separation.

As God's people, we have our times of wondering: "Does God really care about me?"

In slavery, in prison, in exile, during shipwrecks, tornadoes, earthquakes, famine, sickness, and death the questions are asked: "Does God know me? Does God care about me?"

Difficult as they are to keep in mind during severe times, the promises of God are true.

The Lord has us engraved on the palms of his hands. We are part of the Lord, ever before him.

The Lord knows who we are. The Lord never forgets.

We can be assured of the Lord's care and keeping because Jesus keeps us ever before him, where we never are out of sight.

Jesus has promised, "I am with you always."

May I believe the Lord never loses sight of me.

I will believe the Lord never loses sight of me. I will trust the Lord always cares for me. I will give thanks to the Lord who never forsakes me.

Prayer: *May I believe God. May I believe that God never loses sight of me.*

Am I believing the promises of God? Am I believing the Lord never loses sight of me?

Taking Good Care

The children born during your bereavement will yet say in your hearing. "This place is too small for us; give us more space to live in."

—Isaiah 49:20

Taking care of ourselves is our first need and responsibility. Being self-centered and taking care of ourselves are not the same.

If we decide to hold on to our sorrow and enter into morbid grief, we become stifling to relatives, friends, and family.

Self-centeredness makes everything too narrow. Concentrating only on ourselves makes the living space for ourselves and others too small, and is not taking good care of ourselves.

Taking good care of ourselves is constructive, positive, and healing.

Taking good care of ourselves is accepting responsibility for our own health and healing.

Taking good care of ourselves is opening the windows of our hearts and souls.

Taking good care of ourselves is allowing some fresh air of hope, light, and love to enter the atmosphere of our grief and grieving.

Taking good care of ourselves is moving out of our self-centeredness into relationship, when we also are concerned for others, and make room for them.

May I open the windows of my life to others.

I will think of those around me. I will make room for them. I will open the windows of my life and let in new light.

Prayer: *May I take good care of myself. May I open the windows of life to others.*

Am I thinking of those around me? Am I opening the passages between myself and others, letting in the new light of love?

Answering a Question

Was my arm too short to ransom you?

—Isaiah 50:2

Is there something we know of that God cannot do? Do we sometimes feel that God cannot restore our lives from sorrow into joy?

In our darkened moods it seems as though nothing or nobody can ever really help us.

And sometimes we may choose to stay in a darkened place, for reasons of our own.

Sometimes it seems necessary, at least for a time, to pester ourselves with the thought that maybe we are beyond help, that nothing really can be done to redeem us from sorrow and grief.

At such times it can be helpful to consider the possibility that we may actually be choosing to stay in the darkened place.

Because, sometimes, this is true.

However, the Lord is ready to confront us: "Was my arm too short to ransom you?"

Let us think it over again.

Do we really believe God is unable to do for us what we cannot do for ourselves?

Or, are we choosing *not* to think about God's power to save?

May I believe God is able to help me.

I will believe God is able to help me. I will turn my life over to the care and keeping of God. I will give thanks to the Lord.

Prayer: *May I believe God helps me. May I trust the Lord to save me.*

Am I trusting the Lord to help me? Am I believing the Lord is here to lead me through my fear and my sorrow?

Believing the Power of God to Rescue Us

Do I lack the strength to rescue you?

—Isaiah 50:2

There is a question about power and deliverance.

When we are bereaved we may be asking, "Who has the power to deliver me from this agony of grief?"

To some the answer comes rather quickly, to others more slowly, and in some cases, maybe not at all.

However, as God's people we can look back over the centuries and see that the Lord has power to deliver us from any kind of bondage.

Certainly the Lord has strength to deliver us from the bondage of loss, sorrow, and grief.

Believing the power of God to deliver our lives from destruction is essential to our recovery. Believing the power of God to deliver us is vital for our spiritual growth and development.

"Do I lack the strength to rescue you?" is the question for each and every day.

"The Lord has strength to rescue you."

May I believe God has strength to rescue me from loss, sorrow, and grief.

I will believe the Lord has strength to rescue me. I will trust the Lord to deliver me. I will give thanks to the Lord for my deliverance.

Prayer: *May I trust God's strength to rescue me. May I trust God's love to save me.*

Am I believing the Lord has strength to rescue me? Am I trusting God for my deliverance?

Affirming What the Lord Is Doing

Because the Sovereign Lord helps me, I will not be disgraced.
—Isaiah 50:7

Sometimes, with bereavement, there comes a strange sense of having been disgraced. A person can feel shame, guilt, and a sense of being humiliated as though, without the lost loved one, we are no longer acceptable people.

But once we have experienced the help of the Lord in our deliverance from loss, sorrow, and grief, it is easier to go on.

Once we are able to say, "See what the Lord has done to help me," our lives take on more hopeful dimensions, and our recovery is strengthened.

Once we are convinced about help coming from the Lord, we are less confused and confounded about our lives, about our loss, and about the pain we are experiencing.

Let us say, "the Sovereign Lord helps me." Then we will be speaking truth to ourselves.

Let us say it out loud.

Let us hear with our own ears ourselves saying these words.

Let us also be ready to say it to others: "The Sovereign Lord helps me."

Let us recall the many ways the Lord helps us.

By so doing we will strengthen and hasten our recovery.

May I believe the Lord God is helping me.

I will believe the Lord is reaching out to help me. I will trust the Lord to help me. I will give thanks to the Lord for helping me.

Prayer: *May I trust the Lord to help me through my sorrow. May I be grateful for the help that is being given.*

Am I believing the Lord God is helping me along the way? Am I giving thanks for the help being given?

Facing the Accuser

Who is my accuser? Let him confront me.

—Isaiah 50:8

Sometimes it seems as though everything is going against us, if not "everything," then at least a lot of things. Our conscience may be accusing us of negligence in relation to the lost loved one, and we are stuck with feelings of guilt and remorse.

We may feel like running away from our "accuser," our lingering, pestering guilt and remorse. It is better to say, "Who is my accuser? Let him confront me."

Dodging the pain might seem to work for a while, but eventually it catches up with us. Then we pay the much heavier price of more deeply set emotional and spiritual confusion—of "unfinished business."

Not dealing with our pain can leave us with hidden stress and tension, resulting in physical, emotional, and spiritual complications including allergies, high blood pressure, digestive problems, and many other maladies.

Much better is it to face the conscience, the remorse and guilt, and address the pain. It is better to accept responsibility for whatever sins we may have committed, rather than dodging and running, rather than attempting to escape and hide.

The Lord is with us, and we have God's power to help us face our accuser because in Christ there is forgiveness.

May I face the pain of my conscience and deal with it.

I will face the pain of my conscience. I will not try to run away from it. I will believe the Lord forgives all my sins.

Prayer: *May I face my pain. May I believe the Lord is always with me in my sorrow, always forgiving my sins.*

Am I trying to escape the pain of my sorrow? Am I willing to forgive myself as the Lord forgives me?

Being Secure in Ourselves

I will not be put to shame.

—Isaiah 50:7

Not everyone suffering bereavement experiences sensations of shame. But there are those who do.

Particularly this is true when one has been very dependent upon the lost loved one.

Such persons sometimes feel as though they don't deserve to live, and even feel that others agree with them.

If you happen to have such feelings it's important to work on the feelings as soon as you are able.

We must remind ourselves that we are children of God who have value and worth.

We must remind ourselves that God loves us just the way we are.

We must remind ourselves that we have a right and duty to live, and to serve God.

It is important to get on with these reminders as soon as possible.

May I become secure about my value as a person.

I will believe I am God's child. I will not be ashamed of myself. I will serve the Lord by accepting myself as a child of God.

Prayer: *May I not be put to shame. May I accept myself as God accepts me, without shame.*

Am I being kind to myself? Am I accepting myself without shame?

Facing Each Other

Who then will bring charges against me? Let us face each other.
—Isaiah 50:8

Sometimes there are family squabbles and divisions—fear, anxiety, anger, resentment, and unfortunately, permanent breakdowns. People accuse each other of things done and left undone, and perhaps of thievery.

Of course, any breach in a family or between friends is painfully unhappy. It is unhappy because it needn't be—not if people stand before one another and try to work things out.

The worst thing we can do to ourselves is to stuff our feelings, thinking they will go away, together with the stress.

The next worst thing we can do is to hammer on our accuser(s), trying to get even with them for the pain caused.

Certainly we never help anyone by avoidance, by complaining, by talking behind someone's back, by trying to gain outside support for our position.

In one culture there is a tradition in which the family locks itself up together for seven days after the funeral to work things out with one another, to clear the decks. That's how important this matter of honestly facing each other should be taken.

May I face those with whom I have differences.

I will face those with whom I have differences. I will be honest, kind, and above-board with my feelings and concerns. I will listen to others who have differences with me.

Prayer: *May I be ready to settle differences with others. May I be ready to be forgiven and to forgive.*

Am I settling differences? Am I dealing with conflicts as directly as possible?

Believing God's Help

It is the Sovereign Lord who helps me.

—Isaiah 50:9

Does God really help us when we are in need, or is this something we say to ourselves?

There are days when we ask whether anyone really cares for us, days when it feels as though the bottom of everything has fallen out again, even though we thought we were beyond that point in our recovery.

There are days when we feel powerless, as though there is nothing we can do to help ourselves along the way.

These are days of severe darkness.

However, in and through the darkness we can see light—that is, if we are able to look.

We are able to see the light of God's power and love, ready to strengthen us for another day, ready to lead us along the way.

When we are feeling weak, and even helpless, it is important to say to ourselves, "It is the Sovereign Lord who helps me."

We will find this to be true.

The Lord helps us along the way.

May I believe the Sovereign Lord helps me along the way.

I will believe the Lord helps me along the way. I will trust the Lord to give me the help I need for this day. I will give thanks to the Lord for helping me.

Prayer: *May I allow God to help me along the way. May I give thanks to the Lord for helping me.*

Am I believing the Sovereign Lord helps me? Am I trusting the Lord to be with me today, to lead me along the way?

Walking by the Light of Our Fire

Walk in the light of your fires and of the torches you have set ablaze.

—Isaiah 50:11

We have spiritual resources. More than we know. We are urged to draw on these resources, affirming our faith in God. "Walk in the light of your fires and of the torches you have set ablaze."

Let us trust God, and the wisdom God has placed inside us. Let us believe the image of God that is in each of us, since the very beginning of the creation.

God has given all of us resources for recovery. But we have to look for them, affirm them, and put them to work. This is the task of recovery to which God has called us.

Let us believe our capacity to live our lives, with God's guidance. This is God's will, that we be all we can possibly be:

Free from the bondage of fear.

Free to love and be loved.

Free to serve and be served.

Free to be strong in the Lord and in his mighty power. Walking in the light of our fires and of the torches we have set ablaze.

May I walk by the light of my fire, the image of God in me.

I will believe the image of God dwells within me. I will go by the light of God that is given to me. I will trust myself to do what is best for me and my recovery from grief.

Prayer: *May I believe in God's power dwelling within. May I believe I am going to see my way through grief to recovery—the light of a new day.*

Am I trusting my own inner light, the image of God within me? Am I beginning to see the light of a new day for my life?

Remembering Where We Have Come From

Look to the rock from which you were cut and to the quarry from which you were hewn.

—Isaiah 51:1

It's important to remember we come from God.

Before we are anything else, we are children of God. We belong to God.

Christ is the rock from which we have been cut. God is the quarry from which Christ has been hewn.

We come from that quarry, from that rock, which is Christ.

We are part of the original creation; we are at the very heart of God. And our lives are hid with God in Christ.

We have an abundance of spiritual resources available to us—resources waiting to be recognized, uncovered, and put to work, resources for recovery to health and healing.

Therefore, let us turn to the Lord and to God's people to help us in our time of need. Let us remember who we are.

We are part of the eternal family of God, with all of its strength to heal. That is the rock from which we were cut. That is our strength.

God asks us to trust the rock from which we have been hewn.

May I remember who I am and where I have come from.

Am I trusting my relationship to the family of God? Am I trusting the resources that are mine for my health and healing?

Prayer: *May I remember my relationship to God in Christ. May I be confident about myself.*

Am I trusting my relationship to the family of God? Do I believe in myself, and God who dwells within me?

Trusting the Lord to Comfort Us

The LORD will surely comfort Zion and will look with compassion on all her ruins.

—Isaiah 51:3

Of course, there are days when we can hardly believe that things are going to get better.

There are days when it is difficult to see the hand of the Lord.

There are days when we cannot be easily comforted.

However, no matter what our circumstances, God is able to comfort us in our affliction—provided, of course, that we want to be comforted.

The promise is that God will comfort us just as God has comforted the family of God through the ages, in the most trying circumstances, under the most dreadful conditions.

In our bereavement we must believe God in order to heal.

Without faith in God we deteriorate emotionally, spiritually, and physically.

May we trust the Lord to heal and comfort us, turning what seem to be the ruins of our lives into new life, new hope, and new joy.

May I trust the Lord to comfort me.

I will trust the Lord to comfort me. I will believe the Lord is always with me. I will turn my will and my life over to the comforting will of God.

Prayer: *May I believe the Lord wants to comfort me. May I allow myself to be comforted by the Lord.*

Am I trusting the Lord to comfort me? Am I allowing myself to be comforted?

Being Remade into a Garden of God

The LORD . . . will make . . . deserts like Eden, . . . wastelands like the garden of the LORD.

—Isaiah 51:3

One day, in our bereavement, we begin to awaken.

We begin to see that indeed there is new life, and new feelings of hope—faint as they may be.

We begin to sense we are changing for the better.

We begin to feel some new excitement.

We begin to realize that we are getting a taste of new life, that a garden wants to grow in the deserts of our sorrow.

We are wanting to be made new.

We are sensing that God is bringing us into newness of life.

We see the Lord is turning the desert of our sorrow into joy.

Let us picture ourselves as a desert, where nothing is growing, where the pain of loss has left us empty, where there is no hope for new life.

Then let us picture a garden beginning to grow in that desert: new life where there was no life, new life coming into being like the dawn of a new day with beautiful, brightly colored plants, nurtured by God, the master gardener.

May I see the garden of the Lord growing in me.

I will believe the Lord is bringing forth new life in me. I will trust that God is able to make a garden grow in the deserts of my life. I will give thanks to God.

Prayer: *May I trust God for new life and growth. May I see the garden of God growing in my life.*

Am I trusting God to give me new life? Am I seeing the garden of God growing in the desert of my sorrow?

Trusting the Lord to Move and to Save

My righteousness draws near speedily, my salvation is on the way.

—Isaiah 51:5

There are times when everything seems to be going too slowly.

There are times when we are running out of patience with ourselves, with others, and with God.

Nevertheless, the promise is that the righteous salvation of the Lord is speedily drawing near to us, no matter how else it may seem, even though it may seem like an eternity in coming.

But, actually, God's salvation is never as slow as it seems. The Lord always is moving toward us with love, compassion, and eagerness to save.

The Lord is not being slow about this.

The salvation of the Lord isn't tempered or held back by the currents of the times, or by the reality of our loss and grief.

"My righteousness draws near speedily. My salvation is on the way."

May we believe this promise by living it with trust in God's faithfulness.

May I believe the Lord always is moving to save me.

I will believe the Lord always is drawing near to me. I will trust the Lord to save me. I will give thanks to the Lord for my salvation.

Prayer: *May I believe the goodness of the Lord is always moving toward me. May I trust God to save me.*

Am I trusting the Lord to save me? Am I believing the goodness of the Lord always is with me?

Believing the Lord's Unending Faithfulness

My salvation will last forever.

—Isaiah 51:6

In recovery things get better as the Lord works in us, toward our healing. But sometimes there is a problem.

We may be hesitant to accept the goodness of the Lord for fear that the goodness will desert us, leaving us abandoned and alone.

This is especially true when we have been deeply hurt by the sorrow of loss.

So we have to be reminded again that the salvation of the Lord is forever.

Does this mean we are never going to be hurt again, that we won't ever have to suffer the pain of loss once this is over? No, it doesn't mean that.

It means God will always be with us, not only in this experience of loss, but in all experiences that may come in the future. Therefore we need not fear the future because God's salvation is forever.

God does not recall, does not take back salvation.

It is important, for our recovery, to trust the faithfulness of the Lord. God is worthy of our trust.

May I believe the salvation of the Lord is forever.

I will believe the deliverance of the Lord is drawing near. I will trust the salvation of the Lord is forever. I will give thanks for the faithfulness of the Lord.

Prayer: *May I trust the salvation of the Lord. May I believe the unending faithfulness of the Lord.*

Am I trusting the Lord? Am I believing the Lord's salvation is forever?

Being Restored to Joy and Gladness

Gladness and joy will overtake them, and sorrow and sighing will flee away.

—Isaiah 51:11

This promise was given to people in captivity, in exile in a foreign land, when everything that had been near and dear to them was gone. All they were left with were their memories of home, of how it had been for them in happier days.

There was a longing for home.

There were deep feelings of sorrow.

It can be like that in bereavement when we have a taste of separation, similar to exile and captivity.

We remember how things were. We may wish for the opportunity to turn back the clock. But we can't.

There is deep sorrow, an absence of gladness and joy.

But the Lord promises that gladness and joy will return. This promise is true.

When the time comes, when we have been prepared to receive the gifts of gladness and joy, they are given.

May I trust the Lord to restore my life to gladness and joy.

I will believe the Lord is going to restore my life to gladness and joy. I will trust God to mend my broken heart. I will accept the gifts of God with thanksgiving.

Prayer: *May I believe the promises of God. May I believe God is going to restore me to gladness and joy.*

Am I trusting God to restore my life? Do I believe the Lord is going to bring me into gladness and joy?

Turning to the Lord for Comfort

I, even I, am he who comforts you.

—Isaiah 51:12

In times of affliction we all want to be comforted. Our hearts long for comfort.

But where does comfort come from?

There are many places we may look for comfort, only to discover that comfort can be illusive. Perhaps because we are looking in the wrong places.

We may look for comfort in alcohol and other drugs, and in dependency relationships.

We may expect other people to bring us comfort, only to discover that they, like ourselves, also are looking for comfort.

The truth is that everyone is looking for comfort. But where do we find comfort for our souls?

The only real and lasting comfort is in the Word and promises of God.

Only God is able to comfort us in all our afflictions.

Let us turn to the Lord for comfort because with the Lord there is lasting comfort.

May we accept the comfort of the Lord into our lives.

May I accept the comfort of the Lord into my life.

I will not cut myself off from the Lord. I will accept the comfort of the Lord into my life. I will give thanks to the Lord for comforting me.

Prayer: *May I look to the Lord for comfort. May I trust the Lord to bring comfort into my life.*

Am I allowing God to comfort me? Am I accepting the comfort of the Lord into my life?

Being Unafraid

Who are you that you fear mortal men?

—Isaiah 51:12

Every day we are reminded of something or someone to fear, including our own death and our own dying. We deal with it each day whether we know it or not.

Our scripture is almost a reprimand. It is as though the Lord is angry about our fearing anything or anyone, including our death and dying.

There is an old piece of advice which says, "Become friendly with your death, for therein do you find life." Or, "It is better to accept death for what it is and not be overcome by what it isn't."

Death is not the end of life. Rather, death is a transition to new life—just as the gospel teaches. Nevertheless, we find ourselves afraid of death. Afraid because separation can be dreadfully painful. And who needs more pain?

The last enemy, the apostle Paul says, is death. "But thanks be to God. Christ has given us the victory (over death) . . ." No longer need we be afraid of "man who dies," or of death itself. Now we can come to rest in the promises and power of God. "Death is swallowed up in victory."

May I not fear death and dying.

I will turn to the Lord in faith. I will believe there is no need to fear death and dying. I will give thanks to the Lord for my deliverance from fear.

Prayer: *May I turn to the Lord with trust and confidence. May I be relieved of all my fear.*

Am I willing to turn to the Lord for help? Am I turning to the Lord to be set free from fear?

Surrendering to the Power of God

I am the LORD your God, who churns up the sea so that its waves roar.

—Isaiah 51:15

Our perception of God, too often, is too small.

We forget the real power of God, with all its energy and capacity to do all things.

The writer of our scripture attempts to challenge us with the power of the Lord who makes the sea and the waves, so powerful is the Lord.

But there are even more powerful signs of God's power: persons being healed of sorrow and grief, seeing someone coming alive again in the spirit of God with joy and gladness, and newness of life.

That's more than the sea churning.

That's more than the greatest of all waves roaring against the shores.

As we continue in prayer and meditation we begin to know the healing power of God.

May I experience the power of God at work in my life.

I will remember the strength of the Lord my God. I will trust the Lord to fill me with power to overcome my sorrow. I will surrender my life to the Lord for release from fear.

Prayer: *May I surrender myself to the power of God. May I trust the Lord to release me from fear.*

Am I trusting the power of God to deliver me? Am I surrendering myself to the power of the Lord?

Being Hidden in God

I have . . . covered you with the shadow of my hand.
—Isaiah 51:16

What does this mean, that the Lord covers us with the shadow of his hand?

What about the millions of people who are homeless, starving, disease-ridden, hopeless, and dying in so many parts of the earth? Who knows?

And what about ourselves, when we lose a loved one? When we suffer the pain of separation, of loss? Who knows?

Where is the hand of God in our life to protect us from pain, anguish, and danger?

We cannot answer the question for anyone else.

We can only find our own answer as to what this promise means for us: "I have covered you with the shadow of my hand."

No one else can speak for us as to this reality.

However, if we are ready to look closely, we will be able to see the protective hand of the Lord in our lives.

The very fact that we are now reading these words, at this time in our lives, is a sign the Lord is with us. It is a sign our lives are hid with God in Christ, that we are in the process of being born again, daily and richly.

May I see that God protects and keeps me.

I will look for the protective hand of the Lord at work in my life. I will believe the Lord protects me. I will give thanks to the Lord for covering me with the shadow of his hand.

Prayer: *May I believe God is looking after me. May I trust the Lord to protect me.*

Do I believe God is looking after me? Am I trusting the Lord to protect me?

Being Awakened to the Strength of the Lord

Awake, awake, . . . clothe yourself with strength.
—Isaiah 52:1

To clothe ourselves with the strength of the Lord we must be awakened from spiritual sleep, from spiritual unconsciousness, from our blindness to God.

Especially when we are grief-stricken is this important. Especially then, when we need an abundance of strength.

We have to be awakened to the strength of the Lord that is available to us in the times of our distress.

We are like sleepwalkers, walking in darkness.

We are spiritually unconscious.

We are blind to God.

So someone has to awaken us. Someone has to say, so we can hear, "Awake, awake, clothe yourself with the strength of the Lord."

It is only with the Lord that we find what we need in order to heal.

It is only with the Lord that we find the strength to overcome our distress.

It is only with the Lord that we inherit the joy of our salvation from loss, sorrow, and grief.

May I be awakened to the strength of the Lord.

I will believe the Lord is the strength of my life. I will call upon the Lord to be my strength. I will use the strength the Lord provides.

Prayer: *May I become alert to the strength of the Lord. May I ask for strength to be given to me.*

Am I aware of the strength of the Lord for my life? Am I asking for that strength and using it day by day?

Willingness to Accept God's Gifts

Without money you will be redeemed.

—Isaiah 52:3

Recovery from sorrow and grief is deeply emotional. But most of all it is spiritual.

The only cost of our recovery, which we have to pay, is our willingness to participate in the process of healing—our willingness to enter our pain and, with God's help, to work it through.

The good news is we don't have to buy God off to get God to help us.

For God redeems "without money."

Also, there is no need to bargain with God, or to get ourselves in God's good graces.

The Lord freely lifts us when we are unable to stand.

The Lord freely carries us when we are too weak to walk.

All that is required is our willingness to be healed.

The Lord freely heals us.

May I accept the healing of the Lord without price.

I will believe the Lord is good. I will trust God to lift me up. I will give thanks to the Lord for every gift given.

Prayer: *May I believe God redeems my life. May I accept God's redemption without price.*

Do I believe God redeems my life without price? Am I willing to accept the gifts of God offered to me?

Being Surrounded by God

You will not leave in haste or go in flight; for the Lord will go before you, the God of Israel will be your rear guard.

—Isaiah 52:12

As we are working through our recovery with the help of the Lord, there is no good reason to hurry, to rush, to run.

With God as our protector we need not worry about what may be coming at us or catching up to us. We are encompassed by the love and protection of the Lord.

The imagery of our scripture is that of the Lord going before us and the Lord coming after us.

In other words, we are surrounded by the Lord.

This is an important vision to maintain—that of being enveloped by the Lord, of being completely protected. This gives no need to worry about being overwhelmed by circumstances beyond our control.

As the Lord led the children of Israel out of Egypt, and brought up the rear guard so as to protect them from all evil, so it is with us.

The Lord is ahead of us.

The Lord is behind us.

The Lord surrounds us.

We are in the safekeeping of the Lord.

May I believe I am in the safekeeping of the Lord.

I will believe I am in the safekeeping of the Lord. I will trust the Lord to protect me from all evil. I will give thanks to the Lord for protecting me.

Prayer: *May I trust the Lord to protect me. May I give thanks to the Lord for staying with me.*

Am I trusting the Lord to protect me? Am I giving thanks to the Lord for surrounding me with love?

Offering Up Your Sorrow

Surely he took up our infirmities and carried our sorrows.
—Isaiah 53:4

When we consider our own suffering it can be helpful to think about the suffering servant, Christ Jesus, our Lord.

It is through his suffering, on our behalf, that we begin to understand the depth of God's love for us.

When we see this great love, and realize it is given to us for our benefit, we cannot help but be grateful.

If we are not grateful it is because we have not yet seen the love, have not experienced it in our souls.

The Christ knows our sorrow and grief, our own very personal loss.

Christ is willing to receive this sorrow. Christ Jesus even asks us to offer up our suffering to him, so as to heal us.

By making an offering of our sorrow to Christ we begin to heal.

Christ walks with us through the dark valleys. Christ listens to our pain. Christ weeps with us.

Christ is able and eager to be our friend. Christ Jesus is ready to help us along the way of our recovery from loss, sorrow, and grief.

May I believe Christ is with me in my sorrow.

I will believe Christ is with me in my sorrow. I will trust the Lord to walk with me along the way. I will offer my grief into his care and keeping.

Prayer: *May I trust the Lord to walk with me along the way. May I offer my grief into the care and keeping of the Lord.*

Am I willing to turn my grief over to the Lord? Am I ready to let go of the pain of my sorrow?

Accepting God's Forgiveness

He was pierced for our transgressions, he was crushed for our iniquities; the punishment that brought us peace was upon him, and by his wounds we are healed.

—Isaiah 53:5

This scripture is not meant to make us feel ashamed or guilty. It simply is a statement of fact. Because of our condition of sin and separation there is pain and anguish, including the pain of loss, sorrow, and grief.

To recover from grief it is necessary to be honest with ourselves, with others, and to be honest above all with God.

There may be things we have done in relation to the lost loved one that we wish could be undone.

If this is the case, something has to be done, even when it seems too late.

We have to do something with the unfinished business, our shame, and our guilt.

We can't simply shovel guilt and shame under a rug. We can't hide the pain of it from ourselves or God.

We have to deal with the pain of our sins.

But we also are promised that the Lord takes all of our transgressions unto himself, and forgives us all our sins.

May I accept the forgiveness of my sins.

I will accept the forgiveness of God. I will believe my sins are forgiven. I will give thanks to the Lord.

Prayer: *May I believe my sins are forgiven. May I give thanks to the Lord for accepting and forgiving me.*

Do I believe my sins are forgiven? Am I giving thanks to the Lord for the forgiveness of my sins?

Extending Ourselves

Enlarge the place of your tent, stretch your tent curtains wide.
—Isaiah 54:2

One of the difficulties with bereavement is that it can turn us back into ourselves. Sometimes excessively.

Being hurt is frightening, and nobody wants to get hurt again. For this reason we may close the windows and doors of our inner selves and hide.

However, the time comes when we must make a move, make decisions we may not want to make: decisions to extend ourselves, decisions to reach out, to touch others, decisions to relate to those around us, and decisions to dream new dreams.

To recover from our sorrow we must do as this scripture urges: Enlarge our inner life and stretch out with new hope to inherit the kingdom that Christ has prepared for us—the kingdom of life, of love, of joy.

All of this can sound like a lot of words, and nothing more. Especially if our sorrow has deepened over the weeks and months. Nevertheless, the Lord asks us to enlarge, to expand our lives.

To do this we must rest our faith in the Word and promises of God that new life and hope are possible. Then we are able to expand our vision of life in order to heal.

May I open my life to the light of God's promise and hope.

I will open my life to the light of God. I will extend myself outward. I will come out of my shell to inherit new life and hope in Christ.

Prayer: *May I reach out to inherit the kingdom of life, love, and joy. May I dare to hope.*

Am I extending myself outward? Am I daring to hope new life is being offered to me?

Investing Ourselves Completely in Life

Do not hold back; lengthen your cords, strengthen your stakes.
—Isaiah 54:2

The theme for today is an extension of the one yesterday: "Do not hold back," we are told.

Let us invest ourselves in new life, new hope, and new joy.

Lengthening the outreach of our lives, like lengthening the cords of a tent, results in more strength, more capacity to hold against the wind and the storms of life.

"Drive your stakes deeper"—the stakes of faith. This is the conviction that life itself, for its own sake, is worth the effort—as is the willingness to live life with all possible vigor.

In the midst of loss and pain the Lord says, "Do not hold back on your investment in life. Do not hesitate to live vigorously."

It is better to invest our lives than to hold back and simply wither away.

The Lord urges us to press on with our lives, not just endure, to invest, to gain strength, to drive our stakes deeper, to lengthen the ropes of our tents with no holding back.

May I invest myself completely in new life.

I will invest myself in new life. I will not hold back on anything the Lord gives me to do. I will not allow my life to waste away.

Prayer: *May I never hesitate to give life all of myself. May I not allow my life to waste away.*

Am I allowing my life to waste away? Am I hesitating to give myself to the Lord and to life?

Being Unashamed

Do not be afraid; you will not suffer shame.

—Isaiah 54:4

With bereavement there also comes an amount of fear—fear of the past, the present, and the future. Sometimes, there is the fear of trying to do something that needs to be done, the fear of failure and the fear of shame.

Losing a loved one can result in some feelings of shame.

We may feel unacceptable; feel others are looking at us in different ways than before.

No longer are we the wife of, the husband of, the child of, or the parent of. Now we may be a widow or widower, or orphaned or childless. We feel alone and different.

Under such circumstances, going out in public, to groups, even to church, can be difficult.

We may feel naked and stripped; unable to handle the pressure.

The Lord admonishes us: "Do not be afraid, you will not suffer shame."

It's important for us to move out into the world, if at all possible, though we may feel stripped and afraid.

Remembering, when we do, that the Lord is with us.

May I not be ashamed of myself or afraid to be who I am.

I will trust the Lord to be with me. I will move out of myself toward others. I will believe the Lord gives me the strength I need.

Prayer: *May I believe the Lord is with me. May I not try to hide myself from others.*

Am I willing to risk? Am I ready to share myself with others?

Being Called by the Lord

The LORD will call you back.

—Isaiah 54:6

During difficult times there can be hope when we understand who it is that is calling us into relationship, into oneness. It is the Lord Christ himself.

This is the promise, the reality that can overcome feelings we talked about yesterday, including shamefulness.

We are children of the Lord. Our Baptism into Christ is a sign of this reality, this truth.

We belong to the Lord. And, when we believe this to be true, we experience a sense of purposefulness, a deep reason to go on with our lives.

We need not be trapped by the past, for the Lord has called us beyond what is past.

We need not feel trapped by the present, because the Lord walks with us through all of our trials and tribulations.

We need not fear the future, because the Lord goes before us.

Forsaken and grieved in spirit, though we may be, the Lord continues to call us out of ourselves into new life, new hope, and new joy.

May I believe it is the Lord who calls me.

I will believe the Lord has called me into relationship. I will believe the Lord has called me in love. I will serve the Lord with gladness.

Prayer: *May I believe the Lord has called me. May I serve the Lord with gladness.*

Do I believe the Lord has called me? Am I ready to serve the Lord with gladness?

Being Willing to Be Brought Back

With deep compassion I will bring you back.

—Isaiah 54:7

It is not just that the Lord has called us, but also that the Lord brings us back with deep compassion, with everlasting love.

It isn't like going to a party where we really are not wanted, or like being an unhappy burden to someone.

With great compassion Jesus comes to our tombs, and the tombs of our loved ones, knowing it is our time to hurt and to weep.

The Lord brings us back to himself, to comfort us in our affliction.

The problem can be that we may not be ready or willing to see the compassion of the Lord, much less accept it into our sorrowfulness, into our grief. That's all right, too. The Lord waits patiently, with deep compassion, for us to become ready to be brought back.

There is a saying, "We're ready when we're ready." And that's true. That's the way recovery works.

There's nothing we can do until we are ready to do it.

The Lord compassionately wants to bring us back, to heal us—when we are ready.

May I be entirely ready to be brought back by the Lord and healed.

I will remember the Lord loves me. I will accept the compassion of the Lord. I will allow the Lord to bring me back.

Prayer: *May I allow the Lord to bring me back. May I accept the compassion of the Lord.*

Am I willing to allow the Lord to bring me back? Am I ready to accept the compassion of the Lord into my life?

Believing and Building

O afflicted city, lashed by storms and not comforted, I will build . . . your foundations.

—Isaiah 54:11

"What is there that can ever take the place of my sorrow?" Seemingly nothing.

That's the way grief feels. It feels as though there is nothing left, nothing to fill the emptiness, nothing to fill the void.

The Lord promises to build a new foundation for our lives that is precious, that we will cherish, and in which we will rejoice.

If we are having any difficulty being comforted in our affliction, it's important to know God's intention for us, to know the Lord has something in store for us we never imagined possible. New life. New hope. Even some new joy.

Deep and lasting joy.

Foundational and supporting joy.

But to receive the gifts of the Lord, we must first believe the promises as in our scripture for today.

The Lord is faithful. The promises of the Lord are true.

A new foundation is ready to be installed in our lives, a precious foundation of love, hope, and joy.

May I build new life on God's foundation.

I will believe God is able to set my life on a new foundation of hope. I will trust God to provide me with what I need to recover from my sorrow. I will be glad in the Lord.

Prayer: *May I find my gladness in the Lord. May I rest my life on the foundation of the Lord.*

Am I allowing God to give my life new foundations? Am I finding gladness in the Lord my Savior?

Drinking Fresh Water

Come, all you who are thirsty, come to the waters.
—Isaiah 55:1

The "waters" of spiritual refreshment are here for anyone who makes a decision to "come" and drink of God's refreshing spirit.

The invitation rests on the word *come* by which action we declare we want the help and healing of the Lord.

Help and healing can only be experienced by those who desire these gifts of God. If there is no desire to recover from grief, there can be no help. While this may seem like hard love, it actually is the essence of real love: the readiness of God to give help where help is sought.

A blind man called out to Jesus for help. Jesus asked him what he wanted.

Jesus already knew what the man wanted. But our Lord knew how important it was for the blind man to say, for himself, "Lord! I want to see."

Likewise, health and healing depends upon our willingness to come to the fresh waters of God's spirit.

It only is by our "coming" to the wells that the Lord is able to quench our thirst and give us new life—life that never ends.

May I come to the fresh waters of the Lord for my healing.

I will seek the Lord. I will go to the fresh waters of the Lord for my healing. I will trust the Lord to heal my broken heart.

Prayer: *May I go to the Lord to be blessed. May I be healed by the Lord's power to heal.*

Am I seeking the fresh water of God for quenching my spiritual thirst? Am I going to the fresh waters of God to be healed?

Coming to the Lord with Empty Hands

You who have no money, come, buy and eat.

—Isaiah 55:1

How can one buy if one has no money, much less eat what one supposedly has not purchased?

With bereavement there can be the sense of having been wiped out. To be bereft is to have the sense of being deprived, even ruthlessly. Deprived of life, hope, and joy. Made desolate. Without resources to recover by our own reason or strength.

It is to grieving people that God comes with the invitation to heal, with the invitation to be filled and satisfied with the things of God, with God's healing spirit.

It's not like having to go to a temple with an offering in order to gain God's attention.

In fact, there is no such requirement at all.

"Nothing in my hand I bring" is the key to the door of God's grace.

We come with empty pockets, empty purses, and empty hearts. God fills us with new life, with new hope, and new joy.

May I go to the Lord to receive food for my soul.

I will go to the Lord for my healing. I will trust God to mend my broken heart. I will receive the goodness of the Lord without price.

Prayer: *May I receive the goodness of the Lord without price. May I trust the Lord to refresh my soul.*

Do I believe the Lord is ready to refresh my soul? Am I willing to go to the Lord empty-handed to receive the gift of healing?

Eating the Good Food of the Spirit

Listen, listen to me, and eat what is good.

—Isaiah 55:2

There are decisions to be made, and not any of them too easy.

Some decisions are very difficult.

What to do with this and that? What to keep? What to sell? What to give away? Where to stay? Where to go next?

But after a while, we come to understand that what we need most of all is to listen to God. To hear the voice of the Lord, be it ever so quiet.

We must listen carefully, and quietly, allowing God to do the talking, giving direction for our lives.

And we must fervently seek that which is good, that which is of God.

In so doing we find rest for our souls.

We must "eat" what God prepares, what God lays on the spiritual table before us.

It is in eating God's food of the Spirit, in digesting the goodness of God, that we find rest for our souls.

Recovery from sorrow and grief is a spiritual journey.

Recovery takes time and requires patience and, above all, trust in God's ability to heal us.

May I eat the good food of the spirit.

I will listen carefully for the voice of God. I will seek to eat the spiritual food of God. I will trust the Lord's goodness to heal me.

Prayer: *May I trust the Lord's goodness to heal me. May I eat the spiritual food given by the Lord.*

Am I going to the Lord for what is good? Am I eating the good food of God's spirit?

Inclining to the Lord

Give ear and come to me; hear me, that your soul may live.
—Isaiah 55:3

To "give ear" means to focus our attention, to lean forward and concentrate on another, to activate one's self in a particular direction.

To listen in this way is to be ready for change.

To heal, our tangled emotions and disrupted spirits must be attended to.

To heal, we must be put together in a new and different way. Because, there is an empty place.

To heal, we must be changed.

To be changed we must be led, must hear a voice other than our own . . . in order to be healed.

To be healed we must activate ourselves toward the Lord, because healing is a gift from God.

Recovery comes when we are inclined toward the Lord, when we are bowed in meekness and surrender before the healing power of God. Cupping our ear, as it were. Listening very carefully for every word that comes from the Lord who says, "I will not leave you comfortless, I will come to you."

May I give ear and come to the Lord.

I will give ear and come to the Lord. I will listen carefully to the Lord. I will wait for the Lord to lead me.

Prayer: *May I listen for the voice of the Lord. May I hear the leading of the Lord.*

Am I going to the Lord in prayer? Am I listening for the voice of the Lord to lead me along the way?

Seeking the Lord

Seek the LORD while he may be found.

—Isaiah 55:6

There are some things we simply must do for ourselves if we are to recover from loss, sorrow, and grief.

Not only is there the need to wait patiently for the Lord to speak and to move in our lives, but we also must make a decision to go to the Lord—to ask, to seek—in order to find help for our souls.

Also, there is a need for spiritual habits, such as daily prayer and meditation, seeking the Lord.

Without spiritual practice our inner life loses its strength, like unexercised muscles.

Without spiritual exercises such as prayer, meditation, and service, life hardens and loses its resiliency.

Without a healthy spiritual life it is virtually impossible to recover from loss, sorrow, and grief.

The Lord is always available to all who seek.

It is a simple truth that when we seek the Lord, we find healing.

May I seek the Lord and find healing.

I will seek the Lord to find healing. I will pray and meditate on the promises of God to heal me. I will trust God to heal me.

Prayer: *May I trust God to heal me. May I seek the Lord through prayer and meditation day by day.*

Am I seeking the Lord to find my healing? Am I praying and meditating to stay spiritually strong in order to heal?

Calling Upon the Lord for Strength

Call on [the LORD] while he is near.

—Isaiah 55:6

Have we ever doubted the nearness of God? If we are like most folks, we have experienced such doubts.

In bereavement the Lord can seem far away from us, as though we were standing in absolute empty space, with no one near.

It's important to sense the nearness of God—especially when we are suffering bereavement.

There are times when this conviction of God's closeness doesn't come through—times when we feel as though God never will be close to us again. But all of this changes once we begin calling on the name of the Lord.

Calling on the name of the Lord is God's invitation to all of us. It's OK to call when we are in trouble. In fact that is one of the better times to call on the Lord—when we are really hurting.

It is important to get into the habit of seeking the Lord through prayer and meditation. By so doing we build our spiritual muscles so as to grow strong in the Lord.

May we call upon the Lord and be made strong.

May I call upon the Lord and be made strong.

I will call upon the Lord. I will trust the Lord to be with me. I will give thanks to the Lord for making me strong.

Prayer: *May I call upon the Lord to be with me. May I call upon the Lord to make me strong.*

Am I calling upon the name of the Lord? Am I asking the Lord to make me strong?

Believing that God Knows Best

My thoughts are not your thoughts.

—Isaiah 55:8

When we call on the name of the Lord, we begin to learn things we never knew before. We learn that the Lord doesn't think the way we think. We learn that the thoughts of God are not our thoughts.

For instance, we may think of our bereavement as being "bad" because it hurts so much. However, it's in the midst of our sorrow that we are most likely to see the reality of God and deeper aspects of life. The Lord may say, "That's good." Painful as it is, "That's good."

Experience teaches that many memorable and "good" things that happen to us come through pain—including the anguish of loss, sorrow, and grief.

One of the best things we can do for ourselves when suffering bereavement is to take it for granted that God's thoughts are not the same as our thoughts. We should also remember that the thoughts of God are better than our thoughts, more directed toward our health and healing.

God knows what is best for us, and God will do what is best.

May I believe God knows what is best for me.

I will believe the Lord knows what is best for me. I will trust that what is happening is for my own good. I will wait for the Lord to teach me.

Prayer: *May I understand that God's thoughts are not my thoughts. May I trust that what is happening to me is for my own good.*

Do I trust that what is happening to me is for my own good? Do I believe the Lord knows what is best for me?

Going God's Way

Neither are your ways my ways.

—Isaiah 55:8

Yesterday we said God's thoughts are not our thoughts, and today we say that our ways are not God's ways.

This is important to understand and affirm.

God's way is not the way of frenzy, fear, and anxiety.

God's way is the way of trust, of faith, hope, and love.

In our bereavement we can get lost along the way—lost in our pain and sometimes in our self-centeredness.

We worry that nothing but more pain is coming our way.

Our way is to draw back, to recoil, to escape. The way of God is to enter, to accept, to forgive, to release.

In our time of recovery it can be helpful to remind ourselves that God knows the way, that God's ways are not our ways.

God *is* the way.

It makes all the difference to know this and to affirm the ways of God, to walk the path of recovery under the guidance of the Lord.

May I turn myself over to God's way for my life.

I will seek to go God's way with my life. I will believe the way of God is better for me than my own ways. I will seek the ways of peace, joy, love, and ever-growing hope.

Prayer: *May I seek God's way for my life. May I believe the way of God is better than my way.*

Do I believe God's way is better than my way? Do I believe God knows what is best for me and my life?

Seeing the Better Way

As the heavens are higher than the earth, so are my ways higher than your ways and my thoughts than your thoughts.

—Isaiah 55:9

We are considering the thoughts and the ways of God as being not our thoughts or our ways.

How much better is our life with God than without God?

Our scripture for today spells it out: much better indeed, because God is far ahead of us. God knows much more about us than we know about ourselves. God knows the best way for us to be going in our recovery.

However, we don't always want to go along with the reality that God actually knows all that much about our situation, about our sorrow and pain.

Sometimes, however, we hang on to old fears, old resentments, old sorrows, and old self-pity. To find our way through bereavement it is to our best advantage to turn to God rather than to the old self-centered self.

For God's ways are higher than our ways, and God's thoughts are higher than our thoughts.

God knows better than we what is best for us.

May I believe God knows what is best for me.

I will believe God's ways are better than my ways. I will believe God's thoughts are higher than my thoughts. I will believe God knows what is best for me.

Prayer: *May I trust the way of the Lord for my life. May I see the way of the Lord for my life.*

Am I trusting the ways of God for my life? Am I ready to think the thoughts of God for my recovery?

Receiving What Is Given

My word] will not return to me empty, but will accomplish what I desire and achieve the purpose for which I sent it.

—Isaiah 55:10-11

"As the rain and the snow come down from heaven, and do not return to it without watering the earth and making it bud and flourish, so that it yields seed for the sower and bread for the eater, so is my word."

God has an investment in us and our recovery from sorrow. God provides us with the nourishment we need to become whole again.

Whatever God sends in our direction to quench our spiritual thirst is like new rain and snow upon the earth.

Not always do we readily appreciate, much less understand, the gifts of God as being good for us. Sometimes the rain feels like ice, the snow like fire.

However, if we stay with the promises of God we eventually see the nature of the gifts that the Lord bestows upon us, and why some of them are particularly painful; they are helping our spiritual growth and development.

Healing is this way.

Healing doesn't come all at once, nor does it come in ways we might want it to come. But healing does come because the word of the Lord never returns empty.

May I be willing to receive the gifts of God as they are given.

I will receive the gifts of God as they are given to me. I will believe the promise of God that I am going to heal. I will accept the blessings of God as they are offered for my healing.

Prayer: *May I seek the will of God to be done in my life. May I receive what God offers for my healing.*

Am I believing God? Do I believe I am going to heal?

Knowing Joy and Peace

You will go out in joy and be led forth in peace.

—Isaiah 55:12

There are promises we want to believe even when we can't quite bring ourselves to really believe them.

Certainly we would like to "go out in joy." Certainly we want to be "led forth in peace."

However, the fact is that when we are feeling down, when we are depressed in spirit, when our heart is breaking, it is difficult to see the promises of God coming true for us now or in the future.

But let us remember that the promises of God were given to people who were confronted with deep and serious problems; people suffering profound loss of loved ones, of all their possessions, of their freedom.

God's promises are always directed at the pits of our sorrow and suffering.

"You will go out in joy and be led forth in peace."

It is important to hear this promise and meditate upon it.

It is vital to believe the promise, not in order to escape suffering, but rather as a way through the pain, in order to transcend it.

May I believe I will know joy and peace in my life.

I will believe I will know joy and peace in my life. I will trust the promises of God. I will allow the Lord to lead me through my pain.

Prayer: *May I allow the Lord to lead me through my pain. May I know joy and peace in my life.*

Am I allowing the Lord to lead me through my pain? Do I believe I will know joy and peace?

Recovering into Joy

The mountains and hills will burst into song before you, and all the trees of the field will clap their hands.

—Isaiah 55:12

Today's scripture is a takeoff on, an expansion of yesterday's thoughts of promised joy and peace.

This promise includes the entire creation, which gives us another dimension of hope.

Like Isaiah, Paul the apostle also speaks of the whole creation being in "birth pains" as it waits for God to save. Particularly from the visions of prophets before him, Paul picks up the conviction that God is doing a mighty work of which all of us are a part because we actually belong to the creation itself.

Yes, there is sorrow and pain and deeply felt loss. But there is much more.

There is joy in the reality of our healing. Joy in the mending and rebirth of our spirits. Joy in our unity with the entire creation, for the celebration of God's gifts.

If this sounds strange to us right now, even impossible, let us put the promise somewhere in the recesses of our hearts and minds. And let us see, one day, if we don't actually come alive with joy, even with a bit of singing and clapping.

May I trust the Lord for my recovery into joy.

I will believe the Lord is leading me toward experiences of joy. I will trust God to lift my spirit. I will give thanks to God for my recovery from grief.

Prayer: *May I believe I am going to recover from my sorrow. May I find my joy in the Lord.*

Do I believe I am going to recover from sorrow? Am I beginning to find some joy in the Lord?

Surrendering to the Lord

Instead of the thorn bush will grow the pine tree, and instead of the briers the myrtle will grow.

—Isaiah 55:13

Is it a fact that the thorns of life can be replaced by something better, something not so piercingly painful?

Remember Paul the apostle who spoke about his "thorn in the flesh" that was not removed even though, at least three times, he prayed to have it taken away.

The answer Paul was given is a promise: "My power is made perfect in weakness." By not removing the thorn in Paul's flesh, whatever it was, the Lord left him with something greater.

Paul discovered that when he was surrendered to the will of God for his life that he could say, "When I am weak—when I am surrendered to God's way and will—then I am strong." And this belief carried him through the rest of his life.

Paul's experience with his affliction was a spiritual experience known as surrender. True healing actually begins here, when death is replaced by life.

May I surrender my will and life to God's care and keeping.

I will surrender my will and my life into the care and keeping of God. I will trust God to deal with the thorns. I will believe God is going to supply all my needs, that I will experience joy.

Prayer: *May I believe God is more powerful than thorns. May I trust God to supply all my needs.*

Do I trust God to deal with my deepest pain and sorrow? Do I believe the Lord will be with me all the way?

Being for God's Renown

This [salvation] will be for the LORD'S renown, for an everlasting sign.

—Isaiah 55:13

The "everlasting sign" is the recovery of God's people, the building of faith, hope, and love.

This is to the "renown" of God, the very proof, if you will, that God is active in the world, and in our lives.

When we watch the process of recovery unfold in ourselves and others, we can see there is a power greater than ourselves involved.

That power is God.

Think of it this way. Everything really is against us when we suffer loss. Everything has been thrown back upon us.

It doesn't feel as though we are going to make it through the dark valleys.

However, we look around and see that others have come through and recovered.

We begin to see the hand of God at work in the world, with other people who have suffered loss.

The Lord's greatest renown is in the healing of God's people, including our healing.

May I have faith in God's power to save and to heal.

I will believe God's power to save. I will be healed for the renown of God's power. I will believe God never forsakes me.

Prayer: *May I be healed for the renown of God's healing power. May I heal and give all glory to God.*

Am I ready to believe God is able to do for me what I cannot do for myself? Am I ready to be healed for the renown of God's healing power?

Looking for God's Salvation

My salvation is close at hand.

—Isaiah 56:1

Impatience can be a very real problem for our recovery. Also, if we are particularly depressed of spirit there is the feeling that this is the way it is going to be for a long time to come, which can be very discouraging.

In this regard God's promise is always the same: salvation is on the way and it's coming soon. Maybe not the kind of salvation we want but certainly the salvation we need.

Always the salvation of the Lord is in process.

If we look for God's salvation, we will see the pieces of a broken humanity being brought together.

Always the Lord is moving toward us and in us, bringing salvation, establishing our recovery.

Let us take time to look for the saving activity of the Lord in our lives. Let us look into the hidden and quiet places, because that is where we will find God's salvation, always at work.

Let us believe the promise: "My salvation is close at hand."

Let us not be impatient.

Let us wait on the Lord.

Let us see the salvation of the Lord working in our lives.

May I see the salvation of the Lord at work in my life.

I will believe the salvation of the Lord. I will believe the Lord is at work in my life. I will trust God to restore my soul.

Prayer: *May I believe the Lord is at work in my life. May I trust God to restore my soul.*

Do I believe the Lord is at work in my life? Am I trusting the Lord to restore my soul?

Building Up and Preparing the Way

Build up, build up, prepare the road.

—Isaiah 57:14

Taking responsibility for our own lives and recovery is essential; we must say, "This I must do for myself. For this I am responsible. If I want to recover my life, I must make some moves."

Making our own moves doesn't mean that we do it apart from the leading of the Lord, or without trusting the Lord to be with us.

Making our own moves means that we affirm our faith that God will give us the wisdom and strength needed to build our recovery.

The best way to "build up," to "prepare the road" for the Lord, and for decision making, is through prayer and meditation.

When we come before the Lord in quiet expectation, we are not disappointed because the Lord is always ready to guide and direct us.

Another way to "build up and prepare the road" is to be attentive to the promises of God to restore us to new life, new hope, and new joy.

Let us recall the promises of God. Let us prepare the road for the Lord to come into our lives to guide and direct us.

May I prepare the way of the Lord.

I will prepare the way of the Lord through prayer and meditation. I will trust the Lord to be with me. I will accept the salvation of the Lord into my recovery from sorrow.

Prayer: *May I prepare the way of the Lord in my life. May I do this each and every day.*

Am I preparing the way of the Lord in my life? Am I doing this day by day?

Removing Obstacles

Remove the obstacles out of the way of my people.
—Isaiah 57:14

The desire of the Lord is for every obstacle to be removed, every hindrance that would prevent us from relating to God. The desire of the Lord is for us to be set free from all that would keep us encased in sorrow.

The obstacles to rebirth are many and varied: self-will, fear, anger, resentments, self-pity, self-centeredness, hopelessness, depression. These are some of the obstacles to recovery. How can they be removed?

One thing we learn about internal obstacles is that none are removed until we become willing for them to be removed.

Becoming God-centered is essential if we want to recover. This is where spiritual practice comes in.

We have to practice being God-centered. Becoming God-centered requires willingness, time and attention, meditation and prayer—on a daily basis, one day at a time.

God is waiting for us to remove all obstacles that separate us from our recovery into faith, hope, and love.

God waits to give us these gifts, when we are ready and willing to receive them.

May I be ready and willing to remove all obstacles.

With God's help I will remove all obstacles to healing. I will open myself to the gifts of God. I will be filled with faith, hope, and love.

Prayer: *May I open myself to the gifts of God. May I be filled with faith, hope, and love.*

Am I removing all that would separate me from God? Am I opening myself to the gifts of God?

Having a Humble and Contrite Heart

Revive the spirit of the lowly and . . . the heart of the contrite.

—Isaiah 57:15

What does it take to recover from loss and grief?

Some believe recovery demands a lot of willpower; actually, the opposite is true.

Recovery is spiritually based, which means our spirits have to be revived, even reborn.

This requires humility rather than willpower.

It requires willingness to have God's Spirit fill us with needed faith and courage in order to transcend our loss, sorrow, and grief.

We must have a contrite heart to see, accept, and confess our wrongs—not only those we have done to others, but also the wrong we have done to ourselves.

A lowly spirit and contrite heart mean being honest with ourselves, with others, and with God.

With a contrite heart, we are able to accept the goodness of God's forgiveness, which leads to healing and health.

May I have a lowly spirit and a contrite heart.

I will accept myself the way I am. I will trust God to accept me the way I am. I will ask God to give me a lowly spirit and contrite heart.

Prayer: *May I have a lowly spirit and contrite heart. May I be open and receptive to the Lord.*

Am I praying to be open and receptive to the Lord? Am I praying for a lowly spirit and a contrite heart?

Offering Our Brokenness

I will heal [you].

—Isaiah 57:18

The emphasis is on the one who does the healing of our souls, who mends our broken hearts.

While we must accept responsibility for our lives and the way we live them, our healing comes from the Lord who says, "I will heal."

We cannot heal ourselves. The blind cannot lead the blind.

Our help must come from the Lord.

Knowing this can bring relief from feelings of hopelessness.

There is something we can do with our brokenness. We can offer it to the Lord.

Offering our brokenness to God is not the same as quitting or giving up. Rather, it is deliberately doing something positive for ourselves, putting things where they belong so that good can result.

Each day, for the rest of our lives, it will be helpful to make this offering: "Dear Lord, I offer my brokenness to you. My broken heart. My sorrow. The pain of my soul."

Let us give ourselves to the Lord and believe the promise: "I will heal you."

May I offer my brokenness to the Lord to heal.

I will believe the promises of God. I will trust God to heal me. I will give myself over to God's care and keeping.

Prayer: *May I give myself over to God's care and keeping. May I surrender my brokenness to the Lord to heal.*

Am I living in the promises of God to heal? Am I offering my brokenness to the Lord to heal?

Breaking Forth Like the Dawn

Then your light will break forth like the dawn, and your healing will quickly appear.

—Isaiah 58:8

In our recovery there sometimes come experiences of transcendence, when we are lifted above the problems of the day, including our sorrow and pain.

It is like new light breaking forth, like the dawn of a new day.

And even though the sensation goes away, we want to remember how it felt, how at peace we were with ourselves, with others, and with God.

We feel as though we belong, that we are healing, that everything is not only all right, but is precisely as it is meant to be.

Somewhere in our recovery we begin to taste the goodness of God's promises being fulfilled.

The Lord promises new light to dawn in our lives, and healing to come speedily (which doesn't necessarily mean right now—or tomorrow—or the next day).

Speedily means when we are ready, when our souls have been prepared, when it is our time to be healed.

May I trust God for light to break forth in my life.

I will believe God is at work in me. I will look for the new light of God in my life. I will trust God to heal me.

Prayer: *May I believe the promises of God. May I expect new light and healing to come to me.*

Am I believing the promises of God? Am I expecting new light and healing to break forth into my life?

Crying to the Lord Who Answers

Then you will call and the LORD will answer.

—Isaiah 58:9

There is nothing quite as painful as not being heard. One can be talking to another person, and everything is going in one ear and out the other.

Maybe the person to whom we are talking is even looking beyond us at something or someone else, only pretending to be listening. They may say, "I understand," without having really heard us.

There also come times when we feel like calling out loudly, maybe even screaming, for someone to listen to us, for someone to answer. But we are afraid that all we are going to hear is the echo of our own cries; and that isn't enough.

We need something more. We need to be listened to, heard, and understood.

The promise is that when we call upon the Lord with our deepest needs, desires, and fears—the Lord listens.

The Lord answers our cries and heals us.

May I cry to the Lord for the Lord to hear.

I will cry to the Lord. I will believe the Lord hears. I will accept God's answers for my life.

Prayer: *May I cry to the Lord for help. May I accept God's answers for my life.*

Am I opening myself to the Lord? Am I accepting the healing of the Lord for my life?

Coming to Know God's Presence

You will cry for help, and he will say: Here am I.

—Isaiah 58:9

Everyone needs a sense of presence, the presence of someone else in our lives to whom we can relate. We need to let ourselves be known, to be accepted, to be heard.

We also need to "hear" the presence. It is like a child who comes into the house shouting for mother or father, needing to hear the parent say, "I'm here."

This fear of no one being there often comes with bereavement, when it is very difficult to hear the assurance of God saying, "I am here."

Coming to know the presence of God takes time.

It doesn't happen immediately, especially during times of severe stress.

However, as quiet times are practiced, as we remain open to the still small voice, we eventually hear the comfort coming: "Don't be afraid, I am with you always. I am always here. You always are at home with me. I am always here at home, with you."

May I believe the Lord is always with me.

I will believe the Lord is here. I will trust the Lord to be with me. I will come to rest in the presence of God.

Prayer: *May I come to rest in the presence of God. May I trust the Lord to be with me always.*

Am I trusting the Lord to be with me? Am I finding my rest in the presence of God?

Being Poured Out into Service

If you spend yourselves in behalf of the hungry and satisfy the needs of the oppressed, then your light will rise in the darkness, and your night will become like noonday.

—Isaiah 58:10

Getting out of ourselves can be a major chore, with our pain and sorrow and all.

But thank God, the way to healing has been laid out for us and finally is realized when we enter into service. This happens, of course, after we have done some work with our inner pain. We need to look at it, admit it, and work with it.

The time comes for us to spend ourselves in service, for the welfare of others; we thereby take care of our own welfare.

This can be effectively done through intercessory prayer and other activities. The object is to serve rather than be served.

When we enter into service something begins to happen. Light begins to shine, dispersing the darkness. Rather than gloom there comes the warm brightness of a newly dawning day.

The only way to know this for sure is to try it.

"If you spend yourself in behalf of the hungry then your light will rise in the darkness, and your night will become like noonday."

May I spend myself in service.

I will open myself to the Lord. I will accept the service to which I am called. Whatever God gives me to do I will do.

Prayer: *May I open my life to service. May I do the service to which I am called.*

Am I opening my life to the service of others? Am I doing the service to which the Lord calls me?

Being Refreshed

You will be like a well-watered garden, like a spring whose waters never fail.

—Isaiah 58:11

Now and then, but especially during times of bereavement, some of us have sensations of hopelessness.

Grief can leave us feeling dried up and without resources upon which to draw.

"Will there ever be new growth, new hope, new life for me?" Yes—even though sometimes it doesn't seem possible.

Today's scripture is a promise of God.

We are going to become like a well-watered garden, and the resources of God will never fail us.

When we pray and mediate upon the promises of God, we find our lives taking turns for the better, toward renewed faith, hope, and love.

Our lives turn toward a healthy recovery from sorrow.

Every day we need refreshment for our souls; there is no human need as great as this one.

If we are not refreshed, like a garden being watered, we dry up spiritually into deeper sadness and sorrow.

The Lord is eager to refresh our souls, whenever we are ready to be refreshed.

May I believe God is going to refresh my soul.

I will believe God is going to refresh my soul. I will trust God not to fail me. I will give thanks to God for the many offered blessings.

Prayer: *May I give thanks for the gifts of God. May I accept God's refreshment for my soul.*

Am I accepting God's refreshment for my soul? Am I giving thanks to God?

Being Rebuilt

Your people will rebuild the ancient ruins.

—Isaiah 58:12

Nothing lasts forever, as well we know. Everything is in the process of passing. Life is a process of rebuilding.

After World War II we saw ruined cities, completely smashed, and seemingly lifeless. But not many years later, restoration—unbelievable restoration.

Where it seemed that nothing could ever be rebuilt, there arose new life and hope.

In the human spirit is the Spirit of God. This is something we never should forget; but we do.

We forget that the reconstruction of life, the resurrection of hope, is a basic part of the human story.

Throughout history we witness the power of God at work. Rebuilding the ruins goes on and on, almost unbelievably. Where there is no life, there comes forth new life. Where there is despair comes new hope, new joy, and new expectation.

Where nothing seems able to live, there comes newness. Out of darkness, there comes the sunlight of God's grace.

Ruins are rebuilt. Foundations are raised up. People are restored.

Death is overcome by victory.

May I trust my life can be rebuilt.

I will trust God to rebuild my life. I will turn myself over to God. I will believe God can do for me what I cannot do myself.

Prayer: *May I believe the promises of God. May I have faith in the Lord to rebuild my life.*

Do I believe the Lord is able to rebuild my life? Do I believe the promises of God?

Building Firm Foundations

Your people] will . . . raise up the age-old foundations.
—Isaiah 58:12

Each of us, in our own time, is given the opportunity to extend ourselves toward enlarged responsibilities, "raising up the age-old foundations."

Such opportunities also come during times of bereavement when we are deep within our own pain and hardly able to move beyond ourselves.

At such times, as during bereavement, we can make the mistake of trying to set aside our own recovery from grief, for fear of being burdensome to others. This is not productive.

We must come to understand that we have a responsibility to ourselves, first of all, to deal with our own pain as honestly as possible—without trying to be a hero, without trying to avoid our sorrow for the sake of someone else.

By dealing with our own grief straightforwardly we provide a foundation for those close to us. A foundation of hope.

Remember, by honestly dealing with our grief, we are laying foundations of courage and hope for those to come.

May I help to provide foundations of hope and courage.

I will remember my responsibility to myself to recover and heal. I will also remember that I have responsibilities beyond myself. I will attempt to lay a firm foundation of courage and hope that rests on the promises of God.

Prayer: *May I accept responsibility for myself and my recovery. May I lay firm foundations of faith, courage, and hope.*

Am I accepting responsibility for my recovery? Am I laying firm foundations of faith, courage, and hope?

Being Delighted in the Lord

You will find your joy in the LORD.

—Isaiah 58:14

Not only are the promises of God focused on recovery from sorrow but even more so on "finding joy in the Lord."

There is an airiness about the promises like the fluffing of a feathered pillow so as to increase the space between the feathers, to lighten the pillow, to expand it, to make it softer.

Finding joy in the Lord is like young lambs romping and leaping for the sheer joy of being alive.

Finding joy in the Lord is like dancing with light feet. It is like floating. It is like laughter and delight.

Trying to imagine such lightness and delightedness is not easy when we are deep in our sorrow, or even on the edges of it. But such is the promise: "You will find your joy in the Lord."

By entering into prayer and meditation and God's Word day by day, we find the shackles of sorrow beginning to soften, as new light is invited to enter our saddened souls. With this comes joy in the Lord, and delight in God's gifts of goodness and mercy.

May I find my joy in the Lord.

I will seek the presence of the Lord. I will find my joy in the goodness of the Lord. I will celebrate the promises of God.

Prayer: *May I seek the presence of God. May I find my happiness in the Lord.*

Am I finding my joy in the goodness of the Lord? Am I celebrating the promises of God?

Trusting the Lord to Hear and to Save

Surely the arm of the LORD is not too short to save, nor his ear too dull to hear.

—Isaiah 59:1

The Lord is not limited. The arm of the Lord is not too short. There are no hold-backs to the salvation of the Lord. Nor is the Lord dull of hearing.

The Lord is able to hear us, regardless of our condition.

Each day we should remind ourselves of the closeness of the Lord. By doing so we are able to find peace, courage, hope, and the desire to go on.

All of us have to face things that, by ourselves, are too much for us. Therefore, let us remember that the Lord is able to do for us what we cannot do for ourselves.

To live with the belief that the Lord will not come up shorthanded, in our behalf, is our call to faith, hope, and love—to newness of life.

To have faith that the Lord hears and knows us is the healing energy of recovery.

In many unexpected ways we begin to see the hand of the Lord at work in our lives, and realize that the Lord actually is walking with us.

May my hope rest in the promises of God.

I will rest my hope in the promises of God. I will trust the Lord to hear and to help me. I will rejoice in the Lord.

Prayer: *May I see the hand of God at work in my life. May I believe the Lord hears my prayers.*

Am I trusting the Lord to hear and to help me? Am I resting my hope in the promises of God?

Living the Presence of God

My Spirit, who is on you, and my words that I have put in your mouth will not depart.

—Isaiah 59:21

We are not going to be left. Never does the Lord desert us, even though there are times when it seems so.

The Lord stays with us all the way through the dark valleys. The Lord does not run away.

The Lord imparts the Holy Spirit, giving us what we need to go on with our life in order to recover and to grow spiritually.

The important part of this promise, which we tend to forget, is the same as all the other promises: God is always with us.

Not only is the Lord with us, but the Lord empowers us to do what has to be done in order for us to heal.

The Lord never departs from us.

What is of utmost importance for our recovery is to remember the promises of the Lord's faithfulness, to believe that, when we need help, the Lord is present and ready to serve us.

The Lord is not going to abandon us.

The Lord is going to help us enter the light of a new day.

May I believe the everlasting presence of God.

I will trust God never to leave me. I will trust God to help me do what must be done. I will believe the promises of God, and live them.

Prayer: *May I trust God to never leave me. May I believe the Lord's presence will be with me forever.*

Am I believing the promises of God? Am I living God's promises?

Rising and Shining

Arise, shine, for your light has come.

—Isaiah 60:1

We have reason to rise and shine, though often it may not seem that way. There are days when everything is heavy, days when we wonder whether it is worth the effort to even get out of bed—if, indeed, we can.

If someone were to tell us, "Your light has come," we might very well wonder, "what on earth can that possibly mean?"

There are the fears that the light is never going to come into our lives again, that our sorrow and grief is probably forever, that we are not going to come out of our depressed state.

We should remember that the promises of God were always given in times of darkness, even despair, when there was no hope in sight for people in bondage.

The promises became the power for the people to believe that light would dawn, that there would be a new day of hope and joy.

"Your light has come." It already is here.

Now we must open the eyes of our hearts in order to rise and shine.

May I rise and shine in the promises of God.

I will rise and shine. I will give glory to God. I will know the joy of the Lord.

Prayer: *May I trust the promises of God. May I rise and shine to the glory of God.*

Am I trusting the promises of God? Am I ready to rise and shine?

Seeing the Glory of the Lord

The glory of the LORD rises upon you.

—Isaiah 60:1

And then the day comes when someone notices, or we ourselves notice, that something actually is different or is in the process of becoming different.

There is a lighter step when we walk. We are not dragging our feet along the path. We catch ourselves humming a tune. We notice a sunrise or sunset and feel a faint thrill of it.

We begin to feel closer to people.

Also, there is a sensation of creeping gratitude, of thanksgiving to God.

Some of this surprises us, but we don't worry about that.

However, we might wonder if our new feelings are showing, whether others are noticing.

The "glory of the Lord" is the experience of joy and peace and love. This produces an inward radiance which begins to glow.

The "glory of the Lord" is like the rising of the sun. It doesn't come all at once.

But if we watch the horizon, we can see the light coming, like the dawn of a new day.

May I see the glory of the Lord rising in my life.

I will look for the glory of the Lord in my life. I will believe God's glory is coming into my life. I will trust the Lord to bless me with peace and joy.

Prayer: *May I trust God to bless me with peace and joy. May I see the glory of the Lord in my life.*

Am I seeing the glory of the Lord in my life? Am I trusting God to bless me with peace and joy?

Looking and Seeing

Lift up your eyes and look about you.

—Isaiah 60:4

Getting outside of ourselves is a real problem of recovery; it is much easier said than done.

We discover we cannot run from our pain and make a recovery, that we must deal with the deep "inside" pain.

There also is another need.

We need to look up, to look around, relating ourselves to others, and to the outside world of events.

We need to see what is going on with others.

We need to see nature in all of its glory.

We need to feel the energy of creation.

We need to see that in spite of our loss, life goes on.

We need to see that God is still active, that the Lord is working to bring about the completion of creation, which includes our healing.

To come out of our bereavement we must lift up our eyes and look around.

We must see the hand of the Lord at work.

We must believe the Lord is at work in our lives in order to restore and to save.

May I look up and see the hand of the Lord at work.

I will look beyond myself. I will look for the hand of the Lord at work in the world. I will believe the Lord is working to restore and to save.

Prayer: *May I look beyond myself and my sorrow. May I see the hand of the Lord at work in the world.*

Am I looking beyond myself? Am I seeing the hand of the Lord at work in the world?

Becoming Radiant

Then you will look and be radiant.

—Isaiah 60:5

There's something we don't need when we are deep in our sorrow. We don't need someone trying to talk us out of our pain, into feeling better, with promises that one day we are going to be filled with joy and gladness.

But when God promises, "One day you are going to look and be radiant," we might, at least, begin to listen.

When we are in the depths of our darkness it is difficult to imagine ourselves as being radiant with light. And until we want to come out of the darkness we don't necessarily welcome anyone telling us how radiant we, one day, will be.

However, we do need the promises of God whether we are able to hear them right away or not. We do need the voice of hope, including the promise that one day our lives will be filled with new light.

Hear the promise: "You shall see God's deliverance, and you shall radiate God's light in the world."

Not only is it God's will for us to recover from our sorrow, but it is God's intention for us to radiate the love, joy, and peace of the Lord.

May I believe my life will become radiant.

I will believe my life will shine in spite of the darkness. I will trust the Lord to fill me with the light of God's love. I will give thanks to God for bringing light into my life.

Prayer: *May I see the radiant light of God in my life. May I let the light of God shine through me.*

Am I letting the light of God into my life? Am I allowing the light of God's love to radiate through me?

Being Thrilled and Rejoicing

Your heart will throb and swell with joy.

—Isaiah 60:5

We continue with our thoughts from yesterday, the promise that we will come out of our sorrow and radiate light. Let us remember, once again, that these promises were given to people in very deep distress.

Today the promise continues as it will tomorrow and in the days to come. "Your heart will throb and swell with joy." This is a very substantial promise, something more than getting a few little goodies.

We are being told our hearts are going to be filled with deep joy to the extent that we will not be able to contain it. We will rejoice; we will give thanks. We will sing praises to the Lord.

Is this possible?

Down through the ages we see how this was possible. God's people sang praises in very painful circumstances. God's people experienced joy in the midst of deep sorrow, and wept warm tears of healing with gratitude.

This is not because someone demands it of us, but because we have been deeply touched by the healing power of God.

We rise from the ashes of sorrow and feel the warmth of a new day urging us on.

May my heart throb and swell with joy in the Lord.

I will believe that new life and new joy is mine in the Lord. I will trust God to fill me with joy. I will give thanks to the Lord for all of my blessings.

Prayer: *May I give thanks to the Lord for all of my blessings. May I be filled with the joy of the Lord.*

Am I giving thanks to the Lord? Am I rejoicing in God my Savior?

Seeing the Abundance of God

The wealth on the seas will be brought to you.

—Isaiah 60:5

What does this mean, "The wealth on the seas will be brought to you"? Simply stated it means that we are going to receive blessings beyond measure

This is not a material promise. It is spiritual. Inner. Something for our hearts and spirits. A newness of life.

As we have been noting for the past several days, the promises of God are not just for a little bit of relief from sadness and sorrow, but rather they are for the gifts of lasting hope and joy.

Often we must be reminded of the promises because we forget so easily, falling back into old distressful patterns of negativism. Bereavement is distressful and leaves its victims in deep need of hope.

The promises of God are all about hope. A wealth of hope.

There seems to be no end to the sea and its treasures. Even so, we are promised, the abundance of God is turned toward us, offering new life, new hope, and new joy abundantly.

May I see the abundance of the Lord in my life.

I will look for abundance of God in my life. I will believe that God intends for me to have what I need to be restored. I will accept the gifts of healing that are being offered to me.

Prayer: *May I taste the abundance of the Lord. May I accept God's healing.*

Am I open to the wealth of God's gifts? Am I receiving what is being offered to me for my healing?

Seeing the Healing of God in Others

Who are these that fly along like clouds, like doves to their nests?

—Isaiah 60:8

We know of people who have suffered deep-felt loss, yet who are now moving like feathery clouds, like doves of peace. People who have accepted the healing power of God and over a period of time have found peace.

Accepting the healing power of God comes through the surrender of our distress, turning it over to the Lord who helps us work it through.

Acceptance is not quitting or running away from our pain. Acceptance is the joining of ourselves to the power and spirit of God. We do this through meditation and prayer and service.

Who are these people who become healed and whole, made alive and hopeful?

They are those who have accepted the healing of the Lord, who have been brought out of the dark valley by the power of God, who fly like clouds and doves to the nest of God.

In Christ there is healing for life and power over death.

This reality can give us the lightness for which our hearts long, lightness like a fluffy cloud floating above us on a warm summer's day, inviting us to enter into the joy of our Lord.

May I see the hope of the Lord at work in others.

I will look for the work of the Lord in others. I will see what God has done and is doing to bring healing. I will allow God to lift me up from my distress.

Prayer: *May I see how God heals. May I allow God to heal me.*

Am I seeing how God is healing others? Am I allowing God to heal me?

Seeing the Mercy of the Lord

In favor I will show you compassion.

—Isaiah 60:10

Did you ever wonder whether the compassion of God actually is there, especially when you find yourself bereft?

Where is the compassion of God? And what is this talk of lifting up our eyes to see, to be radiant, to have our hearts throb and swell with joy? Is this all make-believe, or is it real?

The collective belief of God's people is to be found in their experiences of God's compassion. God's compassion happens anywhere: in the most dire of circumstances as well as in times of abundant and delightful outpourings of God's grace.

In the depths of deepest pain God's people have found the compassionate favor of the Lord.

While this is foolishness as far as the world is concerned, it is the truth by which we live and breathe.

"I have had compassion on you," says the Lord.

We are favored by God.

We are receiving the Lord's compassionate gifts of healing.

May I see the compassion of God at work in my life.

I will look for the compassion of God in my life. I will believe I am favored by the Lord. I will rejoice in the gifts of God given to me.

Prayer: *May I see the merciful gifts of God in my life. May I give thanks to the Lord, for the Lord is good.*

Am I seeing the goodness of the Lord in my life? Am I giving thanks for the gifts of God given to me?

Opening Up to God and to Others

Your gates will always stand open, they will never be shut day or night.

—Isaiah 60:11

Bereavement tends to shut us down emotionally, spiritually, and sometimes, physically.

With loss comes shock. With shock comes a locking up, a closing off, simply because we are not able to deal with the trauma all at once. So we need time to adjust in order to heal.

There is also depression—another aspect of closing down.

We sense something has to change, that we dare not remain in a closed-down position an overly extended period of time.

We sense that if we stay shut down too long, we may never open up again to ourselves, to people around us, or to God.

We are given a promise that this need not be.

We don't have to remain in the stuck position with the doors of our lives closed. We don't have to build further defenses to ward off danger. We can open up to God, to others, and to the world around us.

God can open us up and keep us that way. But we must decide for ourselves if we actually want this to be.

May I be ready to open myself to God and others.

I will ask the Lord to open my life to receive the gifts of God's healing. I will receive the gifts of God as they are offered. I will share the gifts with others.

Prayer: *May I open myself to the gifts of God. May I open myself to those around me.*

Am I open to receive the gifts of God as they are given? Am I ready to open myself to God and others?

Leaving a Legacy of Hope and Joy

I will make you the everlasting pride and the joy of all generations.

—Isaiah 60:15

Do we have memories of someone, now gone, who inspires us when they come to mind? Have we not been impressed with the ways in which some people, now gone, have dealt with their lives, how they mastered set-backs and suffering?

Remembering the "saints" of yesterday can be very inspiring when we are attempting to deal with our sorrow and grief, when we wonder whether we are going to make it through.

The Scriptures are filled with such stories of suffering and victory—especially in the life, death, and resurrection of our Lord Jesus Christ.

Christ is majestic because of his sacrificial suffering, and the manner in which he did it.

What he did remains with us as well as the memories of others who came and went in his footsteps; people who are the joy of all generations.

In our suffering we also have the opportunity to leave a legacy of hope and joy.

May I leave a legacy of hope and joy.

I will accept my suffering as a task to be done. I will leave a legacy of hope and joy for others to share. I will ask the Lord to help me.

Prayer: *May I accept my suffering as a task to be done. May I leave a legacy of hope and joy for those to come.*

Am I entering into my suffering as a task to be done? Am I leaving a legacy of hope and joy for those to come?

Being Led by Everlasting Light

The LORD will be your everlasting light.

—Isaiah 60:19

Sooner or later we must place our absolute faith and trust and hope in someone. But this is especially difficult since others, like ourselves, are finite. People get sick and die and are killed in accidents, leaving loved ones behind.

The truth is that our basic relationship must be vertical before it can be horizontal. We must be connected to the eternal, and then relate to that which is in the here and now.

The promise is that the Lord will be with us forever. Therefore we are urged to attach ourselves to the Lord in order to receive God's everlasting light.

We need not worry about where light will come from to pierce the darkness of our sorrow. The light comes from God because God is the originator and giver of light to lighten the darkened places in our lives.

As we walk through the dark valleys of sorrow and suffering, we are being led by everlasting light that will not go out; everlasting light that will not leave us alone in the darkness of painful grief.

May I be led into the light of God.

I will seek to be enlightened by the light of God. I will believe God will not forsake me, that God's light is always available to me. I will trust the leading of God.

Prayer: *May I trust the leading of God for my life. May I be enlightened by the light of God.*

Am I trusting God to be with me? Am I allowing myself to be led by the light of the Lord?

Drawing Closer to the Lord

The Spirit of the Sovereign LORD is on me . . . to preach good news to the poor . . . to bind up the brokenhearted, to proclaim freedom for the captives and release from darkness for the prisoners.

—Isaiah 61:1

The work of the Christ is to bring good news to the poor, and we are the poor.

The work of the Christ is to bind up the brokenhearted, and our hearts are broken.

The work of the Christ is to proclaim freedom for the captives, and we are in captivity to the pain of our loss.

Jesus, as the chosen one of God, accepted this mission of healing and salvation. He also accepted us with our sorrows, our afflictions, our broken hearts, and the pain of our captivity.

Drawing closer to the Lord is the most important part of our recovery from bereavement. How we draw closer to the Lord is something each of us must decide and do for ourselves. But let us remember that the Lord is not pulling away from us.

The Lord is always coming toward us, standing at the door of our hearts and knocking. He waits for us to open the door for him to come in and be with us, as our Savior and friend.

May I draw closer to the Lord.

I will draw closer to the Lord. I will trust the Lord to heal me. I will thank the Lord for freeing me from my sorrow.

Prayer: *May I draw ever closer to the Lord. May I be released from my captivity to sorrow and grief.*

Am I trusting the Lord to heal me? Am I drawing closer to the Lord day by day?

Receiving the Comfort of the Lord

To comfort all who mourn.

—Isaiah 61:2

What is this comfort except to know and believe that life goes on in Christ our Lord, that death is a transition into another form of life, world without end?

What is this comfort of our Lord except to know and believe that we are deeply loved, looked after, and cared for by God?

In the pits of our loss, sorrow, and grief, we will hear the voice of the good shepherd calling us by name—that is, if we are listening.

This then is the promise: "The Lord comes to comfort you in your mourning."

The Lord comes to lift us up, to heal our sorrows, to give us new life where there is death.

Let us believe the Lord is ready to comfort us.

Let us receive the comfort being offered.

May I receive the comfort of the Lord into my life.

I will believe the Lord is ready and able to comfort me. I will trust God to help me through the pain of my sorrow. I will give thanks to the Lord for the gift of healing.

Prayer: *May I trust the Lord to help me through the pain of my sorrow. May I believe that the Lord heals.*

Am I trusting the Lord to help me through the pain of my sorrow? Am I believing the Lord has the power to heal me?

Being Repaired and Restored

They will rebuild the ancient ruins and restore the places long devastated.

—Isaiah 61:4

As we have often noted, the promises of God are primarily given during times of devastation, when people are wiped out emotionally, physically, socially, politically, economically, and even spiritually. When we have hit the very bottom of the pits, they are given, when there is no foreseeable way out, no ray of light—only darkness.

Jerusalem is destroyed; people are in exile and bondage. The promise is that they will go home and restore the Temple.

But this seems impossible.

In our bereavement we know the feeling of impossibility, whether we feel that way often, or just now and then.

Particularly, we feel the seeming impossibility of being able to experience a lasting amount of healing joy.

However, what is impossible for us is possible for God. We must remember that in our days of loss, sorrow, and grief.

The devastations of our lives will be restored. We can trust the Lord to bring this about—not necessarily in ways we want to have it, but in forms that ultimately are best for us.

May I believe the devastated places will be restored.

I will believe the devastated places of my life will be restored. I will trust God to heal what has been broken. I will celebrate the goodness of God in my life.

Prayer: *May I celebrate the goodness of God in my life. May I trust God to heal what is broken.*

Am I trusting the Lord to heal what is broken? Am I celebrating the goodness of God in my daily life?

Expecting a Double Portion of Joy

My people will receive a double portion . . . and everlasting joy will be theirs.

—Isaiah 61:7

One thing about the promises of God, which we very likely have been noticing, is that they are not laid back. They are not small in nature.

If someone didn't know the source, one could suppose that the promises are too far out ever to be true.

Perhaps that's the way *we* feel about the promises, at least sometimes. And why not, when the pain still hangs around and there seems to be no end to the sorrow?

The promise for this day is very extensive—"a double portion and everlasting joy"! Who can even imagine such a promise, much less digest and believe it?

Nevertheless this is precisely what happens when we go with the Lord through our recovery.

Not that we feel exuberant or high, but that we come into a time when we experience inner peace as we have not known it before, the basic essence of joy. And we feel that it is ours to have, like a pearl of great price, for which we are willing to give everything we have in order to own it.

May I have a double portion of everlasting joy.

I will believe the promises of God. I will trust the Lord to lead me into a double portion of joy and satisfaction. I will give thanks to the Lord for the Lord is good.

Prayer: *May I be granted a double portion of joy. May I trust the Lord for inner peace.*

Am I expecting joy to enter my life deeply and abundantly? Am I trusting the Lord to be with me?

Waiting for the Garden to Grow

As the soil makes the sprout come up and a garden causes seeds to grow. . . .

—Isaiah 61:11

What we learn about the movement of God in our lives is that it is very natural.

It is natural for the soil to bring forth sprouts, and for planted seeds to grow, given good earth, sunshine, and water coupled with tender care by the gardener.

Then there is the time for waiting, after the field has been ploughed, disked down, seeded, and fertilized. Waiting for rain and sunshine. Waiting for God.

Recovery is like that.

When we have done all we are able to do, we come to the time for waiting. Waiting for the Lord to do the work. Waiting for the Lord to bring forth the new sprouts, the new plants, new fruit, and new life.

It's important to keep in mind not to become impatient or disheartened about the recurring pain and sorrow, or the reappearing tears which we believed were dried and over with.

Let us wait on the Lord.

Let us be patient.

May I believe God is bringing forth new life in me.

I will believe new life is coming. I will trust the Lord to bring about this new life in me. I will give thanks to God for the gift of new life.

Prayer: *May I trust the Lord to give me new life. May I wait patiently for the Lord to heal.*

Am I waiting patiently for the Lord to give me new life? Am I trusting the Lord to give me new life?

Affirming Our Worth

You will be a crown of splendor in the Lord's hand.

—Isaiah 62:3

How are we looking at ourselves? What kind of an image do we see as to who or what we are? What do we see ourselves becoming?

A common response is, "I don't choose to look at myself because there is nothing really worth looking at. I am not much of anything and not very important. I am insignificant, and am never going to be anything special."

Having a poor self-image is quite common, regardless of rank and station in life. This feeling especially grows and pesters when we suffer loss.

The promise is that we are to be crowns of splendor in the hand of the Lord.

This means we have eternal worth, that we are of profound value to God, even when we may be feeling of no importance or value to anyone else, not even to ourselves.

A healing way to start and end each day is to repeat this promise to ourselves: "I will be a crown of splendor in the Lord's hand."

Better still to affirm, "I *am* a crown of splendor in the Lord's hand."

May I see I am a crown of splendor in the hand of the Lord.

I will remember who I am. I will remember what the Lord means to me. I will remember what I mean to the Lord.

Prayer: *May I remember who and what I am. May I remember that I am a person of value.*

Do I remember the Lord loves me? Do I believe I am a person of value to the Lord?

Remembering the Lord's Faithfulness

No longer will they call you Deserted.

—Isaiah 62:4

What possibly could be said for a people who have been forcibly taken from their homeland and enslaved?

And didn't Job also wonder about this as he sat in the ashes and ruins of his life, having lost everything, including possessions and family?

And didn't Jesus feel that way about himself when he cried out on the cross, "My God, my God, why have you forsaken me?"

Wasn't Christ thought of as being deserted by God? Even mocked by his enemies because of it?

So it is with loss, sorrow, and grief.

We can feel utterly deserted by God and everyone else.

We can lose any sense of our value as a human being.

We need to be reassured that we are persons of value, that we are not being deserted.

If we stay close to the word and promises of God, we will come to know and believe that we are not deserted.

The Lord is faithful. The Lord never deserts us.

May I see that I am not deserted by the Lord.

I will believe the Lord has not deserted me. I will trust the Lord to stay close by, never to leave me. I will bless the Lord for staying with me.

Prayer: *May I trust the Lord to stay with me. May I believe the Lord will never desert me.*

Am I trusting the Lord to stay with me? Am I believing the Lord will never desert me?

Accepting God's Delight in Us

The Lord will take delight in you.

—Isaiah 62:4

When was the last time we said to ourselves, "The Lord really loves me; the Lord really delights in me"? Perhaps never.

It sounds brazen.

Besides, "I'm not good enough for that to be true."

That makes it sound as though God is very stern, like a father who doesn't speak to his children except when the time for punishment comes.

That's the image many have of the Lord.

During bereavement, when we are feeling on the outside of deep and warm relationships, it doesn't seem as though anyone could ever be delighted in us, much less even want us around.

So little we may think of ourselves and our self-worth.

It is necessary to be reminded that someone not only wants us, but delights in us.

While this may be a bit too much to believe, it is true.

The Lord delights in us because we belong to God.

May I accept myself as God accepts me.

I will accept the word of the Lord. I will believe the Lord delights in me. I will rejoice in the goodness of God.

Prayer: *May I rejoice in the goodness of God. May I believe the Lord delights in me.*

Am I rejoicing in the goodness of God? Do I believe the Lord is delighted with me?

Passing through the Open Gates

Pass through, pass through the gates.

—Isaiah 62:10

We have those days when we feel as though we don't want to move, or can't. Maybe we feel like holding back because something unhappy will happen to us if we commit ourselves. Or maybe we have simply run out of energy to go on.

Someone may tell us that the gates to new life and hope are open to us; not only are we being invited to go through, we are even being urged to do so.

But we simply don't feel up to it. So we stay inside ourselves and the sorrow deepens.

However, there are some things we must do to help bring about our recovery from loss, sorrow, and grief.

Yes, we must wait on the Lord for strength, but we also must make some moves. For instance, we must seek the presence of other people. We must engage in activities of give and take—of sharing.

One of the better ways to do this is to find something to give to another, going out of our way to be helpful, helping others feel better about themselves, recognizing others as our brothers and sisters in Christ.

The gates are open for our recovery, but only we can go through them—for our own benefit.

May I see the open gates and go through them.

I will extend myself toward others. I will offer myself in service. I will get outside of myself and get going.

Prayer: *May I extend myself toward others. May I offer myself in service.*

Am I going through the open gates? Am I extending myself in service?

Seeing the Prepared Way

Prepare the way for the people.

—Isaiah 62:10

We are not alone. Not only is the Lord with us, but we are a part of humanity for whom God is preparing a new way of life.

The center of God's interest in all creation is humanity, which includes each one of us.

The way is being prepared for us not only to recover from sorrow, but to come into new and expansive possibilities for our spiritual growth and development.

This is not always easy to see. Rather, it can seem as though everything is being blocked off, closed down, and shut off.

However, it is not the will of the Lord for our path to be blocked, or that we should remain in a stuck position.

While we have talked about preparing the way for the Lord, we must also realize that the Lord is preparing a way for us.

There is a way prepared for us to walk, which is God's way.

If we walk with confidence in the Lord we discover that God's way is very good for us and our lives.

May I believe God is preparing a good way for me.

I will believe the Lord is preparing a good way for me. I will trust the Lord to show me the way. I will go where I am being led.

Prayer: *May I see the way prepared for me. May I go where I am led.*

Am I seeing the way prepared for me? Am I going where God wants to lead me?

Dealing with Obstacles

Build up the highway! Remove the stones.

—Isaiah 62:10

The land of our Lord is known for its stones that can make life very difficult.

Stones must be dealt with—lifted and set aside before the ground can be put to use, before crops can be planted.

What is more, stones continue to surface.

"Build up the highway. Remove the stones," means that we must deal with the stones. We cannot simply ignore them—the stones of loss, sorrow, and grief—or hope they go away by themselves.

The "highway" that leads us out of our bereavement doesn't materialize by itself.

There are things we must do in order to move on, dealing with one obstacle to recovery at a time.

We may not like the design of this project, with the work that is involved, but this is the way to recovery: one stone at a time. Before the highway is cleared, before we can move on, it must be done.

There is no one way around the obstacles to recovery. Each one must be dealt with individually.

May I clear the way of every obstacle.

I will not ignore the stones. I will deal with every obstacle to my recovery. I will do the work the Lord gives me to do.

Prayer: *May I work with every obstacle to my recovery. May I do what has to be done in order to recover.*

Am I facing up to obstacles to my recovery and dealing with them? Am I clearing the way for my recovery, one stone at a time?

Believing God's Salvation

See, your Savior comes.

—Isaiah 62:11

With the Savior comes God's salvation. *Salvation* means something more than life after death; something more than the reward of heaven.

Salvation means coming to terms with our life and circumstances as they are right now, in our bereavement.

Coming to terms is no easy task because we have our own ideas about what is good or bad for us. Right or wrong. Helpful and not helpful.

Each of us has our own range of stubborn determination to get what we think we have coming. And, we are this way without knowing it, even when we look like patsies who don't have a will of our own.

The way out of this bindery of self-will and stubborn determination to control things is our surrendering to the leading of God, because that is how salvation comes. That's how we recover from grief and sorrow; how we grow spiritually into newness of faith, hope, and love.

Let us believe God and remember that our salvation is coming. And let us make sure that we do not stand in the way.

May I believe my salvation into new life is coming.

I will believe my salvation from loss and sorrow is coming. I will trust God to deliver me in God's good time. I will wait on the Lord with hope.

Prayer: *May I wait on the Lord with hope in my heart. May I believe my salvation from sorrow is coming.*

Am I seeing the salvation of the Lord? Am I waiting on the Lord with hope in my heart?

Being Sought after by God

You will be called Sought After, . . . No Longer Forsaken.
—Isaiah 62:12

Is anyone interested in me? Really?

Does anyone care for me or about me?

Or am I being forgotten, overlooked, swept under the rug, never to be found again?

As we have been saying, it is understandable that in our bereavement we can feel forsaken, with no one looking out for us. Even though people show us acts of love and concern, even though we may feel their closeness, there still can be that gnawing sense of being forsaken—even forsaken by God.

But the promise is this: "I will not forsake you, I will come to you." Even more so it declares, "I will pursue you. And I will find you. Because you are mine. I have bought you with a price."

Christ has been referred to as the "hound of heaven," reclaiming what belongs to him, never content until every last soul is gathered in, never satisfied until all has been redeemed.

We are sought after by God. We are wanted.

And God will not be content until we are where we belong: in the care and keeping of God.

May I believe I am sought after by God.

I will believe God seeks me. I will believe God does not forsake me. I will rejoice in the goodness of the Lord.

Prayer: *May I believe I am not being forsaken. May I rejoice in the goodness of the Lord.*

Do I believe God is seeking me out? Do I trust the Lord never to forsake me?

Recounting Acts of Love

Tell of the kindnesses of the LORD.

—Isaiah 63:7

We often have indicated the need to look for the hand of the Lord in our lives, to remember the kindness of the Lord.

"Count your many blessings, count them one by one" says an old hymn. There is a reason for doing this in detail; we remember the kindness of the Lord.

Looking back over our lives, tragic as they might have been, there is always the kindness of the Lord.

There is good reason for making this search into the past, to see the love of the Lord at work in our lives.

As we see how the Lord has stayed with us in days gone by, we can also believe the Lord will stay with us now, and will be with us in the days to come.

Remembering the goodness of the Lord leads us into thanksgiving. And gratitude is the attitude that lifts us beyond our sorrow, into the joy of a new day.

Let us remember the kindness of the Lord in our lives.

May I remember the kindnesses of the Lord in my life.

I will remember the acts of God's love in my life. I will trust in the steadfast love of the Lord. I will give thanks for God's faithfulness.

Prayer: *May I give thanks to God for staying with me. May I remember the blessings of the Lord given to me.*

Do I remember the kindnesses of the Lord in my life? Do I trust the Lord to be with me forever?

Sharing Distress

In all their distress he too was distressed, . . . in his love and mercy he redeemed them; he lifted them up and carried them all the days of old.

—Isaiah 63:9

We have the companionship of our Lord who has entered into the pain of this broken world, into our own broken, separated condition.

We have the support of the Lord who suffers with us.

We may not always see what is happening, because of our loss, sorrow, and grief, but the Lord is at work in our lives.

In all our afflictions, the Lord is with us. The cross of Christ reminds us of this reality. Jesus calls us into remembrance.

As we break the bread and share it, one with the other, we are reminded that the Lord is with us, sharing our distresses.

As we drink from the cup, we remember that Christ knows our distress, that the Lord identifies with our suffering—not as an onlooker, but as one who participates with us.

In all our distresses he is distressed. He understands precisely where we are; he knows and accepts us the way we are in our brokenness and separation, in our loss, sorrow, and grief.

May I believe Christ suffers with me.

I will believe Christ is with me in my distress. I will trust the Lord to stay with me all the way. I will give thanks to the Lord for all mercies given.

Prayer: *May I remember the mercies of God. May I believe Christ is with me.*

Am I remembering the mercies of God? Do I believe Christ suffers with me?

Being Formed by God

We are the clay, you are the potter.

—Isaiah 64:8

Where there is confusion there also is anxiety about who we are and where we belong.

Such confusion is very common when we are suffering from loss, sorrow, and grief.

Today's scripture is clear in this regard. We are the clay, God is the potter.

It is God who forms and shapes us. We are in the process of being shaped right now through the experiences of our bereavement, and sometimes the potter doesn't handle the clay delicately.

Preparing the clay for the potter's wheel can be quite wrenching. The clay must be vigorously molded and kneaded; it must be set down firmly on the wheel to be transformed into a usable vessel—perhaps as a dish to hold food, or a cup to hold fresh water.

We might wonder why, at times, we have to be dealt with so firmly. But as with the clay, this is how the best is brought to the surface. This is how we are formed into serviceable tools.

May I see that I am a work of God in process.

I will see myself for what I am, the workmanship of God. I will believe that what God is doing with me is best. I will trust the hand of the Lord in my life.

Prayer: *May I trust the hand of the Lord in my life. May I believe God is doing the very best with me.*

Am I trusting the hand of the Lord in my life? Am I believing the Lord is doing the very best with me?

Knowing the Presence of God

Here am I, here am I.

—Isaiah 65:1

We reach out with our hearts to touch the hand of God, and the hand isn't there—or so it seems.

Then there comes that empty feeling, the sensation that we are alone.

The spiritual walk is like this. Even the greatest of saints periodically experience the emptiness.

But God does not leave us alone in our desolation.

If we are willing to wait quietly, we begin to sense the presence, to hear the assurance, "Here am I, here am I."

We begin to discover the "presence" once more, deep within our souls, in another person, in the unexpected.

We begin to realize that we are being spoken to, that we have not been abandoned, that the Lord is with us.

As we go on with the journey, over the rocky roads and through the dark valleys, we will find the presence of God in unexpected and astounding ways—and the empty feeling lessens.

May I know the presence of the Lord.

I will believe the Lord is present. I will trust that I have not been abandoned. I will wait for the presence of the Lord to speak to me.

Prayer: *May I be open to the presence of the Lord. May I experience the presence of the Lord in my life.*

Am I listening for the presence of the Lord? Am I trusting God to be with me?

Making All Things New

Behold, I will create new heavens and a new earth.
—Isaiah 65:17

Very often, with loss, sorrow, and grief, there comes blurred vision, which leaves us feeling exhausted emotionally, physically, and spiritually.

At such times we are unable to see anything new coming into our lives, which can be quite disheartening, even frightening as the depression deepens.

The Lord, however, offers visions that surpass anything we are able to see by ourselves.

The Lord promises that not only are we going to be given new life, but that the entire world is going to be recreated.

When we consider this promise—and believe it—something has to change inside ourselves.

A new and important hope has to dawn. What is so very dark has to be infiltrated by new light and joy.

Although it may not seem so, everything is being changed for the better. It is God's intended purpose to recreate the world, ourselves included, and bring an end to loss, sorrow, and grief.

May I believe the Lord is making all things new.

I will believe the Lord is making all things new. I will trust God to remake my life. I will try to live my life hopefully and with joy.

Prayer: *May I live my life hopefully and with joy. May I believe God is making all things new.*

Do I believe God is making all things new, including me? Am I living my life hopefully, with joy?

Being Free to Start Again

The former things will not be remembered nor will they come to mind.

—Isaiah 65:17

One of the first reactions to deeply felt loss sometimes is trying to forget what has happened, to blot it out, to not remember. We try to act as though it hadn't happened, as though we only had to open a door and our loved one would be standing there, just like before.

There are other things we want to forget, like mistakes we have made or how we treated the lost loved one badly.

Certainly we don't want our sins remembered. Not only do we want to forget, but we want God also to forget.

At such times it is helpful to understand that the Lord has a deep love relationship with us.

Whatever it is that we have left undone, whatever sins we have committed, "the former things will not be remembered nor will they come to mind." That is the promise.

This means that we can start again right where we are, with no unnecessary baggage of shame and guilt.

The Lord forgives; and we are the forgiven. The Lord releases; and we are set free to live in expectation, hope, and joy.

May I believe I am free to begin again.

I will believe I am free to start again with my life, right where I am. I will believe my sins are forgiven, that God does not hold them against me. I will give thanks to the Lord for all gifts of grace.

Prayer: *May I believe my sins are forgiven. May I feel free to start over again.*

Am I believing God does not remember my sins or hold them against me? Am I feeling free to start my life over again?

Rejoicing in God's Created Order

Be glad and rejoice forever in what I will create.

—Isaiah 65:18

Sometimes, as bereaved persons, we may feel that we dare never enjoy life again, out of respect to the lost loved one.

We may feel guilty about feeling good. Feeling guilty keeps us from participating in the ongoing creation of God's world.

We must remember that God's goodness and mercy is to be enjoyed, as our scripture says.

God has no desire for us to be sad and sorrowful, and certainly does not want us to feel guilty about feeling better.

There is an ancient teaching of the Talmud which says, "In the world to come, each of us will be called to account for all the good things God put on earth which we refused to enjoy."

Perhaps that teaching is our scripture for today.

Our attitudes toward joy and gladness are important. We must give ourselves the right to feel good and to rejoice.

The starting point is to rejoice in the Lord. From there we can go just about any place where joy and gladness invite us to come.

May I be glad and rejoice in God's creation.

I will open my heart to the joy of the Lord and give thanks. I will rejoice and be glad in the goodness of God. I will not be afraid of joy and gladness.

Prayer: *May I experience joy and gladness of heart. May I rejoice and be glad in the Lord.*

Am I opening myself to joy and gladness? Am I allowing myself to have good feelings?

Believing That Life Is Worthwhile

They will not toil in vain.

—Isaiah 65:23

"What am I doing with my life? I feel so useless."

In a bereft state of deeply felt loss and sorrow, many or even most people feel very unsettled, even useless.

What good, then, can come of anything we do, if we are in such a depressed condition? Even if we put our minds and backs to it, and try ever so hard, some say, "Nothing good will come of it anyway."

However, it need not be that way if we can believe and live the promises of God. Living the promises of God is where our new life begins.

For instance, there is the promise we have in our scripture today: It is worth investing ourselves in our tasks, whatever those God-given tasks may be, because we have the assurance that the effort is going to be worth it.

We may not live to see the result of our work, and no one else may be able to see what is happening, but we are contributing to the creation by investing ourselves in it. And thus we are contributing to life.

Once we begin to see ourselves and our daily tasks as being of value, we will know that our labor is not in vain, and our spirits will be renewed.

May I believe my life is worthwhile.

I will entrust my life to the Lord. I will believe my toil is not in vain. I will believe my life is worthwhile.

Prayer: *May I believe my life is not being lived in vain. May I entrust my work to the Lord to be blessed.*

Am I entrusting my work to the Lord? Do I believe my life is worthwhile?

Trusting the Lord to Answer

Before they call I will answer, while they are still speaking I will hear.

—Isaiah 65:24

Someone is ready to listen, to hear, to understand.

Does this sound like a utopian dream?

The promise is that God will hear and answer, even before we have finished speaking.

Is this possible and real?

Have we received blessings for which we have hardly asked, as though God were ahead of us, knowing what we really need?

Does God really know us better than we know ourselves?

Is the promise true, that God is going to help us along the way, especially when the "way" is through the dark valleys?

Does God listen?

Does God care?

Does God act on our behalf, for our welfare?

While at times it may not seem so, eventually we begin to see the promises being fulfilled in our lives, although they may be in unexpected ways.

God is in the process of bringing us into the light—answering our prayers even before we even speak them.

May I believe God is hearing and answering.

I will believe the Lord cares about me. I will believe the Lord is listening to my prayers. I will believe God answers my prayers.

Prayer: *May I trust the Lord to hear my prayers. May I believe the Lord is answering my prayers.*

Do I believe God is listening to me? Do I believe the Lord is answering my prayers?

Realizing Inner Peace

The wolf and the lamb will feed together.

—Isaiah 65:25

How can there be peace for my soul? How can I ever come to rest?

Because of sin, of separation, there is a war going on inside ourselves.

The old flesh and the Spirit battle, darkness against the light of God.

Because of this there can be some very hostile feelings directed at ourselves, at others, at God, at the world around us.

We may feel as though we are being devoured by wolves, that there is no hope for us, that this is the way it is going to be all the time.

The inner conflict can be very severe: feelings of being torn, of not being at ease, of not coming to rest within ourselves, of not quieting down.

Recovery is the quieting down of the inner self, when the wolf and the lamb feed together, finding peace and rest.

The gifts of peace and rest are experienced when we trust the Lord's healing power and surrender to it.

It is then we see the wolf and the lamb lying down together, as our troubled souls are being healed.

May I believe my inner conflicts will heal.

I will believe I am going to heal. I will trust God to heal me. I will rejoice in the promises of God to heal.

Prayer: *May I trust God to heal my inner conflicts. May I believe I am going to be at peace with myself.*

Do I believe I am going to be at peace with myself? Do I trust God to heal my inner conflicts?

Being Comforted

You will be comforted.

—Isaiah 66:13

There is nothing quite like being discomfited. This is more than being just a little bit uncomfortable.

To be discomfited is to feel utter defeat, to be in a state of near absolute perplexity.

To come out of this state of confusion, we need help simply because we are, ourselves, the confusion.

We, ourselves, are the proprietors of inner conflict.

What is more, we cannot heal ourselves because we cannot objectively see what is happening to us.

Left to ourselves, without the guiding hand of God, we are doomed to remain in a discomfited situation, unable to become untangled, remaining confused and afraid.

What is needed, before anything can really be done to bring healing, is hope. That is where the promise comes in.

"You will be comforted."

Let us remember this promise when we are distressed.

May I be comforted by the Lord's comfort.

I will believe God brings comfort. I will trust God to comfort me. I will give thanks for the comfort of the Lord.

Prayer: *May I trust God to comfort me. May I receive the comfort of the Lord.*

Am I trusting God to comfort me? Am I receiving the comfort of the Lord?

Seeing the Healing and Rejoicing

When you see this, your heart will rejoice.

—Isaiah 66:14

There is "clarification" when things begin to make some sense.

In our recovery from bereavement a good sign is when we notice things are coming into focus, when we are beginning to see what has been hidden.

Perhaps we get a sense of unexpected warmth, hope, and wonder.

Then we get a little twinge of joy, as we begin to sense the hand of the Lord at work in our lives.

Then our hearts begin to rejoice (just a bit, at first).

Clarification is a wonderful experience.

Like the blind man Jesus healed, we can rejoice and say, "Once I was blind, but now I see."

God intends that we should gain clarification, that we should be enabled to see beyond the darkness of our sorrow, to see the transcendent power of the Lord reaching to uphold and heal us.

Through the Lord's healing power we become clarified—able to see our healing and to rejoice in the Lord.

May I see the healing hand of the Lord and rejoice.

I will look for the healing hand of the Lord in my life. I will see what God is doing to heal me. I will trust the Lord to do what is best for me.

Prayer: *May I trust God to do what is best for me. May I see the healing hand of the Lord in my life.*

Am I seeing the healing hand of the Lord? Am I trusting the Lord to do what is best for me?

Flourishing with New Life and New Hope

You will flourish like grass; the hand of the Lord will be made known to his servants.

—Isaiah 66:14

With bereavement there is the experience of death and dying—our own emotional and spiritual deaths.

We may hear ourselves saying, "I feel as though there is nothing left of me. I am nothing but bones."

Certainly this is not the same as "flourishing."

To "flourish" is to thrive, to be vigorous, to succeed. These, of course, are not the feelings of bereavement—not at the time of loss or immediately thereafter.

However, if there is a desire to get well, to heal, to become whole again, there also is the promise: "You will flourish like grass." This means we will grow.

God has no intention for us to remain in a bereft condition, without hope or joy.

It is God's desire for us to heal and to flourish.

It is God's desire for us to become healthy and abundant in faith, hope, love, and joy.

May I believe new life is going to flourish in me.

I will believe new life is awaiting me. I will trust God to give me the life of the Spirit. I will become a healed person.

Prayer: *May I become a healed person. May I believe I will flourish in God's Spirit.*

Do I believe I can and will flourish in the goodness of God? Do I trust the Lord to give me new life in the Spirit of God?

Trusting the Strength of the Lord

Today I have made you a fortified city, an iron pillar.
—Jeremiah 1:18

We can be very concerned whether we have enough strength within our souls to stand up against that which is to come.

Once we have been hurt, like it or not we carry the scars with us—especially when we have suffered the loss of a loved one.

We may become so frightened of what might still happen to us that we are unable to venture ahead.

We may even be frightened to the extent of holing up and hiding and keeping everything within.

"I have been hurt and I simply can't stand another loss. I am afraid of what is to become of me."

The promise of God is that we will be fortified, that we will have sufficient strength to deal with any kind of an onslaught.

While this may not seem possible right now, the promise is that we will not be given more than we are able to handle.

Maybe we don't feel like a fortified city or an iron pillar. But because the Lord is with us, that's how strong we are.

Let us trust the Lord to give us the strength we need.

May I have the strength that I need.

I will trust in the strength of the Lord to protect me. I will believe God will give me the strength I need. I will not fear what is to come.

Prayer: *May I not fear what is to come. May I trust in the strength of the Lord.*

Am I fearing what is to come? Am I trusting in the strength of the Lord?

Being Delivered

I am with you to rescue and save you.

—Jeremiah 15:20

Day after day we need the rescue and salvation which comes from God, so we are not overcome by the world.

Many are saying these days, "It's a jungle out there!" And so it seems, like it or not.

Life is tough and life is not fair. So what do we do with ourselves, especially when we are in a weakened condition because of bereavement?

One thing is certain. By ourselves we cannot overcome the world, handle its complications and confusions, or heal the heartache with all its pain.

We need someone stronger to lead us through. Not "around," but "through."

What we need most is assurance that the Lord is with us, to rescue and save us from fear and destruction.

The basic promise of God is, "I am with you," and this is followed by the assurance, "to rescue and save you."

We can take heart in the promises of God because they prove themselves to be trustworthy, especially in the "jungles" of life.

May I believe the Lord is with me to rescue and save.

I will believe the Lord will rescue and save me from destruction. I will trust the Lord to be with me. I will wait patiently on the Lord.

Prayer: *May I wait patiently on the Lord. May I believe the Lord will rescue and save me.*

Do I believe the Lord will save and deliver me from destruction? Am I waiting patiently on the Lord?

Trusting the Strength of the Lord

O LORD, my strength and my fortress.

—Jeremiah 16:19

We find out that we cannot go it alone, in our own strength, under the power of our own will. We simply are not that strong.

We are not strong enough to handle all of the trials and tribulations that come with living in this shattered world.

One of the difficulties, especially during times of bereavement, is that we may get the notion that somehow we have to be strong in and of ourselves: "I can make it! I will make it!"

However, when we turn out the lights and lie down to sleep, there can be an emptiness creeping across our chests, inserting itself deeply into our hearts. Then we may begin to wonder if we are going to make it through the night, much less the day to come—if, indeed, there is to be another day.

Far better it is to turn to the Lord as quickly as possible and stay there.

God isn't asking us to go it alone under our own power.

God is offering to be our strength and our stronghold.

Let us trust the strength of the Lord.

May I ask the Lord to be my strength and stronghold.

I will ask the Lord to be my strength. I will believe God to be my stronghold. I will place my confidence in the Lord God.

Prayer: *May I place my confidence in the Lord. May I trust the Lord to be my strength.*

Am I trusting the Lord to be my strength? Am I placing my confidence in God to be my stronghold?

Being Confident in God

Heal me, O LORD, and I will be healed.

—Jeremiah 17:14

The kind of healing we want, of course, is healing that lasts.

Not that we aren't going to need healing again and again; because every day we're in need of healing.

People may offer many ideas as to what we can do to heal ourselves, to recover, to regain our strength. Some of the suggestions are bound to be good.

But the one that really counts is for us to have confidence in God's healing power.

"Heal me, O Lord, and I will be healed" is a firm statement of faith. First it recognizes where the healing comes from; the healing of consequence; the healing that goes on and on, into the depths of our souls.

Second, such a firm statement of faith is confident: "I will be healed," it says. "I am going to get better."

The best kind of healing comes when our confidence is in the healing that comes from the Lord.

Then we are ready to receive God's power to heal.

"Heal me, O Lord, and I will be healed."

May I be healed and made whole.

I will believe in the healing power of God. I will trust the Lord to heal my broken heart. I will lay down my burdens before the Lord.

Prayer: *May I lay down my burdens before the Lord. May I trust the Lord to heal my broken heart.*

Am I laying down my burdens before the Lord? Do I believe in the healing power of God for my life?

Seeking God's Salvation

Save me and I will be saved, for you are the one I praise.
—Jeremiah 17:14

When we pray for salvation we are agreeing that there is something we cannot do for ourselves.

We cannot recover from loss, sorrow, and grief by ourselves.

We cannot heal ourselves.

By ourselves, we are not able to go on living with any degree of optimism and hope.

We really need something more than bright ideas about how we might make it through the dark valleys.

When we pray for salvation we aren't asking the Lord to rid us of pain.

Rather, we are asking the Lord to help us through our pain in order to transcend it, to go beyond the pain.

We pray for a salvation that will give us strength, courage, hope, and faith—salvation that will provide us with the will and desire to recover, to go on with our lives by serving God.

When we begin to experience the salvation of the Lord, we are able to confidently say, "Save me and I will be saved, for you are the one I praise."

May I be saved by the salvation of the Lord.

I will seek the might and power of God to work in my life. I will seek the salvation of God to heal me. I will trust the power of God to save.

Prayer: *May I seek the might and power of the Lord. May I trust the power of God to save me.*

Am I seeking the salvation of the Lord? Am I trusting the power of God to lift me up?

Asking to Be Heard

Listen to me, O Lord.

—Jeremiah 18:19

There are those times of sorrow when we simply feel like pleading for someone to help us; we want to reach out and grab someone. We want someone to stop and be with us, someone to recognize our pain.

One of the unfortunate realities of our human situation is, however, that many people are so tied up in their own struggles that relatively few are disposed to really hear the pleas of others.

Unfortunately, we sometimes get the notion that God is like everyone else—that God is too busy to listen to us, to hear us.

We are urged to call upon the Lord, even to beg, if that's what we feel it takes. Like the man in one of Jesus' stories who bangs on a neighbor's door to get him out of bed for a loaf of bread.

It doesn't depreciate our value as persons to plead for ourselves.

Rather, when we plead for God's help we uncover more of our pain, with its anguish, and let it drain out.

We open ourselves up for the healing power of God to enter.

May I ask the Lord for help.

I will ask the Lord to listen to me. I will ask the Lord to help me. I will believe the Lord will answer my cries.

Prayer: *May I call upon the Lord to help me heal. May I trust the Lord to heal me.*

Am I calling upon the Lord to help me? Am I trusting the Lord to heal me?

Trusting the Lord's Presence

But the Lord is with me.

—Jeremiah 20:11

With bereavement there is a deep, sometimes completely hidden and painful need to know that the Lord is with us. How else are we going to be able to make it through, into our recovery from loss, sorrow, and grief?

Yes, there are many pains, but the Lord is with us. Many sorrows, but the Lord is with us. Many different kinds of deaths to die, but the Lord is with us.

That's the promise. The Lord is with us!

If we haven't tried, it will be helpful to take time out, to meditate on the theme, "The Lord is with *me.* The Lord *is* with me. The Lord is *with* me."

There are times when the pain is so great that nothing else matters except that the Lord is with us.

The world may collapse around us, and so it has, *but*—and that's where hope begins—*the Lord is with us.* This affirmation of faith becomes the only reality that makes any difference, reaching into the pits of our sorrow and touching us where we need to be touched. Healing us where we need to be healed—in the depths of our souls.

May I remember the Lord is always with me.

I will remember the Lord is always with me. I will trust the Lord's presence in my life. I will turn to the Lord to lift me out of my sorrow.

Prayer: *May I turn to the Lord with confidence. May I trust the Lord's presence in my life.*

Am I believing the Lord is always with me? Am I turning to the Lord with confidence?

Praising the Lord

Sing to the Lord! Give praise to the Lord! He rescues the life of the needy.

—Jeremiah 20:13

In bereavement there come feelings of neediness, the desire for someone to pick us up, to hold us.

On the other hand, we may withdraw into ourselves and keep others away. We may also turn away from God, refusing to be held and healed.

Hopefully, there also come times when we experience the reality of our need for help.

For, in order to heal, we must come to see the nature of our problem. The problem is that we try to be self-sufficient when we aren't.

We need deliverance. Deliverance from the binding of our hearts and minds in loneliness and fear. Deliverance from the pain of loss.

The Scriptures promise deliverance, and Christ was manifested to bring about our redemption from fear and death.

There is no human need that God cannot fill.

Sing to the Lord!

Give praise to the Lord!

May I praise the Lord for deliverance from fear and death.

I will sing praises to the Lord. I will praise the holy name of the Lord. I will give thanks to God for deliverance from fear and death.

Prayer: *May I give thanks to the Lord. May I praise the name of the Lord.*

Am I praising the Lord? Am I giving thanks to God?

Trusting God to Heal

I will restore you to health and heal your wounds.
—Jeremiah 30:17

Within the human experience of life and death there always is the deep need for restoration and resurrection, coming back into life, regaining spiritual health, having our emotional and spiritual wounds healed.

Each of us has our own wounds—specific kinds of wounds, which we may or may not recognize.

When we are wounded we need to be restored to health and healing. Sometimes we have no idea how this is going to be accomplished because everything is so hazy, so much in the shadows.

However, the more we are awakened to our loss, and the deep pain that comes with it, the more we begin to sense our need for outside help.

Trusting the Lord to lead us into our healing becomes a good way to go.

While there is no way of telling, for sure, where the Lord will lead—or how—we can be certain that the Lord will do for us what we cannot do for ourselves.

God will heal us. And God is worthy of our trust.

May I trust God to heal the wounds of my bereavement.

I will trust the Lord to restore me to health. I will trust the Lord to heal my wounds, no matter how deep. I will believe the Lord is with me.

Prayer: *May I trust the Lord to heal my wounds. May I trust the Lord to restore me.*

Am I trusting the Lord to restore me? Am I believing God can and will heal my wounds?

Believing and Belonging

I will be their God, and they will be my people.

—Jeremiah 31:33

There is no greater promise or act of friendship than this: "I will be your God, and you will be my people."

Here we are given the opportunity, the deep privilege, to accept an offer of great significance, to accept this offered relationship of friendship with God.

The promise has no end to it. No time limit. No threat of being nullified, of coming to a halt.

"I will be your God. You will be my people" is forever.

When we find ourselves bogged down in our disappointments, sorrow, and grief, it is helpful to remember how eager the Lord is to have us as friends.

If that doesn't mean much to us at this moment, we can keep the promise somewhere in our memories, for future recall, for a time when we need to hear the promise: "You will be mine and I will be yours."

Lasting recovery from loss, sorrow, and grief comes with this kind of assurance.

May I believe I belong to God.

I will believe the promise of God. I will believe I belong to God. I will believe God is my friend.

Prayer: *May I believe God is my friend. May I believe I belong to God.*

Do I believe I belong to God? Do I believe the Lord really is my friend?

Believing There Is Joy

I will turn their mourning into joy.

—Jeremiah 31:13

Often this state of grief and mourning is submerged and hidden from ourselves and others as we go about our business each day.

With the loss of a loved one, the already existing grief is shaken loose and we experience the pain of separation in greater measure.

Our immediate loss triggers deeper anguish.

We have a deep longing for oneness, to be one with ourselves, with others, with God, and with the universe.

However, because we are separated beings, we find ourselves spiritually and emotionally wounded, fractured and isolated by fear and mistrust.

The whole creation is groaning for unity, as Paul the apostle put it.

The promise is that our mourning shall be turned into joy.

Right now, however, we must work with our sorrow by recognizing that it is there and by dealing with it.

We must also believe our sorrow will be turned into joy.

May I believe my mourning will be turned into joy.

I will believe my mourning will be turned into joy. I will trust God to heal my wounds. I will believe the promises of God.

Prayer: *May I believe my mourning will be turned into joy. May I trust God to heal me.*

Do I believe my mourning will be turned into joy? Am I trusting God to heal me?

Finding Heartfelt Joy

I will give them comfort and joy instead of sorrow.
—Jeremiah 31:13

Yesterday we mentioned the universal sorrow, how the whole creation is in a state of grief and mourning because of separation.

We all are longing for our created unity with God to be restored, to be in fellowship with others, with ourselves, and the creation itself.

Today we are thinking in terms of "joy instead of sorrow" because God gives us joy—while we are still in our bodies, while we still are living on this wounded earth with our wounded lives.

In spite of all the turmoil and pain, we human beings have the capacity to have heartfelt joy, to rejoice in goodness—in God—to rejoice in one another, to rejoice in the creation and our privilege to be part of it.

Even though the sorrow is deep, and the pain severe, there is a reservoir of joy and gladness somewhere within, waiting to be tapped.

We have the comforting word and promises of God to help us find heartfelt joy.

Above all, we have the presence of our Lord Jesus Christ who urges us to be joyful because he is with us.

May I find heartfelt joy.

I will believe God heals. I will trust the Lord to give me joy. I will rejoice in the Lord.

Prayer: *May I have heartfelt joy. May I rejoice in the Lord.*

Am I rejoicing in the Lord? Do I believe my heart can be glad?

Celebrating the Goodness of God

My people will be filled with my bounty.

—Jeremiah 31:14

Everyone is looking for satisfaction, which means, first of all, "freedom from pain." Beyond that satisfaction generally means getting our heart's desire—whatever that may be. Satisfaction also means getting what we want when we want it—regardless of the expense.

Then too, satisfaction is experiencing the joy of doing something well and being rewarded for what we accomplish.

There are many kinds of satisfaction, but the greatest of all is the realization that God's goodness is at work in our lives.

The highest and best of satisfaction is the sense of being in concord with the Spirit of God, of being tuned-in to the working of God in the world, of being a part of God's redemptive work.

When we are conscious of God's goodness at work in our lives we enter a state of gratitude, because goodness and gratitude go together. And gratitude overshadows sorrow.

It is helpful, in the process of our recovery, to look for the bountiful goodness of God at work in our lives, and to be grateful for the Spirit of God alive in us.

May I see the bounty of God in my life and be comforted.

I will believe the goodness of God is in my life. I will accept the comfort of the Lord. I will celebrate the goodness of God.

Prayer: *May I accept the bounty of God into my life. May I celebrate the goodness of God.*

Am I accepting the bounty of God? Am I celebrating the goodness of God with my life?

Giving Thanks to the Lord

Give thanks to the Lord Almighty, for the Lord is good; his love endures forever.

—Jeremiah 33:11

Before and after every meal let us give thanks. Let us give thanks for every breath we are able to breathe, for water to drink, for the sun, for life.

The blessings never end, even when we are wracked with pain. The love of the Lord endures forever. Living this truth is the joy of life and our strength. The need to give thanks, as an aid to healing, is fundamental.

The sooner we give thanks for the goodness of the Lord, the sooner we begin to sense the healing power of God coming to work in our lives; not because God insists that we give thanks, but simply because the giving of thanks is positive energy.

And when the positive energy of thanksgiving is released in our souls, everything begins to take new shape and form.

The way to healing is to give thanks, to build a thankful heart. That is why we are urged not to hesitate in our giving of thanks, and why it is important to express our gratitude in as many ways as possible. It is important to make the best possible use of thanksgiving as a tool for healing.

May I give thanks to the Lord for the Lord is good.

I will give thanks to the Lord for the Lord is good. I will build a life of gratitude. I will open my heart to the goodness of God.

Prayer: *May I open my heart to the goodness of God. May I build a life of gratitude to God.*

Am I building a life of gratitude to God? Am I opening my heart to the goodness of God, and giving thanks?

Taking Refuge in the Lord

Blessed are all who take refuge in [the Lord].

—Psalms 2:12

Life is dangerous, not just because of the big bombs and natural catastrophes, but because we can be hurt in so many other ways, including that of losing someone we love.

When we are hurt, we need somewhere to go with our pain. This doesn't make us strange. This simply is the way human beings are put together.

We are emotional creatures who have feelings. We can be deeply hurt and frightened.

When confronted with the loss of a loved one, we naturally feel like we are going to crack and crumble. There can be times when we actually fall apart under the strain of loss. We need a place of refuge, somewhere to crawl in and hide for a while.

God understands our need and offers refuge.

If we take our pain and sorrow to the Lord, we will find refuge; we will be given all we need to deal with our bereavement and recover from our sorrow.

May I take refuge in the Lord.

I will trust the Lord. I will take refuge in the Lord. I will receive my strength from the Lord.

Prayer: *May I trust the Lord with my life. May I take refuge in the Lord.*

Am I receiving strength from the Lord? Am I taking refuge in the Lord?

Accepting the Shield of the Lord

You are a shield around me, O LORD.

—Psalm 3:3

Yes, there is wishful thinking and false security. There are also times when we are eager to listen to anyone who promises us a less painful way. But this is not the way of the Lord.

It is not God's intention for us to miss the growth experiences which pain affords. Rather, it is the Lord's purpose to go with us through the pain, helping us grow emotionally and spiritually.

But in the course of dealing with our pain, we do need protection. We need help from a power greater than ourselves; that power is God.

This is not escapism offered in the name of the Lord. This is not a promise that we are going to escape suffering because we believe in God.

The promise is that God wants to be our shield. But we still have to get on with our work of recovery, and deal with the pain of separation. We can begin doing so with prayer.

May I accept the shield of the Lord to protect me.

I will accept the protection of the Lord. I will ask the Lord to lead me through the pain of my sorrow. I will believe in the power of the Lord to save and to make me whole.

Prayer: *May I believe in the power of the Lord. May I ask the Lord to shield me through the pain of my sorrow.*

Am I asking the Lord to shield me in the pain of my sorrow? Am I believing in the saving power of God?

Crying Aloud to the Lord

To the LORD I cry aloud and he answers me.

—Psalm 3:4

There are times when it is best for us to cry aloud to God, to hear the sound of our own voice, and to experience the relief that comes from a deep cry.

There are people who say, "If only I could cry. I would feel so much better." This is true because tears release tension.

But too many of us have been socially conditioned not to let our feelings be known; and particularly not to ask, out loud, for help.

However, if we start praying out loud, really opening our hearts to the Lord, even with loud cries of agony, or simple little whimpers, we may be surprised by the relief experienced.

There is a therapy called "the primal scream" in which persons are pressed to recall early traumas until they start screaming from deep within, screaming the pain of fear, anger, frustration, and resentment, releasing internal tension.

Likewise, calling loudly upon the Lord can be helpful for releasing pent-up feelings that come with bereavement. Let us not hesitate to express ourselves "loudly" to the Lord. The Lord will listen. The Lord will hear, and the Lord will respond.

May I not be afraid to call upon the Lord with a loud voice.

I will not be afraid to let my needs and desires be known to God. I will cry to the Lord for help. I will trust the Lord to hear and answer my cries.

Prayer: *May I trust the Lord to hear my cries. May I let my needs and desires be known.*

Am I letting my needs and desires be known to the Lord? Am I trusting God to hear and answer my prayers?

Being Sustained by the Lord

The LORD sustains me.

—Psalm 3:5

When we are in a state of disruption, such as loss, sorrow, and grief, we look for strength and deliverance.

Sometimes we may find ourselves virtually begging for help, spoken or unspoken.

The fear may be that no one will listen, that no one will give us the needed support.

However, as we go along in our life through many experiences of pain, we find we are being supported although we may not immediately recognize it.

We discover that the Lord has been with us all the time.

And we may wonder, "Why haven't I noticed this before? How could I have been so blind? The Lord has been holding me up all the time, and I have been thinking and feeling that I am alone, without support."

Let us look back over our lives and see how the Lord has sustained us.

Let us remember the Lord is going to stay with us all the way.

May I believe the Lord always sustains me.

I will believe the Lord sustains me in my sorrow. I will trust the Lord not to leave or forsake me. I will believe the Lord knows what is best for me.

Prayer: *May I believe the Lord knows what is best for me. May I trust the Lord to sustain me.*

Am I trusting the Lord to sustain me? Do I believe the Lord knows what is best for me?

Accepting the Deliverance of the Lord

From the LORD comes deliverance.

—Psalm 3:8

Recovery from loss, sorrow, and grief, first of all is spiritual—"From the Lord comes deliverance."

The issue is spirituality or the lack of it, the capacity or incapacity to adequately deal with the inner life.

If there is to be recovery it must come through spiritual channels. For one thing, we have to become unhooked from unhealthy desires and attachments that involve us with the deceased.

Since the physical bond has been broken, what is left are the emotional and spiritual aspects of grief.

Emotionally we can find help through counseling and other such activities.

But the deepest of all our wounds are spiritual, which means that we have to turn to the Lord in prayer, because deliverance comes from the Lord.

The Lord is able to deliver us from fear, anger, resentment, and hopelessness.

The Lord is able to heal our broken hearts.

The Lord is able to give us new life because salvation belongs to the Lord.

May I accept the deliverance of the Lord into my life.

I will accept the deliverance of the Lord. I will trust God to deliver me spiritually, to set my feet upon a rock. I will believe the Lord is able to heal me.

Prayer: *May I accept the deliverance of the Lord. May I be delivered from sorrow by the power of God.*

Am I believing the Lord is able to heal me? Am I accepting the deliverance of the Lord?

Receiving the Gift of Peace

I will lie down and sleep in peace.

—Psalm 4:8

When we come into close fellowship with God we should be able to sleep in peace with confidence and contentment that we are being looked after by the Lord.

Sometimes this takes a lot of doing on our part. It takes a great deal of faith and trust, together with the will and desire to change.

For instance, we have to be ready to lay aside anxiety by turning it over to the Lord. Of course, that's easier said than done.

Also, we have to surrender all fear, anger, and resentment to the Lord, which also is easier said than done.

However, if we seek the peace of God by offering ourselves up to the Lord, we will find rest for our souls.

We are invited to turn our troubles over to the Lord as an offering. In return, the Lord will bless us with the gift of peace.

May I receive the gift of peace and rest for my soul.

I will seek peace and rest for my soul. I will turn over my anxiety and fear as an offering to the Lord. I will believe God is able to give me the peace for which my heart longs.

Prayer: *May I believe God is able to give me the gift of peace. May I receive the gift of peace from the Lord.*

Am I turning my fear and anxiety over to the Lord? Am I receiving the gift of peace from the Lord?

Finding Safety in the Lord

You alone, O LORD, make me dwell in safety.

—Psalm 4:8

Looking for safety is a very human reaction. Everyone wants to be in a safe place, to live in safety.

We may become so afraid we will not launch out and try anything new.

However, with bereavement there comes the imposed need for us to do some things differently with our lives than we have done before depending, of course, on the nature of the loss.

We must look at certain things and people in a different light. We must make moves we may have not have made before, some of which seem dangerous.

What we are looking for is safety. We want to be safe.

We want no more harm to befall us, because the pain is too severe, and we have had enough pain.

However, in order to heal, we must reach out beyond our fear, asking God to be with us. We must also ask others to be with us.

There is nothing shameful about wanting to be where it is safe.

May I find my safety in the Lord.

I will rest myself confidently in the Lord. I will believe I am safe in the arms of the Lord. I will venture out beyond myself.

Prayer: *May I rest confidently in the Lord. May I venture out beyond myself.*

Am I resting confidently in the arms of the Lord? Am I ready to venture out beyond myself and my fears?

Becoming Unlocked

I will praise you, O LORD, with all my heart.

—Psalm 9:1

There are times when we simply don't know what to do with ourselves, particularly when we find ourselves in unknown and strange places where we never have been before.

We may see that unless we become unlocked emotionally and spiritually we are going to shrivel up and blow away.

It becomes essential, if we are to recover from our grief, that we make some very bold moves out and beyond ourselves.

We simply cannot stay cooped up in a defensive shell and expect to be restored to faith, hope, and love, in the joy of the Lord.

How then do we begin to move out beyond ourselves, to transcend our loss, sorrow, and grief, and to experience the rebirth of our spirit?

We can begin with the psalmist who makes a decision to praise the Lord with no holding back, with no qualifications. No ifs, ands, or buts.

If we praise the Lord with our whole heart, there is nothing that can stop us from becoming emotionally and spiritually unlocked.

May I praise the Lord with all my heart.

I will praise the Lord with all my heart. I will not hold back on my gratitude. I will become unlocked.

Prayer: *May my heart become unlocked. May I move out beyond myself.*

Am I unlocking emotionally and spiritually? Am I moving out beyond myself?

Rejoicing in the Wonderful Deeds of God

I will sing to the LORD, for he has been good to me.
—Psalm 13:6

How has God "been good" to us? Finding answers to this question will help us gain a new outlook on life.

The problem is that too often we don't want to get out of our stuck positions, don't want to look at other possibilities for our life and development.

That, of course, is a situation which cannot be dealt with by anyone other than ourselves.

Singing praises to the Lord must come from the inner self. We must reach for this kind of song, must look for the hand of the Lord at work in our lives, in order to see the goodness of God and to give thanks.

We must look for the hand of God through our tears. When we find the goodness of God, we must extend ourselves into thanksgiving.

In so doing, we heal.

May I sing praises to the Lord.

I will sing praises to the Lord who has been good to me. I will see the goodness of the Lord in my life. I will give thanks to the Lord with a grateful heart.

Prayer: *May I give thanks to the Lord with a grateful heart. May I see the goodness of God in all of my life.*

Am I seeing the goodness of God in my life? Am I giving thanks to the Lord with a grateful heart?

Sharing the Wonderful Deeds of God

I will tell of all your wonders.

—Psalm 9:1

A very real source of help toward our recovery from loss, sorrow, and grief is to remember the works of God in our lives.

We can do this by looking back in order to see what the Lord has done in, with, and through us.

At first we might not see all that much good upon which to reflect. But this will only be true with a first glance over the terrain. When we look closer we begin to see how God has dealt with us in love.

It is true there have been some difficult and painful times, and we may wonder if looking for goodness isn't simply a bad joke. Or, we may become angry at the mere suggestion that there possibly can be anything worthy of our gratitude and thanksgiving.

However, there is goodness because the Lord is good. If we look closely we see this to be true. Then comes the next step: "I will tell of all your wonders."

It is important to share the news of how the Lord has been dealing with us in love, about the "wonders" of God in our lives. It is by sharing the good news of God's love that we grow in hope and joy.

May I tell of the wonders of God in my life.

I will look for the goodness of the Lord. I will tell of the wonders of God in my life. I will rejoice in the goodness of God.

Prayer: *May I rejoice in the goodness of God. May I tell of the wonders of the Lord in my life.*

Am I rejoicing in the goodness of God? Am I telling the wonders of the Lord in my life?

Taking Refuge in the Lord

Keep me safe, O God, for in you I take refuge.
—Psalm 16:1

Everyone comes to a time when refuge, a place to hide, is needed.

Not to hide away so as to escape, but to hide away in order to be strengthened and refreshed.

A child ventures out into the world, perhaps just beyond the front door of the home. Suddenly something happens that frightens the child—a stranger, a barking dog, a loud noise.

The child runs for cover, grabbing hold of mother or father, asking to be held. Then the child feels safe.

However, the child is going to be put down again, to go out the door once more, to face a hostile world again in an attempt to move beyond fear, to come alive again in hope, expectation, and joy.

There is nothing wrong about seeking refuge.

From time to time all of us have this need to be held, to be protected, to be looked after.

We are invited to take our refuge in the Lord, trusting the the Lord to bear us up, and when necessary, to carry us like little children.

May I take refuge in the Lord my God.

I will take refuge in the Lord my God. I will trust the Lord God with my life. I will believe the Lord God is able to save me.

Prayer: *May I take my refuge in the Lord. May I believe the Lord is able to save me from destruction.*

Am I believing the Lord is able to save me? Am I taking my refuge in the Lord?

Finding Goodness in God

Apart from you I have no good thing.

—Psalm 16:2

Eventually, things get sorted out. What we once thought to be important no longer is of consequence. This becomes quite apparent when we experience severe loss.

"Nothing is important to me anymore." Or, "There are many things I once thought were important which no longer are."

Money? Wealth? Power?

What is worthwhile? What is good?

Only God is good, and without God, there is no lasting good.

Enjoyable things and people, possibly, but no lasting good. Enjoyable people and things don't last.

Only God lasts.

And, as Jesus taught, "Only God is good."

Let us say to the Lord, "I have no good apart from you."

Let us say this with heart, mind, and soul.

By so doing we will become focused emotionally and spiritually.

And with this focus we can move on to find our healing.

May I find goodness in God.

I will find goodness in God. I will trust God's goodness that lasts. I will rejoice in the goodness of God.

Prayer: *May I trust the healing goodness of God. May I live the goodness of God from day to day.*

Am I finding my healing in the goodness of God? Am I living the goodness of God from day to day?

Walking the Pathway of God

You have made known to me the path of life.

—Psalm 16:11

God's purpose is to have us grow in wisdom and knowledge and walk the pathway of life.

The path of life is not somewhere out of this world in which we live. The path includes our journeys to hospitals, funeral homes, and cemeteries.

The path of life goes right through our everyday affairs, with the joy and the sorrow, the victories and the defeats.

The path of life is God's way for us to travel, in and through this world, so we can experience victory over fear and death.

The purpose for God's path of life is to bring us into the realization that we are children of God.

The "path of life" is meant to lead us into the kingdom of God, which is our rebirth into faith, hope, and love.

Without the Holy Spirit leading the way, we are blind to the pathways of God.

Therefore, let us pray for the Holy Spirit of God to make known to us the pathways of eternal life.

May the path of life be made known to me, for me to walk in it.

I will look for the path of life in God. I will seek to walk the pathway of the Lord for all of my life. I will believe the Lord will lead me into the light.

Prayer: *May I be led in the pathway of the Lord. May I walk the path of life, in God.*

Am I seeing the pathway of God for me to walk? Am I ready to walk the path of life as it is given to me?

Accepting God's Deliverance

The LORD is my rock, my fortress and my deliverer.
—Psalm 18:2

Who doesn't want stability? Who doesn't need a firm foundation, something built upon a rock, rather than sand that can be washed away by erosion or a flash flood?

Who doesn't need to be delivered from sorrow, from grief, from all kinds of heartache?

And who doesn't need the assurance that there is stability to be had, together with deliverance from sorrow?

The psalmist saw the Lord as a rock and a fortress, also as the deliverer from the hands of enemies—external and internal enemies.

There's not one of us who doesn't have internal enemies of the spirit. Not one who can't use a fortress built on firm foundations. Not one who can't use deliverance from fear.

The work of the Lord is to provide us with a firm foundation, to be a fortress for us.

The work of the Lord is to be our deliverer from all that would keep us bound spiritually in fear and dread.

May I turn to the Lord to be my fortress and deliverer.

I will turn to the Lord to be my rock of stability. I will turn to the Lord to be my fortress. I will accept the deliverance of the Lord from fear and dread.

Prayer: *May I build on the foundation stone of the Lord. May I accept the deliverance of the Lord, and live it.*

Am I building on the firm foundation of the Lord? Am I accepting the deliverance of the Lord into my life?

Feeling Forsaken

My God, my God, why have you forsaken me?

—Psalm 22:1

The scripture for today is a familiar one.

While dying on the cross our Lord felt the dreaded sensation of having been abandoned by God. "My God, my God, why have you forsaken me?" he cried out in anguish.

There is nothing more frightening to human beings than that of being forsaken or abandoned.

No one can tolerate such feelings for any extended period of time without being overcome emotionally, physically, and spiritually.

As we have said before, with suffered loss, sorrow, and grief, there often comes the feeling that we have been forgotten.

We should not be surprised if we find ourselves feeling that we have been abandoned by God. After all, our Lord felt that way, it certainly can happen to us.

In truth, however, God does not abandon us. The promise remains firm: "I will never leave or forsake you."

It is important to remember this promise when we are in the dark valleys of loneliness and near despair.

May I believe I am not being forsaken by God.

I will believe I am not being forsaken by God. I will trust God never to forsake me. I will believe the promise of God to be with me always.

Prayer: *May I believe the promises of God never to forsake me. May I trust God with my life.*

Am I trusting God with my life? Am I believing the Lord will never leave or forsake me?

Being Drawn Closer to God

Why are you so far from saving me?

—Psalm 22:1

It is not necessarily as though we have been forsaken by God, it's just that sometimes God seems out of reach or too far away to help us.

We may reach out to make contact, but no one answers. Perhaps no one picks up the phone or opens the door to invite us in.

It's not uncommon to feel that God is far from helping, far from even extending a hand. Dreadful experiences can make us feel this way. And why not?

But then if we take another and closer look, we begin to see the loving hand of God at work in our life. Not only in the past, but right here, in the present, in the midst of our sorrow.

God never is far from helping us, regardless of the circumstances in which we find ourselves, painful as they may be.

Therefore, let us draw ourselves closer to God. Or better still, let us allow God to draw us closer.

It works better that way.

May I be drawn closer to God.

I will trust the Lord never to be far from me. I will trust the Lord's faithfulness. I will ask God to draw me closer.

Prayer: *May I believe the Lord is never far from me. May I be drawn closer to the Lord.*

Am I trusting the Lord? Am I believing the Lord is drawing me closer?

Believing that the Lord Is Near

Do not be far from me.

—Psalm 22:11

This scripture says, "Do not be far from me, for trouble is near and there is no one to help."

"No one to help" means what it says.

Everyone is gone.

No one is around to help, and real danger is ahead, waiting to destroy us.

We need help, but it feels as though no one is listening.

There is a vacuum, a void.

Sometimes even friends seem not to be there—not as we might like them to be. Not all the way there. Not really with us, emotionally or spiritually.

As we said yesterday and the day before, sometimes this is the way it is with our feelings.

The Lord can seem very far off. We must pray God to draw us closer, to take us in, to be with us all the way through.

Granted, in our loss, sorrow, and grief it is sometimes very difficult to be conscious of the presence of God. Nevertheless, we should remember that God is not far from us because God is part of us.

And we are part of God.

May I see and believe God is always near to me.

I will believe the Lord is near. I will trust the Lord to stay nearby. I will believe God and give thanks.

Prayer: *May I seek the Lord. May I trust the nearness of the Lord.*

Am I seeking the Lord? Do I believe the Lord is with me always?

Sharing Our Feelings

I am poured out like water, . . . my heart has turned to wax; it has melted away within me. My strength is dried up.
—Psalm 22:14-15

We lose energy in times of stress. Our bodies don't function well because of the added stress. We can be slowed down considerably, not able to work as we would like to. Sometimes there are guilt feelings because we aren't getting much done.

In short, we are in depression.

The psalmist expressed his feelings dramatically: "I am poured out like water. My heart has turned to wax. My strength is dried up." He didn't hesitate to tell the Lord how bad he felt.

There are days when our strength is dried up and we feel melted down emotionally, spiritually, and physically—especially if the grief is exceptionally deep.

It's important not to deny what is happening to us, but to be as open as possible and find someone to talk to. Sharing our feelings is very important for our health and healing.

By sharing our painful feelings with someone who can listen, we open ourselves to be released, to be healed.

May I share my deepest pain with someone else.

I will find someone who will listen to me when I need help. I will seek professional help if necessary. I will trust the Lord to be with me.

Prayer: *May I trust the Lord to be with me. May I find someone to talk to.*

Am I seeking the help I need for my recovery? Am I finding someone to talk to about my sorrow and stress?

Being Cared For

The LORD is my shepherd, I shall not be in want.

—Psalm 23:1

We know what it is to feel deep and heartbreaking sorrow.

What we may not always be able to remember, however, is the Good Shepherd's readiness to help us in our grief, to provide what we need for health and healing.

The psalmist was a shepherd. He knew how much sheep depend upon the shepherd.

Whether the sheep realize it or not, the good shepherd takes care of his sheep.

The good shepherd provides for the sheep, seeing that they have everything they need.

When a single sheep is lost, the good shepherd goes looking for it.

It is the good shepherd's business to be alert to the needs of the sheep, guarding them with his life.

Our Lord says, "I am the Good Shepherd."

The Lord provides what we need for recovery from loss, sorrow, and grief.

We can say, "I shall not be in want."

May I believe I shall not be in want.

I will believe the Lord is my shepherd. I will believe I shall not be in want. I will believe the Lord supplies my every need.

Prayer: *May I believe the Lord supplies all I need. May I believe I shall not be in want.*

Am I believing the Lord supplies all I need? Am I believing I shall not be in want?

Lying Down in Green Pastures

He makes me lie down in green pastures.

—Psalm 23:2

Are we to take this imagery seriously, that the Lord actually leads us to green pastures, where we can find rest for our souls?

The only way to find out is to enter the relationship of trust, believing the Lord will lead us to new life and new hope.

With trust we can turn our wills and our lives over to the care and keeping of the Lord.

The promise is that the Lord will give us all we need for our health and healing.

The "green pastures" may not look very green to us right away. We may be spiritually color blind.

Green looks brown or black. Light is dark. Up is down. Right is wrong. Good is bad.

However, once we establish our trust in the Good Shepherd, things begin to change for the better. Our sorrow turns toward joy, we are able to see the green pastures of God's deep love, and we are ready to let go and lie down, to find rest for our souls.

May I lie down in the green pastures of the Lord.

I will believe the Lord knows best. I will do what the Lord asks. I will take my rest in the green pastures of the Lord.

Prayer: *May I believe the Lord and do his bidding. May I believe the Lord gives me what is best.*

Am I trusting the Lord to do what is best for me? Am I ready to lie down in the green pastures of the Lord?

Being Led to Quiet Waters

He leads me beside quiet waters.

—Psalm 23:2

By ourselves we cannot see our way through the pain of separation. Emotionally and spiritually we can be confused: it becomes difficult to sort things out, difficult to know what to do with our feelings, and impossible to know what to do with the rest of our lives.

We must be led to a quiet place where the turbulence is stilled.

By ourselves we cannot find the resting place. We don't know the way to peace and rest.

Hidden in the rugged mountains of wind and cold and storms is a quiet valley.

In that valley are green pastures beside quiet waters, with room to lie down and rest.

The Lord knows the way to the quiet waters; we don't.

Our task is to follow the leading of the Lord. The Lord always leads us where we need to be led.

When we need the quiet waters, the Lord will get us there.

When we are ready for the turbulence again, the Lord will lead us through.

The Lord will help us to grow in faith, hope, and love.

May I be led to the quiet waters to be refreshed.

I will entrust myself to the Lord. I will be led to the quiet waters. I will come to the quiet waters of the Lord and be refreshed.

Prayer: *May I be led to the quiet waters. May I become calm and peaceful before the Lord.*

Am I allowing myself to be led by the Lord? Am I coming to the quiet waters?

Being Spiritually Restored

He restores my soul.

—Psalm 23:3

Because we are always in the process of rising and falling, we need to be emotionally and spiritually restored; we need to be brought back, made new again, day after day—especially when we are suffering from loss, sorrow, and grief.

Real restoration, the restoration of our souls, is the capacity to relate, to feel, to love, to believe, to have faith, to hope.

Restoration is spiritual.

To be "restored" is to be brought back into existence.

God's restoration is a gift inherited by our willingness to be returned to new hope and new life under the guidance and leading of our Lord.

However, we cannot be restored unless and until we want to be brought back "into existence."

As we noted yesterday, we must be led to restoration because we don't know the way to the quiet waters of the Lord.

Loss, sorrow, and grief can be soul-shattering experiences for many of us. There is no easy way through the darkness.

Nevertheless, the Lord is able to restore our souls, strengthening us in faith, hope, and love.

May I be spiritually restored.

I will be spiritually restored. I will trust the Lord to restore me. I will rejoice in my restoration.

Prayer: *May I be given new life and hope. May I trust the Lord to restore me.*

Do I want to be spiritually restored today? Do I trust the Lord to restore my soul?

Seeking the Paths of Righteousness

He guides me in paths of righteousness.

—Psalm 23:3

As we progress in our recovery from loss, sorrow, and grief, we sense a growing desire for righteousness, the willingness to do what is right, good, and true.

This is because our experienced loss has left us clear about the preciousness of life, and that we must make the most of what little time we have left.

We seek what is real, true, and lasting, and will settle for nothing less.

We become eager to grow in faith, hope, and love.

We become more conscious and concerned about the welfare of others.

In short, we are seeking the paths of righteousness: love, giving, receiving, sharing, and blessing.

So, we pray the Lord to lead us in the paths of righteousness, because therein is new life, new hope, and new joy.

May I be led into the paths of righteousness.

I will seek the paths of righteousness. I will ask the Lord to lead me. I will follow the leading of the Lord.

Prayer: *May I seek the paths of righteousness. May I follow the leading of the Lord.*

Am I seeking the paths of righteousness? Am I asking the Lord to lead me?

Serving His Name

For his name's sake . . .

—Psalm 23:3

While we must do what is best for us, in order to recover from deep sorrow, we also must find reasons for living, growing, and serving—in love.

Within ourselves we cannot find that kind of reason, that much of a pull or draw, because we are locked into self-centeredness and cannot break out on our own.

It is necessary, therefore, to seek a higher good. In our case, that higher good is the Christ, our Lord.

"For his name's sake"—the name of Jesus—we seek the higher good; we do this because Jesus is our Lord.

In Christ, "for his name's sake," we are able to rise above ourselves, and to break out of our shells of self-centeredness, selfishness, and fear. Then it is no longer we who live, but Christ who lives within us.

It is important to become deeply attached to Christ as soon as possible. For it is in the name of Christ that we are able to rise from the ashes of our loss and inherit the new life that is being offered.

May I do what needs to be done in Jesus' name.

I will live my life in the name of Jesus. I will do what I do for Jesus' sake. I will give glory to my Lord in all I do.

Prayer: *May I give glory to the Lord's name in all I do. May I live my life in the name of the Lord.*

Am I living my life in the name of my Lord? Am I giving glory to the Lord in all I do?

Remembering the Presence of the Lord

Though I walk through the valley of the shadow of death, I will fear no evil, for you are with me; your rod and your staff, they comfort me.

—Psalm 23:4

Yes, our life's walk is through the deep valleys of the shadow of death. That shadow is so needlessly feared, because the Lord is with us.

Yes, we are always surrounded by destructive forces.

Yes, we do lose our loved ones and have our connections broken. And yes, we do experience fear.

This is our human condition, which need not be denied.

However, we also have the eternal presence of the Lord: "For you are with me; your rod and your staff, they comfort me."

We need not be afraid because we are being watched over and cared for in God's own way and time.

Regardless how deep, dark, and dangerous the valleys, we have the presence of the Lord to comfort us.

May I be comforted by the presence of the Lord.

I will believe the Lord is with me. I will find comfort in the presence of the Lord. I will believe the Lord protects me.

Prayer: *May I believe the Lord is with me. May I trust the Lord to protect me.*

Do I believe the Lord is with me? Do I trust the Lord to protect me?

Going to the Table of the Lord

You prepare a table before me in the presence of my enemies.
—Psalm 23:5

Enemies. Do we have enemies?

Perhaps not in the sense that someone is trying to destroy us, but enemies of another sort.

Internal enemies such as fear, doubt, anxiety, and dread. And always, there is the potential enemy of hopelessness.

In the face of our enemies, the Lord has a table prepared for us, and the Lord invites us to enter into his feast.

"Come to the table of the Lord," is the invitation.

The Lord is ready to feed us, ready to give comfort and joy.

Our enemies of fear, doubt, anxiety, and dread become lessened as we go to the table of the Lord as we, together with our brothers and sisters in Christ, enter into the presence of the Lord.

Most certainly, the Lord prepares a table before us in the presence of our enemies.

But it is up to us to decide what to do with the invitation: "Come to the table of the Lord."

May I go to the table of the Lord.

I will go to the table of the Lord. I will taste the Lord's goodness. I will rejoice in the Lord.

Prayer: *May I see what the Lord has prepared for me. May I taste the goodness of the Lord.*

Am I going to the table of the Lord? Am I tasting the Lord's goodness?

Giving Thanks for the Overflowing Cup

You anoint my head with oil, my cup overflows.

—Psalm 23:5

The old hymn rightfully says, "Count your many blessings, count them one by one."

In other words, take time to list and look at each and every blessing and give thanks for the overflowing cup of mercy.

The greatest blessings are found in the recognition of God's work being done in our lives in so many unexpected places. God's work is done in hidden ways and hidden places deep within ourselves, where no one but we and the Lord may be able to see.

Where once there was fear, now faith is growing.

Where once there was dread, now hope begins to blossom.

Where once there was deep sorrow, now there are flickers of joy and serenity.

Let us look for the cup that is overflowing and accept the anointing of God's love.

Let us open ourselves to the blessings of the Lord and let the light come into our lives, even into the most painful places.

And, above all, let us give thanks for the overflowing cup of God's love.

May I give thanks for the abundance of the Lord.

I will look for the goodness of the Lord in my life. I will see the overflowing cup of blessings. I will give thanks to the Lord.

Prayer: *May I look for the goodness of the Lord in my life. May I see the cup of overflowing blessings and give thanks.*

Am I looking for the goodness of the Lord in my life? Am I seeing the blessings of the Lord given to me?

Believing the Goodness of the Lord

Surely goodness and love will follow me all the days of my life.
—Psalm 23:6

Recovery depends on how we look at things and react to them, whether we are expecting good or ill to befall us, whether we can believe in God's goodness and love.

If we have gone over our list of blessings, as suggested yesterday, we probably have a different attitude than we had the day before yesterday. Maybe even an attitude of hope and expectation for whatever is to come.

Let us visualize the goodness of the Lord always being with us from this day forward, all the days of our life.

Let us see how that can bring a change of attitude for the better. Let us simply begin to say to ourselves and others, "Surely goodness and love will follow me all the days of my life."

If we are not satisfied with our lives, perhaps we can take a look at our attitudes, asking ourselves questions.

"Am I expecting the best or the worst to happen to me?"

"Am I certain that the goodness and love of God will follow me all the days of my life? Do I know that each time I fall, the Lord is there is help me get up and go on?"

May I believe the goodness and love of God.

I will trust the goodness and love of God. I will believe God is with me all the days of my life. I will look forward to the future.

Prayer: *May I believe God is with me. May I rejoice in the goodness of the Lord.*

Do I believe the goodness and love of the Lord also is for me? Do I trust the Lord to be with me, and bless me, all the days of my life?

Dwelling in the House of the Lord

I will dwell in the house of the Lord forever.

—Psalm 23:6

Everyone is looking for a sense of well-being, for a place where we know we belong.

Where there is no sense of belonging, there is anxiety, unhappiness, and depression of spirit.

Finding a dwelling place with the Lord is finding our location with God.

Unfortunately we often forget God's purpose for us: "To dwell in the house of the Lord forever."

In times of deep sorrow the sense of separation can deepen. We may feel there is no dwelling place for us. No place where we belong.

The truth is that there is no final contentment apart from the Lord. As St. Augustine noted, "Our souls do not find rest until they find rest in God."

To "dwell in the house of the Lord forever" is to be connected to God; it is to seek the Lord's will to be done in our lives, to trust the Lord to do what is best for us in whatever condition we find ourselves, and to live in the Spirit of God.

May I dwell in the house of the Lord forever.

I will turn to the Lord with my whole heart. I will seek the Lord. I will dwell in the house of the Lord forever.

Prayer: *May I seek the Lord's will in my life. May I dwell in the house of the Lord forever.*

Am I turning to the Lord? Am I dwelling in the house of the Lord with my whole heart?

Seeing the Hand of God at Work

The earth is the Lord's, and everything in it, the world, and all who live in it.

—Psalm 24:1

To heal we must be able to see beyond our shells and get out of our cocoons. For this to happen we have to gain a new vision of life and of the creation in which we are trying to live.

Seeing the Lord at work in the world is important for broadening our vision and hope.

Our God is not locked up in a sanctuary. The Lord is active in the world, offering mercy, binding up wounds, putting together what has been broken.

Also, it makes a difference how we view ourselves in relation to God and the creation. For, if we don't see that we are part of the created order, and have no sensation of belonging to the Lord's creation, we are in a very hard place; we are locked into the whimsies of fate.

There are vital questions to ask ourselves: "Do I believe the earth is the Lord's and everything in it, including myself? Do I believe the Lord is paying close attention to me and my pain?"

May I see God at work in the world and in my life.

I will look for the hand of God at work in the creation. I will see myself as part of God's creation. I will trust God with my life and give thanks.

Prayer: *May I see the love of God at work in the world. May I celebrate the gifts of God given to me.*

Am I looking for the love of God in the world around me? Am I experiencing the workings of God in my life, day by day?

Lifting Our Souls to God

To you, O LORD, I lift up my soul.

—Psalm 25:1

Several times in past meditations we have pointed out the need to get outside of ourselves, to see beyond ourselves.

How is this possible when we are feeling so bad, in our loss, sorrow, and grief?

We have our better days and our not-so-good days. It's all part of everyday life and the process of recovery from loss, sorrow, and grief.

Life has its ups and downs, and we can always use just a bit of a spiritual lift, or sometimes, a substantial boost.

When we are "down" it is natural to look for a "lifter upper."

Some seek a "lift" through the use of alcohol or other drugs, by overeating, or by an excessive use of caffeine. But "lifters" finally leave us emotionally and spiritually depressed.

The only real "lift" comes from above, as we lift up our souls to the Lord in prayer, praise, and adoration.

The promise is that when we lift up our souls to the Lord we are not disappointed.

The Lord hears, the Lord responds, and the Lord heals.

May I lift up my soul unto the Lord.

I will lift up my soul to the Lord. I will sing praises to the Lord with my heart and my life. I will serve the Lord with gladness, and I will heal.

Prayer: *May I turn to the Lord with praise and thanksgiving. May I serve the Lord with gladness.*

Am I lifting my soul up to the Lord? Am I serving the Lord with gladness?

Being Established in Trust

In you I trust, O my God.

—Psalm 25:2

Hopefully, in our bereavement we come to discover the basic need to trust.

When we are shattered by grief there is a strong tendency to lose heart and to lose trust in ourselves, in others, and in God.

However, if we don't establish and build trust there can be no lasting recovery.

Trust is the building block for quality recovery from loss, sorrow, and grief.

When we are being hurt by circumstances beyond our control, it can be very difficult to place our trust anywhere—in ourselves, in others, or in God.

Losing a loved one is a circumstance beyond our control.

With the loss of a loved one there also can develop a loss of trust.

In order to heal we must build our trust in God. Only then are we able to begin trusting ourselves and others.

May I place my trust in the Lord.

I will trust God. I will believe the Lord is going to show me the way I am to be going. I will go where I am led.

Prayer: *May I believe the Lord will show me the way. May I go where I am being led.*

Am I trusting the Lord? Am I going where I am being led?

Being Led and Taught

Show me your ways, O LORD, teach me your paths.
—Psalm 25:4

There are times when we simply get lost, when we don't know where we are or where we are going. Such confusion results in more fear and anxiety.

We try our old ways of doing things, but nothing seems to work. We walk the same paths we have been walking for years, but we get lost and upset.

It should become obvious to us that there has to be a better way for us to go, and better paths to follow. But sometimes, we are very slow learners, and too filled with false pride to ask for help.

We say, "I'll figure this out for myself. I can do it on my own. I don't need anyone to help me."

The truth is this: When we are suffering loss, sorrow, and grief, we don't know where we are. We can't figure things out for ourselves, or recover on our own. We need outside help in order to heal.

The psalmist knew he needed outside help when he prayed, "Show me your ways, teach me your paths." He was not too proud or too stubborn to ask God for help.

May I be led and taught by the Lord.

I will be shown where I am to be going. I will trust the pathways of God. I will go where the Lord leads me.

Prayer: *May I be shown the pathways of God. May I go where I am led by the Lord.*

Am I seeing the pathways of God? Am I going where the Lord is ready to lead me?

Seeking the Guidance and Teaching of God

Guide me in your truth and teach me.

—Psalm 25:5

To ask to be guided and taught is either something we generally forget to do, or don't do at all, for fear of losing face or for other senseless reasons.

However, the truth is that we human beings need teachers.

To learn, we have to be taught.

Self-teaching goes only so far and often is filled with self-deception.

We have to be taught how to recover from loss, sorrow, and grief.

We also have to be guided out of the dark valleys.

Praying for the guidance and teaching of the Lord can be very productive for our recovery. And the sooner we pray, the better—the sooner our sorrow will be turned into joy.

The Lord is ready to guide and to teach us when we are ready to be guided and taught.

Until we are "ready" to be guided and taught, there is nothing the Lord can do to help us heal.

May I be guided and taught by the Lord.

I will turn to the Lord in prayer. I will ask the Lord to lead me into truth. I will ask the Lord to teach me the way of life.

Prayer: *May I ask the Lord to teach me the way of life. May I ask the Lord to lead me into the light.*

Am I asking the Lord to lead me? Am I ready to have the Lord teach me?

Hoping in the Lord

You are my God my Savior, and my hope is in you all day long.
—Psalm 25:5

Is there anything more difficult or emotionally draining than trying to have hope when we are feeling hopeless or when we are frightened by what may happen next?

Waiting and trying to be hopeful about what is happening, or about to happen, can be painful—like when we are in the waiting room of a hospital while a loved one is in surgery.

During such times it can seem as though even God has deserted us. We simply may not sense the presence of the Lord.

It's as though God has gone into hiding. It's as though everything is going to be over and done with forever, before the Lord comes to save us.

Why do we have to wait? Why the hopeless feelings? Why can't the Lord come right away and make everyone well? Why do we have to endure more suffering and sorrow? Why do I have to be left behind alone?

Obviously there is just too much for more than one day at a time, but when we place our hope in God our Savior, all day long, the questions asked begin to find their own answers, and we begin to have hope; we begin to heal.

May I place my hope in the Lord day after day.

I will place my hope in the Lord. I will be ready to receive what the Lord is ready to give. I will give thanks to the Lord.

Prayer: *May I wait for the Lord with hope and expectation. May I be ready to receive the Lord's help for my healing.*

Am I hopeful? Am I ready to receive what the Lord is ready to give?

Trusting the Steadfast Love of the Lord

All the ways of the LORD are loving and faithful for those who keep the demands of his covenant.

—Psalm 25:10

We need love and faithfulness. This is true for all human beings, particularly when we are bereft. We need the assurance of a love and a faithfulness having a real sticking quality.

We need someone we can trust without reservations. Apart from the Lord, who is worthy of such love and faithfulness?

Do we know this faithfulness to be true for ourselves?

Is it our experience that the Lord is faithful and loving?

Let us take a long and deep look into our lives and see how the Lord has always been loving and faithful to us.

Has there ever been a time when we can honestly say we actually have been forsaken by the Lord? Or that we ever have been lacking in God's love?

While at times it may seem we have been forsaken, a closer look tells us this is not true. Even in the most trying and desperate times we are surrounded by the love and faithfulness of the Lord.

As we faithfully live in the covenant of the Lord, we find healing for our souls.

May I see the love and faithfulness of the Lord.

I will look for the love and faithfulness of the Lord at work in my life. I will trust the Lord to love me forever. I will give thanks to the Lord.

Prayer: *May I trust the faithfulness of the Lord. May I believe God loves me deeply and richly.*

Am I trusting the love and faithfulness of the Lord? Do I believe the Lord loves me deeply and richly?

Seeing New Light and Salvation

The LORD is my light and my salvation—whom shall I fear?
—Psalm 27:1

When we are in the pits of our sorrow and grief, we need to see light to find a salvation from the pain of our loss.

But this isn't easy.

We may reach in many different directions for salvation, looking for someone or something to give us new light, new insights, new directions to travel.

Or we may come to believe that new light is impossible, that there is no salvation, no hope, no joy.

However, in order to heal it is necessary to see new light and salvation. Otherwise we are doomed to live in fear, dread, and hopelessness.

In and of ourselves we are not able to see our way through. Without the light and salvation of the Lord we remain stuck in ignorance and fear.

The psalmist recognized his need for outside help.

Except for the light and salvation of the Lord, he saw himself locked up in ignorance and fear.

Except for the light and salvation of the Lord, we too remain locked up in ignorance and fear.

May I see the Lord's light and salvation.

I will see the light and salvation of the Lord. I will believe the Lord is going to take care of me. I will fear no evil.

Prayer: *May I believe God's light and salvation is for me. May I fear no evil.*

Do I believe the Lord is near to me? Do I see the light and salvation of the Lord at work in my life?

Being Kept Safe by the Lord

In the day of trouble he will keep me safe in his dwelling . . . and set me high upon a rock.

—Psalm 27:5

The scripture for today is an affirmation that the Lord keeps us safe in days of trouble.

The Lord is ready to "keep us safe in his dwelling" in the day of trouble, ready to place us "upon a high rock" where it is safe.

Let us think of ourselves as being lifted out of a madly rushing river and being placed on a high rock.

The river is still there, with all of its danger, but we are in a safe place.

We likely will be back in the rushing river again, but the Lord will go with us.

Let us trust the Lord to be with us all the way through these turbulent times, to give us shelter when we need rest for our souls.

May we find shelter in the dwelling of the Lord.
May the Lord set us upon a high rock.
May we find a hiding place in God.
May the Lord go with us all the way.

May I find my hiding place in God.

I will find my hiding place in the Lord. I will allow myself to be sheltered by the Lord. I will trust the Lord to be with me.

Prayer: *May I believe the Lord will give me shelter. May I forever trust the Lord to be with me.*

Am I trusting the Lord to be with me? Am I allowing myself to be sheltered by the Lord?

Making Music to the Lord

I will sing and make music to the LORD.

—Psalm 27:6

There are many ways to express ourselves that assist in our healing. One way can be singing. Making music to the Lord.

Why is this important?

Because singing can release tension.

Singing can help clear energy passages for the Spirit of God to flow for healing.

In the most trying of circumstances, people have turned to singing for strength to rise above their travail.

Slaves have sung their way through merciless cotton fields and other miseries.

Prisoners have sung hymns to God.

Songs of hope and joy can be heard where there is deep sorrow and suffering.

Singing heals.

Let us open our hearts to the Lord, and may music rise to the Lord.

May I sing and make music to the Lord.

I will sing and make music to the Lord. I will open myself to the goodness of God and give thanks. I will praise the Lord with a grateful heart.

Prayer: *May I praise God with a grateful heart. May I open myself to the goodness of God and give thanks.*

Am I opening myself to the goodness of God? Am I praising the Lord with a grateful heart?

Seeing and Celebrating the Goodness of God

I am still confident of this: I will see the goodness of the LORD in the land of the living.

—Psalm 27:13

Comfort is knowing that there is eternal life and that one day we shall see our loved ones again. But there also is the here and now in which we are called to live.

Is the goodness of the Lord still here? Did we miss it? If so, where did it go?

There are times when everything seems so dark, so hopeless, as though nothing good can come out of this life on earth, "in the land of the living."

The psalmist had a different vision.

The psalmist believed the possibility of seeing the goodness of the Lord in the here and now.

He was determined to invest himself in living his life to the fullest extent possible, to know the goodness of the Lord on this side of the grave. That is a good sign of health.

The only way we are going to be able to inherit the joy of the world to come is to inherit it now, where we are.

We must be confident of the goodness of the Lord in the here and now, and live and celebrate that goodness.

May I see the goodness of God and celebrate it.

I will believe the goodness of God. I will see the goodness of the Lord in my life. I will live and celebrate God's goodness with joy.

Prayer: *May I believe the goodness of the Lord. May I accept the goodness of God and celebrate it.*

Do I believe the goodness of the Lord is mine to have? Am I ready to accept the goodness of God, to live and to celebrate it?

Waiting for the Lord to Move

Wait for the LORD.

—Psalm 27:14

Sometimes we are impatient.

Impatience is destructive, especially when we are determined to get something done which doesn't flow and fit together the way we want. When we insist on getting our own way. When our self-will pushes, and tires us out.

Learning to wait for the Lord is a spiritual commitment that has to be developed.

However, almost everything we are taught in our culture is against waiting.

In fact, waiting often is considered to be a real cop-out, something for lazy people who don't have any ambition to get ahead.

But if we listen carefully to the spiritual wisdom of the ages, we always bump into the word *wait.*

"Wait for the Lord."

Another way of saying this is "Go with the flow."

Or, "Let go and let God."

This wisdom can be of great help in our recovery.

May I wait patiently for the Lord to move in my life.

I will be patient. I will wait for the Lord to move in my life. I will believe the Lord is intent on doing what is best with me and for me.

Prayer: *May I believe the Lord intends the best for me. May I wait patiently for the Lord to move in my life.*

Am I waiting patiently for the Lord to move in my life? Am I confident the Lord knows what is best for me?

Being Strong in the Lord

Be strong and take heart.

—Psalm 27:14

To be strong and take heart is to have courage.

Courage is the quality of mind and heart that enables us to encounter difficulties and dangers with confidence, hope, and firmness.

When we are bereft, in the depths of our sorrow, we don't feel very courageous.

There are times when it seems as though we have no courage at all, no capacity to endure, to carry on.

This can be quite frightening.

When the psalmist speaks about being strong and taking heart, he means "in the Lord," not in ourselves.

When we are urged to be strong and take heart we are not being told to become heroes, nor are we being asked to do something we can't do.

Rather, we simply are being urged to turn our wills and our lives over to the care and keeping of God, for the Lord to lead and guide, for the Lord to help us through the dark valleys.

May I be strong and may my heart take on the courage of the Lord.

I will be strong in the Lord. I will find my courage in the power of the Lord. I will believe the Lord is able to strengthen me.

Prayer: *May I be strong in the Lord. May I find my courage in the power of God.*

Am I finding my courage in the power of God? Am I being strong in the Lord?

Being Shielded by the Lord

The LORD is my strength and my shield; my heart trusts in him.

—Psalm 28:7

The Lord is our strength.

The Lord is our shield, our protector.

Therefore it is possible for us to trust the Lord.

When we do this, we are led through our recovery from loss, sorrow, and grief into wholeness of life.

In and of ourselves we have little strength to deal with the tumults of life. We simply are not put together to live as isolated beings.

We always are in need of relationship, in need of grace, in need of God's protection, to carry us through.

Insisting on trying to make it through the dark valleys without the help of the Lord is wasteful.

If we want the strength and protection of the Lord, they are always there, waiting for us to be reclaimed by them.

We never need be without these gifts.

We can always trust God to protect us, to be our shield.

May I trust the Lord to be my shield.

I will turn to the Lord for strength. I will accept the Lord as my shield. I will place my trust and confidence in the Lord.

Prayer: *May I turn to the Lord with trust and confidence. May I be protected by the shield of the Lord.*

Am I trusting the Lord to be my shield? Do I believe the Lord will protect me?

Rejoicing in the Goodness of God

I am helped and my heart leaps for joy.

—Psalm 28:7

When we trust the Lord with our lives we are helped. When we reflect on the help the Lord has given us, we experience a sense of well-being and of joy. This is the major part of our recovery—being helped, feeling joy, giving thanks to God.

It is important to say, "I have been helped by the Lord." It is important to hear ourselves affirm the help of the Lord.

It's also important to give thanks. When we do we experience the joy of the Lord. Gratitude and joy are partners, one going with the other.

If we want joy, we must have gratitude and give thanks. This will be followed by quiet sensations of serenity, and sometimes even exciting displays of celebration.

Our hearts may leap with a lively and triumphant joy. This is difficult to imagine when we are deep in our loss, sorrow, and grief.

Nevertheless, we have the promise that joy comes to those who seek it, who bring it about through the giving of thanks.

It is not always easy, but giving thanks to the Lord is the way to healing and health of the spirit—then our hearts will leap for joy.

May I rejoice in the goodness of God.

I will trust the Lord to help me. I will be grateful for the gifts of God given to me. I will praise the Lord with my whole heart.

Prayer: *May I give thanks to the Lord with my whole heart. May I trust the Lord to bring me joy.*

Am I trusting the Lord to give me new life? Am I praising the Lord with my whole heart?

Seeking the Lord's Help

O LORD my God, I cried to you for help and you healed me.
—Psalm 30:2

The psalmist is reporting something that happened to him: he was in trouble; he cried to the Lord for help; the Lord healed him.

This is not easy for many of us to do—to cry for help when we need it. But there come times when we run out of strength, when joy is hidden somewhere in the deepest reaches of our souls, when we are unable to feel gratitude or give thanks.

However, once we consciously experience the healing hand of the Lord, we begin to take another look at our situation. We become more comfortable about asking, even crying for help.

We begin to understand we do not heal ourselves, but the Lord heals.

The truth is the Lord hears our cries.

The Lord hears and heals. Perhaps not as we believe we should be healed, but, nevertheless, healed in ways most beneficial to us and our spiritual growth.

The question is always the same: "Am I ready to let the Lord heal me, to bind up my wounds, to set me free?"

May I seek the healing of the Lord.

I will seek the healing of the Lord. I will let God bind up my wounds. I will trust the Lord to heal me.

Prayer: *May I turn to the Lord for healing. May I trust the Lord to heal my sorrow.*

Am I turning to the Lord for healing? Am I trusting God to heal my broken heart?

Seeing a New Day

Weeping may remain for a night, but rejoicing comes in the morning.

—Psalm 30:5

Disturbed sleep can be a real part of the bereavement experience. During the night there may be tossing and turning.

There also may be an abundance of tears, with deep lamenting and weeping, such as we have never known before.

The "night" can be extended periods of time: days and months of darkness, because it takes time to recover and heal.

The promise is that "rejoicing comes in the morning"—not the immediate morning, necessarily, or not for many mornings, but eventually.

Joy comes when we have worked our way through our pain with the help of the Lord.

It is then we find our morning dawning with renewed light, renewed brightness, and renewed warmth.

The Lord brings us into the new day one step at a time.

May my joy come in the morning.

I will turn to the Lord. I will look for the joy of the Lord. I will see my weeping turned into the morning of a new day.

Prayer: *May I see my weeping turned into joy. May I see the dawn of a new day for my life.*

Am I ready to see the dawning of a new day for my life? Am I ready to let the Lord heal me?

Giving Thanks to the Lord Forever

O LORD my God, I will give you thanks forever.
—Psalm 30:12

Once we enter into a state of thanksgiving we are well on our way to recovery. However, getting there can be difficult because we have so much of ourselves standing in the way of God's grace.

As long as our self-centeredness is in the way, there is little God can do to bring us peace of mind and heart.

But when we release ourselves from self-centeredness, the healing of God is able to enter and rebuild our souls. With this comes the song of the psalmist, "O Lord my God, I will give you thanks forever."

When healing is experienced there is relief. But relief doesn't last long without ongoing gratitude and the giving of thanks.

If we hold back on the giving of thanks we quickly are back under the burden of sorrow and grief.

There are spiritual exercises which strengthen us spiritually, and giving thanks is one of the most vital and health giving.

To give thanks forever means we recognize where our help comes from, and everything we receive from God is a gift of grace.

May I give thanks forever to the Lord.

I will remember the goodness of the Lord. I will give thanks to the Lord. I will bless the name of the Lord with my whole heart.

Prayer: *May I bless the Lord with my whole heart and life. May I give thanks to the Lord forever.*

Am I giving thanks to the Lord? Am I blessing the name of the Lord with my whole heart?

Committing Ourselves to the Lord

Into your hands I commit my spirit.

—Psalm 31:5

When we enter into the act of surrender, as our Lord demonstrated with his life and death, we are well on our way to recovery.

Turning ourselves, our wills, and lives, over to God is most helpful for recovery from loss, sorrow, and grief.

"Into your hands I commit my spirit."

As usual, this isn't as easy as it may sound.

When we come right down to it, we tend to hang on to our "old" stuff: old fear, old anger, old resentments, old grief.

We must become ready to do something else with our lives than hanging on to what has been and cannot be again.

Of course, letting go is painfully difficult.

However, when we are ready, God is ready to receive us.

With Jesus we too can say, "Into your hands I commit my spirit." When we do we place ourselves where we have always belonged, from the foundation of the world—with God!

Then, at last, we are "at home" where there is a resting place for our souls.

May I commit my spirit to the Lord.

I will commit my spirit to the Lord today. I will entrust my life to the care and keeping of God. I will receive the strength of God's love into my life.

Prayer: *May I entrust my life to the mercies of God. May I receive the strength of the Lord.*

Am I committing my spirit to the Lord? Am I receiving the strength of the Lord into my life?

Rejoicing in Steadfast Love

I will be glad and rejoice in your love, for you saw my affliction and knew the anguish of my soul.

—Psalm 31:7

One of the most painful experiences of life is to be ignored—not to be seen, heard, or cared about. Left alone and unrecognized, we human beings become emotionally disturbed, sometimes seriously.

On the other hand, when we know someone cares about us, and is interested in our welfare, and even more particularly, loves us, we become glad of heart. We feel uplifted.

In bereavement, feelings of insignificance can develop, and we may feel as though no one is seeing or hearing us, as though no one really cares what is happening to us.

However, when it becomes clear the Lord hears, sees, and cares, we begin to feel better.

It is very important to know we are not being ignored.

God doesn't ignore us.

It is important that someone hears and sees us.

God hears, sees, and responds to our cries for help.

It is important that we are not left alone and abandoned.

God doesn't forsake or abandon us.

Therefore we can be glad and rejoice in the Lord.

May I be glad and rejoice in the Lord's love.

I will rejoice in the love of the Lord. I will believe the Lord does not overlook my needs. I will trust the Lord to see and hear me when I cry for help.

Prayer: *I will trust the Lord to see and hear me. I will rejoice in the love of the Lord.*

Am I trusting the Lord to see and hear me? Am I rejoicing in the love of the Lord?

Being Confident in the Hands of the Lord

My times are in your hands.

—Psalm 31:15

The psalmist finds himself surrounded by many enemies and is depending on the protection of the Lord.

He is saying his life is in the hands of the Lord each moment, each hour, every day, and in all circumstances.

The length of his time on earth is determined by the Lord: how long he is to live in his body, when his end will come, and how.

Although he is a king, with armies at his command, his confidence is in the Lord. As enemies, even within his own household, are trying to destroy him, the king places his trust in the care and keeping of God.

Like the king, we too must place ourselves in the hands of the Lord in order to heal and to be made whole—regardless of other resources such as people, power, or money.

When we say, "My times are in your hands, O Lord," we are committing ourselves to the care and keeping of God, who determines the length of our days.

May I believe my times are in the hands of the Lord.

I will believe my times are in the hands of the Lord. I will trust the Lord with my life. I will believe the Lord, whose mercy endures forever, is good.

Prayer: *May I believe I am in the hands of the Lord. May I believe the Lord is being very good to me.*

Do I believe my times are in the hands of the Lord? Do I believe the Lord is being very good to me?

Living the Gratitude

Praise be to the LORD, for he showed his wonderful love to me.
—Psalm 31:21

How has the Lord shown his wonderful love toward us? Have we taken time to reflect upon the goodness of the Lord at work in our lives? Even in the midst of our pain?

Many of us don't do this very well; we don't think about God's goodness, don't recall the blessings of the past, don't see the current blessings, and therefore, don't feel gratitude toward the Lord, or show it.

We may even be singing songs of praise, but not with our hearts, not really offering our thanksgiving.

Gratitude is the missing link between unhappiness and happiness, between spiritual development and underdevelopment, between recovering from sorrow and not recovering.

The psalmist was deeply aware of the work of the Lord in his life. He saw the goodness of the Lord as being wondrous, staggering, exceptional, beyond expectation, and awesome.

Let us also sing: "Praise be to the Lord, for he showed his wonderful love to me."

May I live a life of gratitude to God.

I will see the goodness of the Lord. I will count my blessings, one by one. I will live a life of gratitude to God.

Prayer: *May I remember the goodness of God in my life. May I live a life of gratitude to God.*

Am I remembering the goodness of God in my life? Am I living a life of gratitude to God?

Singing a New Song

Sing to [the Lord] a new song.

—Psalm 33:3

We know the feelings that come with radical change, when a loved one leaves us.

The shock and the fear of it.

The sorrow and the grief.

Sometimes the anger, resentment, and guilt.

Having lost part of ourselves to the past, we become afraid of losing more, or even everything, to the future.

If there is a new song to sing, we don't know where or what it is.

Out of fear we want to cling to the past, to what we think we know and believe and understand. But we also know we must do something new with ourselves. However, we are not at all that sure we can.

Change can be so very radical and painful, and "new songs" don't come easily to shattered lives.

However, in the midst of our loss, sorrow, and grief, there is a new song to sing. It is a new song of new hope and new joy, in the Lord's continued and unchanging presence.

A new song of gratitude to God who stays with us through the changes we must make, in order to heal.

May I sing a new song to the Lord.

I will look for newness in my life. I will look for the goodness of God. I will sing a new song of joy and thanksgiving to the Lord who never leaves me.

Prayer: *May I see God at work in my life. May I find a new song of thanksgiving and sing it.*

Am I seeing God at work in my life? Am I singing a new song of thanksgiving?

Extolling the Lord at All Times

I will extol the LORD at all times.

—Psalm 34:1

Certainly the writer of our scripture for today can't be speaking about singing, dancing, and giving thanks without ceasing. He too had his ups and downs. Like ourselves, he too had his very dark and gloomy days, when life didn't seem worth living.

Nevertheless he was willing to extol the Lord "at all times," in all the circumstances of his life, willing to give thanks to God even during the lowest ebbs of his life.

"Extolling the Lord at all times" is affirming that the goodness of God is always at work in our lives, whether we are able to perceive it or not.

In the midst of our loss, sorrow, and grief, the Lord is at work. In the midst of very troubled days the Lord is bringing about our opportunity to heal, to be made whole. But this also requires some doing on our part, some resolution.

Like the psalmist, we too must be ready to say, "I will extol the Lord at all times." We do this not because God demands it of us, which God doesn't, but because we must, with God's help, release ourselves from the bindings of loss, sorrow, and grief by extending ourselves outward.

May I extol the Lord at all times.

I will see beyond my sorrow. I will extol the name of the Lord. I will rejoice in the goodness of God.

Prayer: *May I look beyond myself and my sorrow. May I give thanks to the Lord.*

Am I looking beyond my sorrow? Am I extolling the Lord at all times?

Seeking the Lord

I sought the LORD and he answered me.

—Psalm 34:4

When we are too tired, emotionally and spiritually, we generally don't have the energy or desire to seek help from anyone.

Nevertheless it's important to continue asking God for help.

By asking for help, we bring our hidden inner self to the surface for healing.

Sometimes, however, it may seem as though no one is there when we knock, that there is nothing to be found when we seek, and no one to answer when we ask. Such experiences belong to all seekers.

This doesn't mean, however, that God is not there. Or that the Lord is not hearing us.

It only means that we are not yet ready to see or hear the answer as it is being prepared for us.

Eventually, however, if we continue to seek, knock, and ask, we see and hear the answer for which we have been looking.

May I seek the Lord and hear the answer.

I will seek the Lord. I will wait for the Lord's healing power. I will believe the Lord will answer my call.

Prayer: *May I believe the Lord listens when I call. May I believe the Lord answers my prayers.*

Do I believe the Lord listens when I pray? Do I believe the Lord answers my prayers?

Being Delivered from Fear

The Lord] delivered me from all my fears.

—Psalm 34:4

Denying our fear can hinder our recovery from bereavement.

It is far better for our health and recovery to admit our fears and to share them with God through prayer, and with others who can listen without making judgments.

And yet, because we are afraid of fear, there are fears we can hardly share with ourselves, much less with others.

We may be afraid that if we admit our fears to someone else, the worst will happen. People will leave us. What we fear will all come true. We will be deeply hurt again, perhaps even destroyed.

Can we be delivered from our fear and fears? Maybe not all fear, not while we are still in our bodies, but we can have our fear diminished by the power of God's love.

When we are in harmony with God we need not be bound by fear. Therefore, our recovery depends upon our coming into harmony with God.

May I be delivered from fear.

I will seek the Lord. I will trust the Lord with my life. I will be delivered from fear.

Prayer: *May I come into harmony with God. May my life be set free from fear.*

Am I coming into harmony with God? Am I being delivered from fear?

Allowing the Lord to Heal

The LORD is close to the brokenhearted and saves those who are crushed in spirit.

—Psalm 34:18

Why do we keep on returning to the thought of broken hearts and crushed spirits? Simply because there always is a residue of pain from loss and separation; the sorrow wells up again, after we thought it gone, and there is another wrenching of the spirit.

When sorrow surfaces, again and again, we may come to wonder if something is radically wrong with us.

We may be afraid that we are going to experience the same pain of loss that we had in the early days of our bereavement.

At such times we must remember the promise of God: "The Lord is always close to the brokenhearted and the Lord saves."

This being true, we can come to believe that the Lord is always with us.

Other than the Lord, no one can save us from a crushed spirit. There is no human power able to do this.

People can bring Band-Aids, but only God can heal. Broken hearts belong to God.

We must take our broken hearts and crushed spirits to the Lord. For the Lord binds up and the Lord heals.

May I always be bound up and healed by the Lord.

I will turn to the Lord with my broken heart. I will share my pain with the Lord who heals. I will allow the healing of the Lord into my life.

Prayer: *May I allow the healing of the Lord to come into my life. May I turn to the Lord with my broken heart.*

Am I turning to the Lord with my broken heart? Am I allowing the healing of the Lord to come into my life and to heal me?

Searching for the Unfailing Love of the Lord

How priceless is your unfailing love.

—Psalm 36:7

In the most severe times of suffering, people are still able to say, "How priceless is your unfailing love." How is this possible?

The truth is we are able to find the unfailing love of the Lord especially in times of deep loss, sorrow, and grief.

To an outsider, an unbeliever, this sounds like sheer nonsense, or even worse. It can also sound like a flat-out lie.

However, believers have personal experiences with the love of the Lord which cannot be denied.

Down through the centuries believers have experienced the love of the Lord who has never deserted them.

There comes, to believers, a sense of preciousness: the pricelessness of one's relationship with God, and the depth of the Lord's love that is able to heal broken hearts and shattered spirits.

It is important, again and again, to search our experiences, looking specifically for the priceless and unfailing love of God in our lives.

If we do this, we are brought into remembrance of the Lord's faithfulness—and into healing.

May I search for the unfailing love of the Lord in my life.

I will search for the unfailing love of the Lord in my life. I will remember that God's love has been with me in the past. I will believe God's love is with me now, and will be with me in the future.

Prayer: *May I see the unfailing love of the Lord. May I give thanks for God's love.*

Am I seeing God's love in my life? Am I giving thanks?

Being Still and Patient

Be still before the LORD and wait patiently.

—Psalm 37:7

There are times when we need to cry, even loudly to the Lord, in order to cleanse our souls.

But more often it is important to be still before God, with no second guessing as to what the Lord is supposed to be doing with or for us.

Being patiently still before God is a spiritual exercise that produces many internal rewards which we must discover for ourselves.

One such reward is that of yoking or bonding with the Lord; that's when there is no anxiety, no fear we are going to be left alone and abandoned, without resources to cope.

When we learn the value of stillness before the Lord and are able to exercise patience, we discover the promised peace of God that keeps our hearts and minds at rest.

Let us take time each day to be still before the Lord.

Let us wait patiently for the Lord to come to us.

Let us be silent before the Lord who brings peace to still and patient souls.

May I be still and patient before the Lord.

I will be still before the Lord. I will wait patiently on the Lord. I will trust the Lord to show me the way I am to be going.

Prayer: *May I trust the Lord to show me the way I am to be going. May I be still before the Lord, with patience.*

Am I being patient and still before the Lord? Am I trusting the Lord to show me the way I am to be going?

Trusting the Lord's Salvation

Be pleased, O LORD, to save me.

—Psalm 40:13

Salvation, of the Lord's making, is a certainty.

How salvation comes is only clear to the Lord who understands all the conditions of our loss and bereavement, who understands all our needs.

When we say, "Be pleased, O Lord," we are also praying, "according to your specifications and on your terms."

Because we don't know what the exact conditions and specifications for our healing should be, we pray this.

We may not even have the slightest notion what they are.

"Be pleased, O Lord" is also a petition for the Lord to "will" our recovery.

The Lord knows what is best for us.

The very best we can do for ourselves is to pray for the Lord to deliver us from sorrow and grief.

The Lord will be "pleased" to do so—in God's good time, in God's own and best way.

May I trust the Lord's salvation.

I will trust the Lord to save me from my sorrow. I will believe the Lord is pleased to help me. I will give thanks to the Lord for healing me.

Prayer: *May I believe the Lord wants to help me. May I trust the Lord to heal me.*

Do I believe the Lord wants to help me? Am I trusting the Lord to deliver me?

Making Haste with Patience

O LORD, come quickly to help me.

—Psalm 40:13

There are times when waiting is very difficult: when we feel as though everything is too heavy for us to bear, when we want to get out of the pits as soon as possible.

Certainly there's nothing wrong with wanting the Lord to hurry to help us. However, by being in too much of a hurry, we can miss what is better, even best, for us.

What we are concerned with today is not the urgent cry for help, because such cries are normal and understandable. Nevertheless, haste can make waste, and impatience does not really promote healing.

Being in an urgent condition can increase stress, thus keeping wounds open rather than binding and healing them.

While it can be healing to voice our urgency, it also is good that the Lord does not respond to us with undo haste. After all, healing is a process in which we have to take one step at a time, through the dark valleys of pain and sorrow, before we can see the light of day.

Let us cry to the Lord for help! Then, let us wait on the Lord with patience for the Lord to heal.

May I be quick to cry to the Lord and wait with patience.

I will cry to the Lord for help. I will trust the Lord to answer my cry. I will believe the Lord is going to heal me.

Prayer: *May I believe the Lord is healing me. May I patiently trust the Lord to answer my cry for help.*

Do I believe the Lord is going to help me? Am I waiting patiently for the Lord to help me?

Accepting the Pain

Why are you downcast, O my soul?

—Psalm 42:5

Today we have a good question with good reason to address it. The question has to do with our states of feeling, and the fact that some days we wake up and don't feel all that well.

Worse yet, we feel quite bad, maybe even terrible.

Then we may begin to wonder about ourselves, asking, "What's wrong with me anyway?"

We may begin to say, "I should be over this by now. I should be feeling better."

With these painful feelings there sometimes can also come feelings of shame and guilt.

We might think of our feelings as being signs that we have not grown or matured spiritually—at least not to the extent we may have wished.

While we don't want to settle for feeling bad, there are times when it is necessary to do precisely that.

Sometimes we need to enter into our depression and let it hurt, yet placing our hope in the Lord.

May I not be afraid of my painful feelings.

I will not be afraid of my painful feelings. I will accept my pain and work with it. I will believe the Lord will lead me through the dark valleys.

Prayer: *May I accept my pain and deal with it. May I trust the Lord to lead me through.*

Am I accepting my pain and dealing with it? Am I trusting the Lord to lead me through?

Placing Our Hope in God

Hope in God.

—Psalm 42:5

Without heaping any guilt or shame upon ourselves for not being as faithful as we might, we can openly admit that we are not always placing our hope in God. And sometimes, hardly ever.

But how do we place our hope in God?

Do we just decide to turn over a new leaf, and then suddenly it happens, once and for all? Hardly.

We have had too much practice placing our hope elsewhere, looking for hope in the things of this world.

How do we turn away from the world and place our hope in God? Make a new year's resolution? Not when we already know how far they don't go and what they don't do.

To place our hope in God we have to surrender to God; turning over our wills and our lives to the care and keeping of the Lord. Then hope will follow. Our hope will be where it belongs—in God.

Then we will recover from our loss, sorrow, and grief because hope also is life, even eternal life. Eternal life for ourselves and our lost loved ones.

May I place all of my hope in the Lord.

I will place my hope in God. I will believe the Lord is with me. I will trust the Lord to help and to heal me.

Prayer: *May I wait on the Lord. May I trust the Lord to heal me.*

Am I placing my hope in the Lord? Am I trusting the power of the Lord to save me?

Knowing Who's in Charge

Be still, and know that I am God.

—Psalm 46:10

Again, we come to the subject of stillness, but with another focus. Today the stillness has to do with "knowing," or coming into realization and into consciousness, of who really is running the world.

We get seriously confused about this, even to the extent of believing we are in charge, that we are running the world, that we are in the driver's eat. This is an illusion.

The fact is we are not in charge, we are not running the world, and we are not in the driver's seat—not even for our own recovery. Responsible for our behavior? Yes. In charge of the outcome? No.

Knowing God is in charge brings about an emphatic change in attitude.

To begin with, we don't get caught up in things beyond our capacity to do. We don't make assumptions about having power we don't actually have.

And thus we don't get into a lot of avoidable confusion about ourselves. We know God is God, and we aren't.

May I know that God is God.

I will place my hope in God, where it belongs. I will trust God with my life. I will believe the Lord is in charge.

Prayer: *May I believe the Lord is God. May I find my hope in God.*

Am I believing God is the Lord? Am I finding my hope in God?

Being Delivered and Honoring God

I will deliver you, and you will honor me.

—Psalm 50:15

The promise is for deliverance. The question may be "When? When, Lord, are you going to deliver us from conflict and pain, from sorrow and grief?"

The answer always is the same: "Be patient. Wait. Trust. Believe. Never lose hope."

If we don't lose hope, we find this to be true: God does deliver us, maybe not as we would have delivered ourselves, but in far more productive, growth-giving ways.

Once we begin to see what God is doing for us, in its fulness, there comes a deep sense of gratitude and thanksgiving. We may even suddenly feel like honoring God, giving thanks and praise to the Lord.

We are destined to know the Lord is with us, that the Lord delivers us from our loss, sorrow, and grief.

In the power of the Lord we will experience deliverance.

And, because of the Lord's deliverance, we shall honor God.

May I see the deliverance of the Lord and give God honor.

I will look for the deliverance of the Lord. I will see how the Lord is delivering me from the pain of loss. I will believe God is working miracles in my life.

Prayer: *May I believe God is working miracles in my life. May I honor God for working miracles in my life.*

Do I believe God is delivering me from loss, sorrow, and grief? Am I giving glory to God?

Purifying and Renewing

Create in me a pure heart, O God, and renew a steadfast spirit within me.

—Psalm 51:10

When we become downcast by circumstances beyond our control, when our life is cluttered with pain and sorrow and disappointments, we may take on a lot of excessive baggage—emotional, spiritual, and physical.

Emotionally, there is sadness and often, depression. Sometimes, there is also anger, fear, and resentment.

Spiritually there are questions about God, and whether we believe there is a God, or believe the promises of God. There is the sense of isolation, of being alone, even abandoned.

Physically, there is stress: the buildup and clustering of tension, and the attack of stress upon our organs, which short-circuits our systems.

What is needed is a flushing out of all that brings about the congestion of mind, body, and spirit. As long as we are bound up emotionally and spiritually, nothing else is going to work right for us.

Therefore, it is necessary to get ourselves straightened out, to find the spiritual channels, and to flow with the river.

Once our spirits are renewed, everything else begins to improve.

May I permit God to renew a steadfast spirit within me.

I will open my heart to the Lord. I will ask God to renew my spirit. I will seek the healing of the Lord.

Prayer: *May I seek the healing of the Lord. May I ask God to renew my spirit.*

Am I seeking the healing of the Lord? Am I asking God to renew a steadfast spirit within me?

Being Willing to Be Restored

Restore to me the joy of your salvation, and grant me a willing spirit to sustain me.

—Psalm 51:12

The prayer of the psalmist is that of a believer, of someone who had known the joy of the Lord, but then experienced loss, sorrow, and grief. He is asking for restoration, to be given new life.

As with the psalmist, it is necessary to ask for help in order to get ourselves involved with our recovery.

The Lord will not infringe on us, will not try to force salvation upon us.

Healing cannot be forced.

Neither can the good will of God be forced.

We must pray for the goodness of God to heal us.

The time comes to ask and to keep asking with a willing spirit.

It is the "willing spirit," the spirit that is ready to be restored, with which the Lord is able to work to bring healing.

Without a willing spirit there is nothing God can do to help us heal.

The question is whether we are ready to ask for help, whether our spirit is willing to receive the healing the Lord offers.

May my spirit be willing to be restored and renewed.

I will commit my spirit to the Lord. I will open my heart to the healing of the Lord. I will believe I can be restored to joy.

Prayer: *May I believe I can be restored to joy. May I open my spirit to the healing of the Lord.*

Am I opening my spirit willingly to the Lord? Am I being restored to the joy of God's salvation?

Trusting the Steadfast Love of the Lord

I trust in God's unfailing love for ever and ever.
—Psalm 52:8

Granted, "for ever and ever" is a very big statement. Also it is something we have no way of predicting. And there are times when it's better not to be so sure of ourselves.

Words really don't mean much of anything, for that matter. What counts is what we do with our lives, how we invest them.

When we invest ourselves in the Lord, things immediately begin to change for the better, whether we can see it or not.

This is because the act of trust opens us up to healing, making way for the energy of creation to flow into us and heal.

Lack of trust blocks the gates to our hearts, closes the doors, shuts the windows, and prevents healing.

The way to restoration is through trust.

May I trust the unfailing love of the Lord to heal.

I will trust the unfailing love of the Lord. I will believe the Lord is going to heal me. I will be healed by the power of God.

Prayer: *May I believe the Lord is able to heal me. May I trust the Lord to heal my troubled spirit.*

Am I trusting the Lord to heal me? Am I allowing God to help me?

Trusting the Lord to Sustain

Surely God is my help; the LORD is the one who sustains me.
—Psalm 54:4

We are created to be in relationship, and to work in relationship. We need to be helped along the way of life, especially in times of upset, turmoil, and the confusion of loss, sorrow, and grief.

Everyone needs support. None of us can really go it alone, simply because we are put together to "be" together.

Our help comes from the Lord. Others may also be helpful, but the deepest help is from God, who sustains us.

Down through the ages it has been noted and affirmed that true help comes from the Lord: comfort, consolation, guidance, and the strength to go on.

The faithful have not been slow to admit, to openly confess, where true help comes from.

Like those who have gone before us, we too have a need to be sustained, to be supported.

With the support of the Lord we are able to deal with the pain of our sorrow, regaining hope and the will to go on with our lives.

Let us place our trust in the Lord who is our helper, who sustains us.

May I allow God to help and sustain me.

I will open myself to the Lord. I will allow the Lord to sustain me. I will trust the Lord to help me.

Prayer: *May I trust the Lord to sustain me. May I open myself for the Lord to help me.*

Am I opening myself to the Lord for help? Am I trusting the Lord to sustain me?

Finding Rest for Our Souls

Oh, that I had the wings of a dove! I would fly away and be at rest.

—Psalm 55:6

Jesus said to his disciples, "Come with me by yourselves to a quiet place and get some rest."

All of us need to find a place of rest, somewhere to be alone with ourselves and the Lord.

But too often we let this need slip by to be replaced by busy things that get in the way of our rest, of our being alone with God.

For our recovery it's essential to find a place to rest, a place to be silent, to be at peace with ourselves and the Lord in prayer and meditation.

Let us not take lightly the need for doing this, even if we find it difficult to do so, because of other demands or because, from time to time, we may find it uncomfortable.

Like the psalmist and our Lord, we also need to "fly away and be at rest."

Let us make a decision to go somewhere and shut a door. Let us find a place where we are alone with ourselves and the Lord in prayer and meditation.

Let us do this, as "on the wings of a dove," finding rest for our souls regularly.

May I find rest for my soul.

I will find a time and place to be alone. I will find a time and a place for meditation and prayer. I will find rest for my soul.

Prayer: *May I find a time and place to be alone. May I find rest for my soul.*

Am I taking time for myself? Am I finding rest for my soul?

Looking to the Lord to Be Saved

He ransoms me unharmed from the battle waged against me.
—Psalm 55:18

There are many ways for us to get deeply hurt. And some of the hurts go with us for the rest of our lives.

This is part of what it means to be human beings, part of the risk, and the danger. It is as though we are in a battle, on a battlefield, with an enemy or enemies raging against us: "powers of this dark world" and "spiritual forces of evil," as Paul the apostle described them.

But in spite of the attack, as it were, it is possible to find safety and serenity in the Lord, and in this sense, to come through unharmed.

However, developing confidence in God, as we know well from personal experience, can be difficult in good times and bad.

Try as we may to have confidence in the Lord, we often find ourselves slipping back again and again into fear.

Real confidence, however, is a gift from God for which we must pray. The more we turn to the Lord in prayer for deliverance into peace and serenity, the more our fear lessens.

The Lord delivers us in safety from the ravages of fear.

May I be safely delivered from the ravages of fear.

I will look to the Lord for deliverance. I will trust the Lord to keep me safe from fear and hopelessness. I will believe the Lord is able to deliver my soul from the darkness of fear.

Prayer: *May I look for safety in the Lord. May I trust the Lord to deliver me from fear and dread.*

Am I looking to the Lord for deliverance? Am I placing my confidence in the Lord?

Giving Over Our Cares

Cast your cares on the Lord and he will sustain you.
—Psalm 55:22

Do we ever feel like "throwing in the towel," like quitting, giving up, not going on?

If we have never felt this way, we probably are one of a kind. For most of us there are times when enough is enough, when we feel that we can't take it any more, when we are in an attitude of near despair.

What to do with cares?

The psalmist decided to lighten his burden of cares by casting them on the Lord.

While that may not seem right or fair, perhaps it may seem even immature, it is precisely what the Lord invites all of us to do.

"What do I do with the burden of this loss?" asked a man about to lose his leg. "Give over your leg to the Lord," someone suggested. He did so. And, when he did, he experienced nearly immediate relief from his burden of loss, sorrow, and grief.

He found that the Lord accepts burdens and sustains. He discovered that the Lord upholds, that the Lord gives comfort.

Whatever cares we have today, we can, by divine invitation, give them over to the Lord.

May I cast my cares on the Lord to find relief.

I will take my cares to the Lord in prayer. I will offer my cares to the Lord. I will ask the Lord to lead me along the way I am to be going.

Prayer: *May I turn to the Lord with my cares. May I trust the Lord to help me along the way.*

Am I turning to the Lord in prayer? Am I trusting the Lord to help me along the way?

Turning Over Our Fear

When I am afraid, I will trust in you.

—Psalm 56:3

Fear must be dealt with. It cannot be healthily escaped, or harmlessly hidden.

The only known remedy for fear is trust—faith that a power greater than ourselves can lift us beyond fear.

Even Jesus knew what it was to be afraid. His last night in the garden of Gethsemane was about fear and what to do with it.

There was the sweat of fear, "like drops of blood." There was the anguish of spirit, and the reality of being abandoned: "Could you not stay awake with me for one hour?" he asked his disciples.

Being afraid isn't the problem.

Deciding what to do with our fear is the problem.

Jesus put his trust in God: "Not my will, but yours be done," he prayed. Then he was ready to face his enemies.

"When I am afraid, I will trust in the Lord." That's the simple answer that has come down through the ages. It is just as valid today as it has ever been.

It is the best way, and perhaps the only way, through fear and into healing and wholeness.

May I trust the Lord to deliver me from fear.

I will trust the Lord to deliver me from fear. I will believe the Lord is able to do for me what I cannot do for myself. I will rest myself in the care and keeping of the Lord.

Prayer: *May I rest myself in the care and keeping of the Lord. May I trust God to do what I cannot do for myself.*

Am I turning my fears over to the Lord? Am I trusting the Lord to deliver me from my fears?

Depending on God for Salvation

My salvation and my honor depend on God.

—Psalm 62:7

The psalmist speaks about "honor," which suggests pride, even vain glory. He is looking to God to vindicate him before the world, to make him acceptable in order to be adulated.

In our recovery from loss, we need the salvation of the Lord, but for a different reason than that of being acceptable, even adulated: "My, but you are brave. My, but you are doing well. How did you ever do it? I certainly could never have been as brave as you are."

The salvation we need, and the salvation that is given, is to be found in God's leading us from the darkness of gloom into the sunlight of faith, hope, and love. And this God certainly does when we are ready to be led. But all honor belongs to God, and our honor has nothing to do with this saving act of grace.

Understanding our dependency upon God is necessary for our healing and health. Giving all honor and glory to God is equally vital.

Let us remember that we are honored by God's salvation, which comes to us as a free gift of grace. Let us remember this is the highest honor we ever can receive.

May I rest myself in the salvation of the Lord.

I will pray for salvation from the bondage of fear. I will trust the Lord to free me from the bondage of fear. I will accept the healing of the Lord.

Prayer: *May I be saved from the bondage of fear. May I trust the Lord to save me.*

Am I turning to the Lord in prayer? Am I trusting the Lord to save me from the bondage of fear?

Seeing What God Has Done

Come and see what God has done.

—Psalm 66:5

While hope is the substance of things yet unseen, there must be experiences of deliverance before there can be hope.

Hope rests on the fact of deliverance already experienced.

There is a history of God's deliverance: deliverance of individuals and deliverance of multitudes from all imaginable and unimaginable kinds of distress.

However, when we are in a state of loss, sorrow, and grief, it isn't always easy to remember what the Lord has done.

We can be bogged down in the immediate pain of our distress, unable to see or hear the deliverance of the Lord.

We may even resent any suggestion that we should "come and see what God has done."

However, the sooner we are able to look at the work of God, the better. It is then we begin to see.

We begin to see we are not forsaken or abandoned by God.

We begin to see how God is working our deliverance in ways which we could not have imagined possible.

May I see the work of the Lord being done in my life.

I will look into my life for the hand of the Lord at work. I will see what the Lord has done and is doing for me. I will trust the Lord to be with me all the days of my life.

Prayer: *May I see what the Lord has done for me. May I trust the Lord to be with me.*

Am I seeing what the Lord has done for me? Am I trusting the Lord to be with me all the days of my life?

Turning to the Lord for Help

Praise be to the LORD, to God our Savior, who daily bears our burdens.

—Psalm 68:19

There is daily need for God.

Moment by moment there is need for God.

We are never without a need for the presence of the Lord.

When we are afraid of what is to come, and how we are going to fare, and whether we are going to be able to bear the burdens that come our way, it is important to remember the words of our scripture: Praise be to the Lord, who daily bears our burdens.

The Lord feels no tedium when it comes to being with us and helping us along the way.

God does not resent us for being in need.

God does not get tired of our dependency upon the Lord.

The Lord is ready to bear our burdens each and every day.

Let us go to the Lord in prayer and without apology.

Let us ask the Lord to be with us, to bear our burdens.

Let us remember the promise, "I am with you always."

May I turn to the Lord for help.

I will place myself in the care and keeping of the Lord. I will trust the Lord to bear my burdens day by day. I will have faith in God.

Prayer: *May I place myself in the care of the Lord. May I trust the Lord to bear my burdens day by day.*

Am I placing myself in the care of the Lord? Am I trusting the Lord to bear my burdens day by day?

Being Honest About Our Feelings

I have come into the deep waters; the floods engulf me.
—Psalm 69:2

There are times when we feel overwhelmed by circumstances beyond our control.

If we could do something about what is happening to us—to prevent the suffering—we would do so.

However, there is nothing we can do to actually escape the suffering, nothing to stop the pain of our loss, sorrow, and grief, nothing we can do to replace what we have lost.

In our bereavement it is necessary to be honest about what is happening to us and, when appropriate, to admit it to others.

Certainly, we should be honest with God.

It is in our being honest about how we feel that we begin to see light at the end of the tunnel.

The psalmist was bold to report his deep feelings of fear: "I have come into the deep waters; the floods engulf me."

He is saying he is helpless in and of himself. There is nothing he can do to save himself. Without God's help, he is lost.

This kind of honesty about fearful feelings is important for our recovery from loss, sorrow, and grief.

May I be honest about my feelings.

I will be honest about the way I feel. I will admit when I am afraid and hurting. I will trust the Lord to be with me in my loss, sorrow, and grief.

Prayer: *May I be honest about my feelings. May I turn to the Lord for help.*

Am I being honest about the way I feel? Am I turning to the Lord for help?

Drawing Nearer to God

As for me, it is good to be near God.

—Psalm 73:28

It never is that God is far from us, but we can be far from God. At such times we become fraught with anxiety and filled with tension.

We may think we are distressed because of circumstances beyond our control, because things have gotten out of hand, but the real distress is spiritual—the conscious or unconscious sensation that we have been distanced from the Lord.

Because we have been created to be with God, we come into severe distress of spirit when we sense separation.

There is a longing within every human being to be near God, even though this longing may be deeply hidden from our consciousness.

Consciously or subconsciously we are always longing for and seeking oneness with God.

We may attempt to attach ourselves to people and things that cannot satisfy this deepest longing of our souls, but only God can provide true satisfaction.

May I draw nearer to God.

I will turn to the Lord. I will draw nearer to the Lord through prayer and meditation. I will relax myself in the care and keeping of God.

Prayer: *May I seek the presence of the Lord. May I draw nearer to God.*

Am I seeking the presence of the Lord? Am I drawing nearer to God?

Taking the Cup of Blessing

In the hand of the LORD is a cup.

—Psalm 75:8

Some days it may seem the Lord has anything but a cup in his hand. It is easier to see something else. Maybe an axe. Perhaps a club, a crown of thorns, or something of that nature. But goodness and mercy?

The question is not what *we* think the Lord is offering, but what actually is being held out to us as a gift. We may see a crown of thorns when actually it is the cup of blessing. We may see a club when it is a warm embrace. So much depends on where we are with ourselves, at any given moment, and the condition of our feelings.

What we need to take hold of is the assurance that the Lord always comes with cup in hand, offering us the chance to partake of goodness and mercy, and other gifts of the Spirit: love, joy, peace, patience, and the like.

Remember this: "In the hand of the Lord is a cup," and it is being offered to us. But we must decide what to do with that cup. Neither the Lord, nor anyone else, can make the decision for us.

May I accept the cup of blessing from the Lord.

I will see that the Lord is offering me a cup of goodness and mercy. I will reach for the gift and receive it. I will bless the Lord for the gift.

Prayer: *May I see the cup of blessing. May I receive the cup and drink of it.*

Am I seeing the goodness of the Lord? Am I drinking of the cup of goodness that comes from the hand of the Lord?

Seeking the Lord to Help

When I was in distress, I sought the LORD.

—Psalm 77:2

Life is a series of problems to be solved, and often problems include an amount of distress.

In days of distress we need somewhere to turn. More importantly, we need someone to whom we can turn.

It is fortunate to have friends who are willing to be with us, to offer assistance.

However, not everyone has friends who are able to help.

Even the best of friends are not necessarily able to bring us out of our bereavement.

Also, there are places within ourselves where other human beings are not able to reach. Only the Lord is able to reach us in the very depths of our souls.

There need be no shame about seeking the Lord in our loss, sorrow, and grief. In fact, we are invited to call upon the Lord and to ask for strength to go on, and to ask for courage, faith, and hope.

In the days of our distress let us turn to the Lord. Let us seek the strength of the Lord, and believe that, together with the Lord, we are going to solve the problems that confront us.

May I seek the Lord in the days of my distress.

I will believe the Lord is able to help me in days of distress. I will trust the Lord to help me. I will rest myself in the care and keeping of the Lord.

Prayer: *May I trust the Lord to be with me. May I share my troubles with the Lord.*

Am I turning my troubles over to the Lord? Am I seeking the Lord to help me in my distress?

Remembering the Deeds of the Lord

I will remember the deeds of the Lord.

—Psalm 77:11

As we must continue to remind ourselves, it is very helpful to remember the deeds of the Lord in our lives. By so doing, we gain confidence to face the future, knowing the Lord is going to be with us all the way.

Regardless of the condition in which we find ourselves, the Lord is able to help us along the way. We know this because of what the Lord has done in the past.

As the people of God we have a wealth of experiences of the Lord's faithfulness. In fact, all our experience as congregations, and as the church, is based on the deeds of the Lord, the faithfulness of the Lord, his power to save and heal.

Our hymns and our community prayers are about the deeds of the Lord, which sermons of hope and life affirm.

Calling to mind the deeds of the Lord in our own lives can help bring healing, as we gain confidence in the power of God.

Let us take time to reflect upon the working of God in our lives and in the lives of others.

Let us remember the deeds of the Lord and rejoice in the truth that the Lord is with us, all the way through.

May I remember the deeds of the Lord in my life.

I will not forget the Lord. I will remember all the Lord has done for me. I will trust the Lord to always be with me.

Prayer: *May I remember the deeds of the Lord. May I believe the Lord will bless me.*

Am I remembering the deeds of the Lord in my life? Am I believing the Lord is blessing me?

Crying to Be Heard

In your distress you called and I rescued you.

—Psalm 81:7

During bereavement, the question of the Lord's faithfulness may come up many times over, consciously or subconsciously.

We may feel as though there is no one to hear us. Or, if someone is there, they don't really care.

Once more we must be reminded of the promise: "You called and I rescued you." This has been the experience of God's people.

God hears and answers our cries.

However, when we are in very dark valleys, we tend to forget God hears and answers our cries.

There are times when we are unable to cry for help. Our mouths are stopped.

Perhaps we feel of little worth to the Lord or to anyone else. And how could God or anyone else hear the cries of a worthless person?

Regardless how worthless or insignificant we may feel, God promises to hear us.

God promises to know our pain.

God promises to deliver us in God's own way, and God's own time.

May I call on the Lord to save.

I will share my distress with the Lord. I will hold nothing back. I will cry to the Lord, and the Lord will answer me, in the Lord's own way and time.

Prayer: *May I cry out my distress to the Lord. May I trust the Lord to hear and to heal.*

Am I crying my distress to the Lord? Am I trusting the Lord to hear and to heal me?

Receiving the Very Best There Is

You would be fed with the finest of wheat; with honey from the rock I would satisfy you.

—Psalm 81:16

Getting the very best out of life is a noble ambition, something too many of us give up on too soon.

We may feel too insignificant to have anything good coming our way. Maybe a few scraps here and there, but nothing lavish, nothing fine, really beautiful, or good.

However, according to our scripture for today, the intention of the Lord is to give us the finest, the best, the most lasting, and most valuable.

Even though this may be difficult to believe, the promise remains: "You would be fed with the finest of wheat; with honey from the rock I would satisfy you."

The Lord desires to give us the finest of gifts—gifts that uplift the soul, that add to faith, hope, and love.

What we need for life and growth will be given, perhaps not in the form we would choose, but in ways best for us.

Our task is to be ready to receive the Lord's gifts, in whatever form they come.

Our challenge is to believe the gifts of the Lord are always what we need for our recovery from loss, sorrow, and grief.

May I be ready to receive the Lord's finest gifts.

I will believe the Lord wants to give me fine gifts for my soul. I will trust the Lord to provide what I need. I will accept the gifts of God and rejoice in the goodness of the Lord.

Prayer: *May I be ready to accept the gifts of God. May I rejoice in the goodness of the Lord given to me.*

Am I accepting the gifts of God as they are offered? Am I rejoicing in the goodness of the Lord?

Hearing the Word of Peace

I will listen to what God the Lord will say; he promises peace to his people, his saints.

—Psalm 85:8

In times of distress and confusion we need to hear something other than our own voices crying to be heard. And we need more than the silence of God. But before we can receive the gifts of God, we must become clear about what it is we want and need from the Lord.

The psalmist wants the word of peace from the Lord. Not only is this his desire, but also his conviction, that the Lord is going to bring peace.

Isn't that what we are looking for in our times of sorrow, distress, and pain?

Don't we want a word of peace, an invitation to peace, a promise of peace?

What is more important for our troubled souls than the peace of the Lord?

The promise is that the message of the Lord is the message of peace. Peace within ourselves, peace with others, peace with God, and peace with the universe.

Let us turn to the Lord for the gift of peace.

May I hear the word of peace coming from the Lord.

I will turn to the Lord with my whole heart. I will listen for the word of peace coming from the Lord. I will trust the Lord to bless me with the gift of peace.

Prayer: *May I be open to hear God speaking to me. May I believe what God is saying to me.*

Am I listening for the word of peace? Am I trusting the Lord to give me the gift of peace?

Affirming Ourselves as Children of God

You are "gods"; you are all sons of the Most High.
—Psalm 82:6

People have been known to go into hiding after losing a loved one; they may feel like freaks.

Sometimes there is the feeling of no return, of never being able to regain one's dignity and worth.

Self-worth is important. Not that we are great or good or terribly smart, or beautiful to look upon, or rich and powerful in the world. Rather, we have intrinsic value simply because we are human beings who have been created by God, and because we are sons and daughters of the Most High.

There is nothing to brag about here, but much for which to give thanks, praise, and adoration. Because as children of God, we have all there is, all we need. There is nothing that can surpass what we already are.

Let us think of ourselves as children of the King. The King of the universe.

Let us affirm it for ourselves, and own up to who we really are: "You are 'gods'; sons and daughters of the Most High."

May I see myself as a child of the Most High.

I will affirm who I really am. I will see myself as a child of God. I will be positive about myself because of who I am.

Prayer: *May I affirm myself as a child of the Most High. May I rejoice in the Lord my God.*

Am I rejoicing in the Lord my God? Am I affirming myself as a child of the Most High?

Trusting the Goodness of the Lord

The LORD will indeed give what is good.

—Psalm 85:12

"What is good for me?" Easy as it may sound, this is a very difficult question.

We have many ideas about what is not good for us. Suffering and death are not good for us, we think.

Not having enough money, going hungry, coming down with cancer, or getting in a fight with someone we love is not good for us—so it seems.

But the truth is we don't really know all that much. We don't always know what really is good or bad for us.

How can we know what is good or best for us, especially when we are out of sorts with ourselves, with others, and with God? When we are confused and destabilized by sorrow and stress?

Coming to believe the Lord knows what is best for us is an important step toward healing.

Trusting the Lord to give what is good for us is important if we are to find rest for our souls.

May I believe the Lord always gives what is good.

I will believe the Lord gives what is good. I will trust the Lord to give me what is good. I will accept what the Lord gives, regardless of how it comes to me.

Prayer: *May I trust the Lord to give me what is good. May I accept the goodness of the Lord as it comes.*

Am I trusting the Lord to give what is good? Am I accepting the goodness of the Lord as it comes to me?

Trusting God's Power to Restore

Love and faithfulness meet together; righteousness and peace kiss each other.

—Psalm 85:10

There is a deep human need to know things are going to come out all right.

Particularly in times of bereavement we need to have confidence that everything is going to be resolved, that "righteousness and peace will kiss each other."

We need to believe there will be a bringing together of all that is good: mercy, love, forgiveness, trust, and faithfulness.

We may be splattered, broken in pieces, needing to be brought back together again. So it shall be.

With God's help, we will be restored—to our best benefit—because of God's love and faithfulness, because God is making everything right, because God is restoring peace in our souls.

Let us remember we are in the process of being brought together and healed.

Because God promises it shall be so, there is good reason to believe things are going to come out all right.

May I believe the love and faithfulness of the Lord.

I will believe everything is working together for good. I will trust the love and faithfulness of the Lord. I will have faith in God.

Prayer: *May I have faith in God. May I trust the love and faithfulness of the Lord.*

Am I trusting the love and faithfulness of the Lord? Am I resting my faith in God?

Giving Praise with a Joyful Heart

Bring joy to your servant, for to you, O LORD, I lift up my soul.

—Psalm 86:4

There is nothing as beautiful as a joyful soul. Nothing that feels better than the serenity of spirit that comes when we surrender our wills and our lives into the care and keeping of the Lord.

The psalmist goes to the Lord when his spirit is low. He doesn't feel well. He is sad and disappointed. He hurts deeply.

He isn't necessarily asking that the circumstances of his life be changed, except that he wants his soul to find peace, to find contentment.

If there is anything we want for ourselves, it is a peaceful soul, a sense of contentment.

Unrest of the spirit, especially the unrest of fear, doesn't leave us feeling well.

Turning to the Lord in prayer is the lifting up of our souls to God; it prepares the way for a gladdened heart; it is the giving of praise to the Lord. We can do this with a favorite hymn, with acts of service, by praying for others, and by making an offering of ourselves to God.

Let us lift up our souls to the Lord with joyful hearts; and let us be healed.

May I lift up my soul to the Lord and become joyful.

I will turn to the Lord. I will lift up my soul to God, my creator. I will become joyful of heart.

Prayer: *May I turn to the Lord with praise. May I become joyful of heart.*

Am I lifting up my soul to the Lord? Am I giving praise to the Lord with a joyful heart?

Believing the Lord Hears and Answers

In the day of my trouble I will call to you, for you will answer me.

—Psalm 86:7

There are those who believe that once we have made peace with the Lord our days of trouble should be over. This, however, is a shallow and unrealistic piece of wishful thinking. The truth is, the closer we are to the Lord, the more we get worked over spiritually, as gold being refined by fire.

Acknowledging trouble as a real and regular part of life is important for the welfare of our souls.

There simply is going to be trouble and more trouble, pain as well as pleasure.

Sometimes it seems we get just enough recess from trouble so as to be strengthened for the next episode.

Troubles often come in "batches." Troubled times are good times to turn to the Lord.

The Lord doesn't always deliver us from trouble, but the Lord leads us through our pain and difficulties.

The Lord is always with us, always suffers with us, weeps with us, and comforts us. The Lord always hears, always answers, always attends to us.

May I call on the Lord to hear and to help me.

I will trust the Lord to hear me. I will call out my troubles to the Lord. I will believe the Lord hears and helps.

Prayer: *May I believe the Lord is with me. May I call out my troubles to the Lord.*

Do I believe the Lord is with me? Am I believing the Lord hears and answers me when I call for help?

Being Taught How to Walk

Teach me your way, O LORD, and I will walk in your truth.
—Psalm 86:11

We have to be learners because that's what we are here for—to learn.

We know very little by sheer instinct of what we have to know in order to operate in this life.

Each step of the way we have to be taught what to do next and why, to be taught what is real, what is true, what is important.

Without truth we are always in a state of confusion. Confusion breeds fear together with conflict.

We have to learn how to walk in the path of the Lord, which is the pathway of truth.

This pathway of truth is not easy.

It makes demands of us.

There are rough spots on the path.

Sometimes, like chopping our way through the jungle, we need to clear away a lot of rubbish in order to see the path.

God teaches us what to do next, and we can only take one step at a time. That's when God leads us best.

May I take one step at a time.

I will walk the path of truth. I will let God teach me. I will take one step at a time.

Prayer: *May I let God teach me. May I take one step at a time.*

Am I letting God lead me on the pathway to recovery? Am I taking one step at a time?

Finding Fulfillment in Giving Praise

It is good to praise the LORD and make music to your name, O Most High.

—Psalm 92:1

What makes us feel good or better or best? Is it when someone is delivering what we want, filling our stomachs, telling us things we want to hear? Or do we feel best when we are giving of ourselves to others, and thus, to God?

There are people who don't know about giving. In fact, many of us don't. Not in the best sense of giving. With no thought of getting something in return.

There is a lot of conditional giving: "I give to you, you give to me, and we try to make each other happy."

But what the scripture is about today is the fulfillment of our deepest need for joy, which is in our praising the Lord.

There is deep fulfillment in praising the Lord unconditionally. Our souls find rest, peace, and contentment when we do so.

When we are able to praise through our tears in times of deep disappointment and sorrow, we learn how such praise is good for us and to us.

May I discover how good it is to praise the Lord.

I will believe it is good for me to praise the Lord. I will remember the goodness of God and praise the Lord. I will help myself to heal by praising the Lord.

Prayer: *May I remember the goodness of God. May I praise the Lord.*

Am I remembering the goodness of God? Am I praising the Lord?

Being Cheered and Consoled

If the Lord had not been my help, my soul would soon have dwelt in the silence of death.

—Psalm 84:17

As a shepherd boy the mighty King David fought the bear and the lion; and, with a mere slingshot, the giant Goliath.

It was out of real-life experiences, and not from an ivory tower, that David openly confessed, "If the Lord had not been my help, my soul would have dwelt in the silence of death."

The mighty king of Israel knew that apart from the Lord his life was out of control, he would be walking in darkness.

Haven't there been times when we couldn't see light at the end of the tunnel, when our lives were out of our own control, when the Lord stepped in to lead, to help, to hold, to direct?

Particularly in our loss, sorrow, and grief, we have the sensation of being out of control, and lost—as though everything is over and done with for us. But the Lord has stepped in to help and to heal: "If the Lord had not been my help, my soul would soon have dwelt in the silence of death."

Let us remember how the Lord has helped us along the way, and see how the Lord is helping us now.

May I be cheered and consoled by the Lord's leading.

I will remember how the Lord has helped me. I will trust the Lord to restore my soul. I will believe the Lord will lead me where I am to be going.

Prayer: *May I trust the Lord to help me along the way. May I believe the Lord will stay with me no matter where I am.*

Do I believe the Lord is with me? Am I being cheered and consoled by the presence of the Lord in my life?

Being Lifted Up Again and Again

When I said, "My foot is slipping," your love, O Lord, supported me.

—Psalm 94:18

The human condition is such that we don't go straight ahead all the time, which also is true of our recovery programs. There is an advance here and there, little by little.

Then there are the level places which last for only short periods of time.

Then comes the slip, before we get our footing again. Then we move on.

That is the process.

It isn't helpful to deny the process, or how it works. Nor does it help to become distraught when we slip back, although we do become frightened when we lose our footing.

Another mistake is that of trying to pull ourselves up by our bootstraps. There is no way, really, to do this—to pull ourselves out of emotional and spiritual slumps. We need someone to help us.

Rather than punishing us for slipping or falling out of faith and breaking the covenant of mutual trust, the Lord reaches out to lift us once more, and over and over again.

The Lord's love supports us.

May I trust the love of the Lord.

I will turn to the Lord for help. I will be supported by the love of the Lord. I will be restored to hope.

Prayer: *May I turn to the Lord for help. May I be restored to life and hope.*

Do I believe I can be restored to life and hope? Am I turning to the Lord for help?

Going to the Lord for Consolation

When anxiety was great within me, your consolations brought joy to my soul.

—Psalm 94:19

There are days when it is difficult to find something to be joyful about—not even so much to be joyful, but just to feel better, even just a little bit better.

Sometimes there is the strong need to be consoled, like a child being held on a parent's lap after being hurt.

We may not like to see ourselves with childlike needs, but that's the way we are. We are God's "little" children, and sometimes God's "very little" children. Even, at times, God's very little and very helpless children.

There need be no shame in affirming who and what we are—unless, of course, we want to feed our false pride.

When we need to be consoled, the Lord is ready to hold us, to stroke us, to lead us through the dark valleys.

It isn't that God is going to enable us to stay in a helpless place, but rather God is going to show us the way out when we are ready to be consoled and led.

May I allow myself to be led and consoled by the Lord.

I will seek the Lord who will console me. I will open my broken heart and sorrowing soul to the Lord. I will ask the Lord to lead me.

Prayer: *May I go to the Lord for consolation. May I allow the Lord to help me through my sorrow.*

Am I going to the Lord for consolation? Am I allowing the Lord to help me through my sorrow?

Seeing the Salvation of the Lord

All the ends of the earth have seen the salvation of our God.
—Psalm 98:3

Joy and excitement fill the psalmist because of a battlefield victory for the Israelites: "All the ends of the earth have seen the salvation of our God."

The real salvation of the Lord is not on the battlefields, not in the places of power, in politics, economics, or government. The real salvation of the Lord is inner peace and contentment on the part of the believers.

Believers are all over the earth, and in this sense the entire earth has seen the salvation of the Lord.

What is important in our scripture is written between the lines: the excitement of having seen the joy of the Lord, not only by the writer himself, but also by others.

Yes, he may have been talking about salvation by military victory, but certainly more than that. He is talking about spiritual victories.

His psalms are filled with thanksgiving for spiritual victories, also about recovery from loss, sorrow, and grief. In this regard it is true that "all the earth has seen the salvation of the Lord."

Let us look for the salvation of our Lord over sin and death—over loss, sorrow, and grief.

May I see the salvation of the Lord in my life.

I will look for the salvation of the Lord in my life. I will look for the victory over loss, sorrow, and grief. I will praise the Lord for salvation from sin and death.

Prayer: *May I see the victorious work of the Lord in my life. May I praise God for my salvation from endless sorrow and grief.*

Am I seeing the salvation of the Lord in my life? Am I praising God for the victory of hope in the world?

Worshiping the Lord with a Thankful Heart

Worship the Lord with gladness.

—Psalm 100:2

There are different ways of going about life—*at* it or *with* it. But the most spiritually productive way of life, given us by the Lord, is that of gratitude in service, worshiping God.

When we enter into selfless service, life begins to take on new shape, form, content, and meaning.

The offering of service, as worship, with no demand for a return, is the way of peace and serenity.

When we are pressed down with sadness and self-pity, it can be helpful to look for our service, to see what we can do for someone else.

There is a spiritual exercise that says, "Do something helpful today for someone, without their knowing." This is true worship of God when done with gladness.

There is nothing as personally rewarding and healing as unconditionally worshiping God through selfless service.

Selfless service can be difficult when we are down in our sorrow but it is one sure way to help ourselves through our loss, sorrow, and grief.

May I worship the Lord through selfless service, with gladness.

I will look for my service. I will worship the Lord by serving others. I will do so with a glad and thankful heart.

Prayer: *May I worship the Lord with a glad and thankful heart. May I give of myself to selfless service.*

Am I giving of myself to others in selfless service? Am I worshiping the Lord with a glad and thankful heart?

Knowing and Belonging

Know that the LORD is God. It is he who made us, and we are his.

—Psalm 100:3

We are children of God, and of the universe. We belong in this creation because God has placed us here, and God identifies with us. Yes, we belong to God. But we forget.

Forgetting is painful because with forgetfulness there comes the pain of isolation, of being separated. We have not been created to be isolated and separated.

Rather, we have been created to be with God and be related to one another.

In our loss, sorrow, and grief it sometimes feels as though there is no chance that we ever will feel located again; ever able to trust God again.

Bereavement wrenches us in the deepest reaches of our souls, especially when we are unable to believe we belong to God.

But those days pass and, by God's grace, we find our way into a deeper faith in God who has made us and always is with us.

Let us remember the scripture and say it aloud to ourselves many times over: "It is he who made us, and we are his."

May I know, for certain, that I belong to God.

I will believe the Lord is God. I will believe God has made me. I will believe I belong to God.

Prayer: *May I believe God has made me. May I believe I belong to God.*

Do I believe God has made me? Do I believe I belong to God?

Being Remembered the Way We Are

The Lord] knows how we are formed, he remembers that we are dust.

—Psalm 103:14

The Lord is not confused as to who and what we are. Nor does the Lord expect us to be what we are not.

The Lord has formed us out of dust.

The Lord remembers that from dust we came and to dust we return.

The Lord has made a covenant of love with this dust; "I will be your God and you shall be my people."

Being "dust" is not the same as being "nothing."

Being "dust" means that we are an intimate part of the earth, and of the whole creation.

This also is true for our lost loved ones.

Together we are part of God's eternal, created order, and are never actually separated, one from the other.

We are all of the same substance.

We all are intimately connected to the Lord.

Furthermore, the Lord always remembers and accepts us just the way we are.

May I believe God remembers me the way I am.

I will entrust myself to the Lord. I will believe the Lord remembers and accepts me just the way I am. I will trust the Lord to give me eternal life.

Prayer: *May I believe the Lord loves me just as I am. May I believe the Lord will give me eternal life.*

Do I believe the Lord loves me just as I am? Do I trust the Lord to give me eternal life?

Coming to Rest in the Presence of God

Look to the Lord and his strength; seek his face always.
—Psalm 105:4

There are things we can do for ourselves which help us along the way to recovery from loss, sorrow, and grief.

The most important spiritual exercise is that of seeking the Lord: seeking the Lord's strength, seeking the Lord's face—his presence.

There are as many ways to seek the face of the Lord as there are persons: prayer and meditation, service, quiet times, reflection, and remembering what God has done and is doing in our lives.

It's not how we seek the Lord, but that we do so, that makes a difference for our health and healing.

Our souls find no satisfaction until they come to rest in the heart of God.

That is where we have come from—the heart of God.

That is where we belong—in the heart of God.

Until we allow ourselves to be immersed in God, we are not where we have been created to be.

May we seek the Lord's strength and the Lord's face—his presence—day by day.

May I seek the strength and presence of the Lord.

I will seek the strength and presence of the Lord through meditation and prayer. I will immerse myself in the heart of God. I will come to rest in the presence of God.

Prayer: *May I seek the Lord. May I rest my soul in God.*

Am I seeking the strength of the Lord? Am I resting my soul in the presence of God?

Remembering God's Deliverance

Then they cried to the Lord in their trouble, and he saved them from their distress. He sent forth his work and healed them, and rescued them.

—Psalm 107:19-20

The salvation of God cuts across the pages of history in boldfaced, capital letters for anyone to see.

The Lord brought the people out of slavery, leading them through the wilderness to the promised land.

At another time the Lord brought them back from captivity in Babylon to rebuild the Holy City "whose builder and maker is God."

The Lord kept every promise for salvation, and continues to do so.

Resting our hope in the word and promises of God is essential for our health and healing.

Remembering the salvation of the Lord is important for strengthening our faith, hope, trust, and love.

By seeing the salvation of the Lord in our own lives, and in the lives of others, we receive new strength and courage to go on.

May I remember the Lord will save me from sorrow.

I will remember the salvation of the Lord. I will celebrate the strength of the Lord to rescue. I will trust the Lord to save me from my sorrow.

Prayer: *May I trust the salvation of the Lord. May I celebrate the salvation of the Lord.*

Am I remembering the salvation of the Lord? Am I giving thanks for the faithfulness of the Lord?

Being Lifted Out of Affliction

The Lord] lifted the needy out of their affliction.
—Psalm 107:41

We need confidence in the Lord. We need to believe the Lord can lift us out of our affliction.

The problem is placing our trust where it belongs, giving our afflictions over to the care and keeping of God. Not to escape them or run away from our pain, but rather for the Lord to walk with us through the dark valleys and to raise us up when we fall.

Needy doesn't mean "whimpering."

Needy simply means those who have been deeply hurt, who need help in order to go on.

Without exception, we all have our needy times when we can't find our way through by ourselves.

Not to affirm this condition when we are deep in sorrow and grief is wasteful—especially when the Lord is ready and eager to help us along the way.

The Lord will lift us up when we are down.

May I be lifted out of my loss, sorrow, and grief.

I will turn to the Lord for help. I will ask the Lord to lift me up and to walk with me. I will trust the Lord to be faithful.

Prayer: *May I turn to the Lord to be lifted up. May I trust the Lord to go with me.*

Am I turning to the Lord? Am I trusting God to lift me up?

Finding Our Rest in God

Be at rest once more, O my soul, for the LORD has been good to you.

—Psalm 116:7

People in prison have said so.

People on their death beds with cancer, and people in abject poverty, and in other severe distresses have said so: "The Lord has been good to me."

Our souls also know this to be true.

What is more, our souls long to be where we belong: "Near the heart of God."

We long to be with God because that is where our home is. That is where we have come from.

God is our origin.

God is our home.

The whole creation is moving in that direction and is returning to the heart of God.

The design of God's creation is for everything and everyone to return home, finding rest in the heart of God.

May my soul find rest in the heart of God.

I will seek rest for my soul in the heart of God. I will go to the Lord in prayer. I will bless the name of the Lord.

Prayer: *May I find rest for my soul. May I rest my soul in the heart of God.*

Am I finding rest for my soul? Am I finding my rest in God?

Taking Refuge in the Lord

It is better to take refuge in the LORD than to trust in man.
—Psalm 118:8

Sometimes we feel a void, as though the whole world is empty, with nothing to fill it.

Sometimes we are feeling hollow, frightened, and forsaken.

Sometimes we have to look for someone to trust.

And who else is there but God?

Have we not discovered God is sufficient for all our needs?

Shall we not place our trust where it belongs, with the Lord?

Have we not learned it is better to take refuge in the Lord than to place confidence in others?

Where else shall we place our trust than with the Lord?

Doesn't experience tell us our firm foundation is in the Lord our God?

Isn't it true the Lord never is fickle, the Lord never just up and disappears when we are in need?

May I place my trust in the Lord.

I will place my trust in the Lord. I will trust the Lord to be my refuge and strength. I will fear no evil.

Prayer: *May I place my trust in the Lord. May I trust the Lord to be my refuge and strength.*

Am I placing my trust in the Lord? Am I trusting the Lord to be my refuge and strength?

Being Kept from Falling

I was pushed back and about to fall, but the LORD helped me.
—Psalm 118:13

Sometimes, taking a firmer grip on ourselves simply doesn't work because we are the bridge that is collapsing. We are the ones who are falling.

This sensation of falling may come alive in dreams.

We are on a very high place, with nothing to hold on to, and no one to hold us. Then comes the moment when we know we are going to fall.

We fall—but not to the very bottom.

Something interrupts the fall before we hit the ground or the floor, the river or the ocean.

We return to consciousness.

"I was pushed back and about to fall, but the Lord helped me," says the psalmist. This also is true for us.

We are pushed by stress and find ourselves about to fall. But the Lord interrupts our fall.

The Lord catches us.

The Lord saves.

May I believe the Lord will catch me when I am about to fall.

I will trust the Lord to catch me when I am near falling. I will believe the Lord will save me. I will trust the Lord to be with me always.

Prayer: *May I trust the Lord to be with me always. May I trust the Lord to catch me when I am about to fall.*

Am I trusting the Lord to be with me always? Am I trusting the Lord to catch me when I am about to fall?

Rejoicing and Being Glad in the Lord

This is the day the LORD has made, let us rejoice and be glad in it.

—Psalm 118:24

There are certain foods cooked with hot spices. One result of the hot spices is opening circulation of the blood stream.

Another result is opening the pores so as to help flush the body of contaminants. So it is with our spirits which have to be opened and flushed of loss, sorrow, and grief.

This is helped a great deal by rejoicing in the Lord.

However, sometimes overt rejoicing and being glad can be very difficult.

But the outward expression of joy and gladness, the actual giving of praise in songs and hymns, is helpful for strengthening our recovery systems. Even praising the Lord with a loud voice, as the psalmist also says, is helpful.

Expressing joy and gladness helps to open us emotionally and spiritually, making room for the new energy of the Spirit to be released within us, like hot spices.

Let us rejoice and be glad in the Lord.

Let us live this day as fully as possible, holding nothing back.

May I rejoice and be glad in this day of the Lord.

I will rejoice and be glad in this day of the Lord. I will open my heart and give praise to the Lord. I will praise God with my whole heart and soul.

Prayer: *May I open myself to the Lord. May I praise the Lord with my whole heart.*

Am I ready to praise the Lord? Am I willing to open my heart and soul to the Lord, rejoicing in the goodness of God?

Seeking the Lord with a Whole Heart

I seek you with all my heart.

—Psalm 119:10

There is only one good way to do anything worthwhile: with the fullness of our being, with our total self, our whole person. Seeking the Lord can be that way; it is the most rewarding way of all.

However, because of loss, sorrow, and grief it can be difficult to seek the Lord with all our heart. We may seek the presence of the Lord partly, in bits and pieces, now and then, but not with all our heart.

Our scripture is strong in its determination: "I seek you with all my heart." We might ask whether there is any way that does any real lasting good, other than "all the way."

Let us ask: "Have I been seeking the Lord with all my heart?" "Have I been making the Lord the primary treasure of my life, setting everything else aside as being secondary, of lesser importance?"

"Have my heart and mind come to rest in the Lord?"

"Have I been experiencing the peace of God that passes all human understanding?"

"Am I at peace with myself, with others, and with God?"

May I seek the Lord with all my heart.

I will seek the Lord with all my heart. I will hold nothing back. I will give myself completely to the care and keeping of God.

Prayer: *May I give myself to the Lord's care and keeping. May I hold nothing back.*

Am I seeking the Lord with all my heart? Am I giving myself completely to the Lord?

According to God's Promise

May your unfailing love be my comfort, according to your promise to your servant.

—Psalm 119:76

The time comes for us to suffer, to be dislocated in heart and spirit, to not know what to do with ourselves.

Such experience is common to all human beings. But the promise of the Lord is certain: "I will comfort you."

Because the Lord has invited us to do so, we also can pray and sing, "Make all my wants and wishes known. . . . Sweet hour of prayer."

We can freely ask to be comforted, "according to your promise."

We can believe the Lord will never leave or forsake us, "according to your promise."

We can rest assured that the promises of God are being fulfilled.

We can find comfort for our souls.

We do not have to look for another.

The love of the Lord is "unfailing." It doesn't go away.

The love of the Lord doesn't dry up and leave us; "according to your promise," it stays.

May I allow the unfailing love of the Lord to comfort me.

I will turn to the Lord with confidence. I will let the unfailing love of the Lord comfort me. I will celebrate the promises of God.

Prayer: *May I believe the promises of God. May I accept the comfort of God with thanksgiving.*

Do I believe the promises of God? Am I allowing the unfailing love of the Lord to comfort me?

Growing in Knowledge, Wisdom, Understanding

The Lord gives wisdom, and from his mouth come knowledge and understanding.

—Proverbs 2:6

As we go through the process of our recovery, we gain new wisdom, knowledge, and understanding of many things.

We find ourselves saying, "I never saw. I never knew. I never really understood."

But now we begin to see and know and understand, even though it is only in part.

We begin to understand, somewhat at least, what suffering is about, and what can be gained from entering into our suffering.

Experience with the promises and the healing of the Lord brings gifts of wisdom, knowledge, and understanding.

Wisdom says, "This too shall pass."

Knowledge says, "I am certain that the Lord is with me."

Understanding says, "I am beginning to see the benefits of this experience."

Enlightenment doesn't come quickly or easily. Rather, it comes through the "process" of recovery, one step at a time, one day at a time, trusting in the mercy and power of the Lord to lead us through.

May I come to see, to know, and to understand.

I will seek the Lord to know wisdom. I will seek the Lord to gain knowledge. I will pray for understanding of God's will for my life.

Prayer: *May I be given the gift of wisdom. May I gain knowledge and understanding.*

Am I seeking the gifts of wisdom, knowledge, and understanding? Am I ready to live and to share the gifts as they are given to me?

Trusting God with a Whole Heart

Trust in the LORD with all your heart and lean not on your own understanding.

—Proverbs 3:5

The investment of faith is to be complete: "With all your heart." That is how we experience the deliverance of the Lord.

Relying on our own strength proves to be not enough. In and of ourselves we are incomplete, without the necessary spiritual resources to make our way through the trials and tribulations and sorrows of life.

There come times when we must make a "total" investment of ourselves in the promises of God if we want to be healed. We must do so with "all our heart," with no holding back.

There are good reasons why Jesus always asks for a total commitment from those who want to follow him.

Without "all our heart," the investment of our total selves, we still are relying on our own understanding and power. As such, we are unable to do what must be done to heal.

Without trust in the Lord we are unable to completely invest ourselves in a life of faith, hope, and love, the elements of salvation that lead to healing, health, and new life in the Lord.

Let us place all of our trust and confidence in the Lord.

May I trust the Lord with all my heart.

I will trust the Lord with all my heart. I will not rely on myself. I will believe the Lord gives the strength I need.

Prayer: *May I not rely on my own strength. May I trust the Lord to give me strength.*

Am I trusting the Lord to give me the strength I need? Am I relying on God's power to be with me throughout my life?

Placing Our Confidence in the Lord

The LORD will be your confidence.

—Proverbs 3:26

When it seems as though the bottom has dropped out of our lives, leaving nothing to take hold of, that is the time we need lots of assurance.

That is the time we need to know we are not alone, that we don't have to make it on our own power.

Neither do we have to whistle in the dark, pretending that we have complete confidence in ourselves, trying to prove we have the power to make it on our own.

We can place our confidence in the Lord and find the needed strength to do what has to be done to recover from loss, sorrow, and grief.

Not only can the Lord be the confidence we need, but the Lord will be our confidence and hope.

Placing our confidence in the Lord is putting it where it belongs. Where confidence will do us the most good. Where we are provided with the best return on our investment.

In the depths of our suffering let us place our confidence in the Lord and not try to rely on our own strength.

For in so doing we will find healing for our souls.

May I place my confidence in the Lord.

I will place my confidence in the Lord. I will not rely on my own strength. I will believe the Lord is going to see me through.

Prayer: *May I place my confidence in the Lord. May I trust the Lord to help me.*

Am I trusting the Lord to help me? Am I placing my confidence in the Lord?

Finding Peace in the Lord

A heart at peace gives life to the body.

—Proverbs 14:30

All of us are looking for peace of mind and soul, longing for a quiet place where we can be at peace with ourselves, longing for spiritual energy, emotional zest, and physical strength, longing for wholeness.

What do we do with ourselves when our minds are wandering and racing in circles? When we are feeling agitated, nervous, and upset? When our emotions are bouncing around trying to find a peaceful place?

There are ways into tranquility, all of which can be summed up in little phrases like "Let go and let God."

"Turn it over."

"Easy does it."

"One day at a time."

"Trust and obey."

Any one of these admonitions, when put into practice, will put our heart at peace. But, of course, this is easier said than done. However, doing something, even a little bit, is better than doing nothing.

Why not, then, get started?

Let us turn ourselves over to God. Let us remember that easy does it, and not try to live more than this day.

May I find my peace in the Lord.

I will live one day at a time. I will turn my will and my life over to God. I will not try to push life along, rather, I will join it.

Prayer: *May I take it easy. May I live one day at a time.*

Am I letting go and letting God? Am I living one day at a time?

Using the Gifts of God

I am sending you grain, new wine and oil, enough to satisfy you fully.

—Joel 2:19

The promise is this: the Lord gives. The Lord is always in the process of sending us gifts to satisfy. However, to be satisfied we must accept and use the gifts.

Often the gifts of God are not recognized and not used. This is especially true of spiritual gifts.

Unlike grain, new wine, oil, and other material gifts, spiritual gifts come in packages we don't readily recognize.

However, if we are open enough to expect God's gifts—because they have been promised—we begin to see the gifts little by little, in and through our suffering.

Slowly but surely we see how God is working to help us grow spiritually, to become stronger persons—not in and of ourselves, but in the Lord, in faith, hope, and love.

It's when we are living in expectation that we begin to see the hand of the Lord at work in our lives.

The Lord promises satisfaction. Not that everything is going to be painless and nice, but that we will receive the gifts we need in order to heal.

May I see and use the gifts of God given to me.

I will believe God is sending gifts to satisfy my soul. I will open my eyes to see the gifts of the Lord. I will use the gifts of healing as they are given.

Prayer: *May I believe God is sending gifts to heal. May I use the blessings of God to grow.*

Am I expecting God to bless me? Am I putting the healing gifts of God to work in my life?

Watch for the Lord

But as for me, I watch in hope for the LORD."

—Micah 7:7

Micah adds something important to his decision to watch for the Lord: "I wait for God my Savior; my God will hear me."

He expects something to happen when he watches for the Lord to help. He is confident the Lord answers his prayers, and believes he isn't going to be forsaken.

If we state our desires to the Lord—"I want to recover from my bereavement, to experience joy again—and if we really mean what we are saying, very likely our prayers will be answered. Perhaps not in the form we imagined, but nevertheless, answered.

If we ask the Lord to be with us, to uphold and save us from depression and feelings of hopelessness, the Lord will answer.

Are we talking ourselves into a better frame of mind and spirit?

What if that is the way the power of God works: in and through our strongest desires for faith, hope, and love?

Don't we know, from past experiences, that God can bring hope only to open hearts?

Let us look to the Lord in prayer. Let us believe God hears our prayers. Let us wait patiently for God to answer.

May I look to the Lord in prayer and wait for answers.

I will look to the Lord in prayer. I will believe God hears my prayers. I will wait for the Lord to answer my prayers.

Prayer: *May I believe the Lord hears my prayers. May I wait for the Lord to answer my prayers.*

Am I believing the Lord hears my prayers? Am I waiting patiently for the Lord to answer me?

Turning Fear Over

My Spirit remains among you. Do not fear.

—Haggai 2:5

Have we ever felt God's presence in our lives, perhaps in "strange" ways which we never have felt comfortable reporting to others?

Perhaps it came to us when we were by ourselves, in one of our favorite places—or not so favorite places.

There came this sense of "divine presence" that infiltrated our spirit. Then we felt strong, even fearless.

Life took on a deeper sense of beauty and belonging.

We felt a unity with ourselves, with others, with God, and with the universe.

We knew the Lord was with us, and we were in the presence of the Most High.

From actual experience, then, we can come to know there is freedom from fear, because the Spirit of the Lord abides among us.

The Lord speaks to our common human dilemma: fear.

The Lord says to us, "Do not fear."

May I not fear.

I will believe the Lord remains among us. I will trust the Lord to protect my life from destruction. I will turn my fear over to the Lord.

Prayer: *May I turn my fear over to the Lord today. May I trust the Lord to abide with me.*

Am I trusting the Lord to abide with me? Am I turning my fear over to the Lord?

Finding Spiritual Renewal

Man does not live on bread alone, but on every word that comes from the mouth of God.

—Matthew 4:4

During the pain of bereavement we may look for something to fill the void.

We may eat too much, drink too much, or do anything else to soften the gnawing emptiness.

But there is no lasting help apart from God, because we are spiritual beings who must be fed spiritual food.

If the spiritual diet is cut short, we are filled with anxiety, fear, apprehension, and other such maladies.

Because feelings of insecurity are strengthened during times of bereavement, we may find ourselves reaching for temporary solutions to fill the void that comes with loss, sorrow, and grief.

But nothing satisfies except God's Word and the promises of God:

"I am with you always."

"I will not leave or forsake you."

"I will come to you."

As Jesus said to Satan, "Man does not live on bread alone, but on every word of God."

Only the "poor in spirit" know what this means. Only the "poor in spirit" find their way into newness of life.

May I be spiritually renewed.

I will seek spiritual renewal. I will turn to Christ for renewal. I will open myself to the gifts of God.

Prayer: *May I be open to the gifts of the Spirit. May I seek spiritual renewal.*

Am I opening myself to the gifts of God? Am I seeking spiritual renewal day by day?

Being Poor in Spirit

Blessed are the poor in spirit, for theirs is the kingdom of heaven.

—Matthew 5:3

Being poor in spirit is anything but giving up.

Being poor in spirit is our act of giving over to God our loss, sorrow, and grief.

Being poor in spirit is being receptive to God's gifts of healing, regardless of the forms in which they come.

When we are poor in spirit we are open to God's love and leading.

When we are poor in spirit we are turning our wills and our lives over to the care and keeping of God.

When we are poor in spirit we don't have to know all the answers because God knows the answers.

And that is sufficient.

When it is our time to know the answers, answers will be given.

When we believe everything is working for good, it no longer is necessary to discern what God is doing with and for us.

We are poor in spirit when we are ready to accept what God gives—believing that what God gives is for our own good.

May I be poor in spirit, trusting the Lord with my life.

I will be open to God. I will wait for the Lord to help and to heal. I will trust God with my life.

Prayer: *May I be open to God. May I trust God with my life.*

Am I open to the leading of the Lord? Am I trusting God with my life?

Mourning and Being Comforted

Blessed are those who mourn, for they will be comforted.
—Matthew 5:4

God does not forsake us in our loss, sorrow, and grief.

The Spirit of the Sovereign Lord is on me,
because the Lord has anointed me
to preach good news to the poor.
He has sent me to bind up the brokenhearted . . .
to comfort all who mourn.
Isaiah 61:1-2

You will grieve, but your grief will turn to joy.
John 16:20

For the Lamb at the center of the throne will be their shepherd;
he will lead them to springs of living water.
And God will wipe away every tear from their eyes.
Revelation 7:17

Blessed are those who mourn, for they will be comforted.

May I find comfort for my soul.

I will trust the Lord to comfort me. I will receive the comfort of the Lord. I will give thanks for the Lord's consolation.

Prayer: *May I be comforted. May I give thanks to God.*

Am I opening myself to receive the comfort of the Lord? Am I giving thanks for the comfort of the Lord?

Being Fulfilled

Blessed are those who hunger and thirst for righteousness, for they will be filled.

—Matthew 5:6

Although it is often hidden, we human beings have a strong inner spiritual desire for righteousness, a strong will to justice, and a deep hunger for God's will to be done.

But when circumstances arise, such as an "unfair" loss of a loved one, we may become confused, angry, and resentful.

We may feel as though we have been cheated, even robbed.

We may feel, "God didn't treat me right. I didn't have this one coming. There are others who deserve this more than I do."

Understandably, we want a fair deal. Who doesn't? And a loss doesn't always seem like a fair deal.

Sometimes a loss can seem exceedingly unfair. And with this feeling comes other feelings: fear, anger, resentment.

But if we place the pain of our loss in the hands of the Lord, we no longer are plagued with fear, anger, and resentment. Rather, we are filled with the goodness of God.

Rather, we have become content with the righteousness of God, leaving it to the Lord to determine what is fair or unfair, good or bad, right or wrong.

In short, we become fulfilled.

May I find my fulfillment in God.

I will trust God to do what is right for me. I will surrender to the will of the Lord. I will be fulfilled.

Prayer: *May I desire the will of God to be done in me. May I be fulfilled by the goodness of the Lord.*

Am I trusting God with my life? Am I finding fulfillment in God?

Receiving and Giving Mercy

Blessed are the merciful, for they will be shown mercy.
—Matthew 5:7

The emphasis of our scripture for today seems to be reversed. The first move is up to us: the giving of mercy.

Of course we know only God is truly merciful, and without a revelation of true mercy, we could not know what mercy is.

In times of loss, sorrow, and grief we may very well want to know if there is such a thing as mercy. Many wonder where mercy has gone. Or who has it. And where we can get some.

As we said yesterday, we can be burdened with fear, anger, and resentment because of our suffered loss: "Someone else deserves this more than I do."

We may be looking for someone to punish, just as we feel we are being unjustly punished. Who is responsible for our pain? Who needs to be taken down a peg or two?

But deep within, under the painful feelings, the spirit of God is stirring: the Spirit of mercy, of benevolence, of kindness.

If we listen to the urging of the Spirit toward mercy, we are able to give, and receive mercy, and heal.

May I be merciful to myself and others.

I will be open to the mercy of God. I will gratefully receive God's mercy. I will be merciful to others as God is merciful to me.

Prayer: *May I give thanks for the mercies of God. May I be merciful as the Lord is merciful to me.*

Am I gratefully receiving the mercies of God? Am I gratefully sharing the mercies of God with others?

Seeing God with a Pure Heart

Blessed are the pure in heart, for they will see God.

—Matthew 5:8

To be pure in heart is to desire God.

To be pure in heart is to desire to do God's will, to have the best intentions for ourselves and others.

To be pure in heart is to see God at work in the world, in others, in our own life.

To be pure in heart is to be ready and willing to serve God by being helpful to others.

To be pure in heart is to trust God with our lives.

To be pure in heart is to see God in ourselves, in others, and in the world around us.

To be pure in heart is to be open to God, to receive the healing of the Lord.

To be pure in heart is to give, even in the midst of our loss, sorrow, and grief.

To be pure in heart is to be healed.

May I be pure of heart.

I will pray for a pure heart to serve God. I will pray for a pure heart to serve others. I will pray for a pure heart to see God.

Prayer: *May I have the gift of a pure heart. May I offer myself in compassionate service.*

Am I praying for a pure heart? Am I seeing God in others?

Being A Peacemaker to Heal

Blessed are the peacemakers, for they will be called [children] of God.

—Matthew 5:9

Often, during times of bereavement, there is a real need for peacemaking.

People can get into each other's hair.

Unresolved conflicts and unsettled business can come to a head.

Anger and resentment can surface. Feelings can get hurt.

The first impulse may be to strike out, or to sweep everything under the rug.

But this is not the way to healing.

The best way to peace is to be a peacemaker, to constructively deal with conflict rather than trying to ignore it.

Peacemaking is a time for people to talk and listen without judgment, a time to hear one another's feelings without trying to put them down.

Of course, peacemaking is not easy, especially if one wants revenge, or has a need to straighten others out.

The better way of peacemaking is to ask God for guidance, to listen, and to share—without judging one another.

May I be a peacemaker.

I will be a peacemaker. I will listen and learn. I will quietly attempt to do God's will—to accept and forgive, as I am being accepted and forgiven by God.

Prayer: *May I listen and learn and heal. May I be at peace with myself and others.*

Am I being a peacemaker? Am I listening to others?

Being Extensions of God

You are the salt of the earth. . . . You are the light of the world.
—Matthew 5:13

There are the poor in spirit and those who mourn. There are those who thirst for righteousness and the merciful. There are the pure of heart and the peacemakers.

These are the salt of the earth who keep the light of God active in the world. They are the ones who bring healing.

Those who do the work of God in the world are the salt of the earth and the light of the world.

In our recovery it is helpful to be reminded of who we are in relation to our Lord, Jesus Christ. Christ tells us, "You are the salt of the earth and the light of the world."

We are the salt of the earth and the light of the world because we have been brought into eternal fellowship with God in Christ. This is not because of something we have done, but because of what God has done and is doing.

Remember what Jesus says: You are a preserver of life, an extension of divine light and life into the world. Keep this ever before you, and move on.

May I live as a little Christ in the world.

I will do what the Lord gives me to do. I will be a little Christ to those around me, offering love, joy, and peace. I will be a preserver and extender of God's light and life.

Prayer: *May I be a little Christ in the world. May I extend the light and life of God.*

Am I serving the purpose to which I have been called? Am I being an extension of God's light and life in the world?

Hallowing the Lord's Name

Hallowed be your name.

—Matthew 6:9

May the name of the Lord be made holy in our lives, as we live them.

May the name of the Lord be made holy as we work through our bereavement.

May others see, in us, the love of Christ radiating and extending itself in service.

May all our testimony be pointed toward Christ who is our hope and salvation, who walks with us through the dark valleys.

May we live the prayer, "Hallowed be your name."

May the Lord's name be praised as we give ourselves to God and others in selfless service.

May we hallow the name of the Lord by entering into selfless service.

May my life hallow the name of the Lord.

I will seek to be the love of Christ to others. I will glorify the name of Christ through selfless service. I will give thanks to God.

Prayer: *May I hallow the name of the Lord by serving others. May I live the love of Christ by giving it.*

Am I living the love of Christ and giving it? Am I hallowing the name of the Lord through selfless service?

Praying for God's Kingdom to Come

Your kingdom come, your will be done on earth as it is in heaven.

—Matthew 6:10

Deep within all of us there is a desire for the will of God to be done on earth as it is done in heaven. There is a hunger for God's kingdom to come.

The coming of God's kingdom will be the time of resolution, when all that is separated will be brought together and united into oneness.

Also it will be the time, according to our faith, when we shall see our loved ones again.

When we actively pray for the coming of the kingdom we are uniting with millions and millions of petitioners all over the world.

Together we pray the healing prayer: "Your kingdom come, your will be done on earth as it is in heaven."

We pray that we may be healed daily and richly.

We pray that others may be healed daily and richly.

We pray for the whole world to be healed forever.

May the kingdom of God come, the will of God be done.

I will pray for the kingdom of God to come in me. I will pray for the kingdom of God to come in others. I will pray for the kingdom of God to come to the whole world.

Prayer: *May I be united with the will and purpose of God. May I pray for God's kingdom to come.*

Am I praying for the kingdom of God to come? Am I being united with God's will and purpose for me and my life?

Living One Day at a Time

Give us today our daily bread.

—Matthew 6:11

Let us live one day at a time. One need at a time. One prayer at a time.

Let us pray for what is immediately needed, and no more.

Let us not get ahead of ourselves, or try to manage God.

Let us surrender to what is simple and direct and helpful for our healing.

Let us remember that our recovery can't be done in leaps and bounds.

Let us see our needs as being one loaf of bread at a time.

One day at a time.

No more, and no less.

Let us lay aside any fear about tomorrow's bread.

Let us trust God with our lives.

May I live one day at a time.

I will live one day at a time. I will ask for no more than I need today. I will settle for whatever God gives me for this day.

Prayer: *May I live one day at a time. May I pray only for the needs of this day.*

Am I praying only for immediate needs? Am I living one day at a time?

Forgiving Ourselves

Forgive us our debts as we also have forgiven our debtors.
—Matthew 6:12

To forgive is to release ourselves from the stress of fear, anger, and resentment.

Stress results from disappointments and anger that have not been honestly dealt with.

Healing doesn't materialize as long as we hold grudges.

Until the heart is opened by forgiveness, and the poison released, there can be no healing.

If we find ourselves angry at anyone, it is time to resolve the conflict.

Also, if we are angry with ourselves, it is time to forgive, to release, to let go of the anger, and to turn ourselves over to the forgiveness of God.

Let us remember we are forgiven.

Let us remember we are released from the bondage of fear and anger when we let go of all negative intentions and desires.

With forgiveness there is healing.

Let us pray to the Lord for the healing of forgiveness.

May I forgive as I am being forgiven.

I will release myself from all hard feelings and anger. I will turn my ill feelings over to God for disposal. I will forgive as I am forgiven.

Prayer: *May I release myself from all that binds. May I carry no grudges or hard feelings.*

Am I carrying any grudges or hard feelings? Have I released myself from all fear, anger, and resentment?

Being Delivered from Falling Away

Lead us not into temptation, but deliver us from the evil one.
—Matthew 6:13

Always there is the temptation to escape the pain of loss, sorrow, and grief rather than working our way through.

Yes, we want to be delivered from evil.

Yes, we want to be fortified by that which is good.

Yes, we want to be healed.

Yes, we must pray to the Lord to deliver us from all that might cause us to stumble and fall along the way.

Yes, we can believe the promise of the Lord that we will be given no more than we are able to bear.

We will not be led into places too dangerous for us to travel.

We are not going to be given more than we are able to handle.

We are being led and cared for by God. God will deliver us from evil.

May I be delivered from temptations to fall away from God.

I will pray for God's care and keeping. I will pray to be delivered from temptations to fall away from God. I will trust God to answer my prayers.

Prayer: *May I trust God to deliver me from falling away. May I trust God to deliver me from evil.*

Do I believe God is carefully watching over me? Am I trusting God to keep me from falling away?

Seeking First the Kingdom

Do not store up for yourselves treasures on earth, where moth and rust destroy, and where thieves break in and steal.

—Matthew 6:19

"But store up for yourselves treasures in heaven, where moth and rust do not destroy, and where thieves do not break in and steal."

If there is anything that becomes clear, with the loss of a loved one, it's that there is something of greater importance than material possessions.

How many have said, "I would chuck everything else if only I could have him or her returned to me"?

We see how fragile life is, how delicate—and how important it is to keep things in perspective. "First things first."

Moth and rust and thieves cannot destroy our relationship with God in Christ.

Moth and rust and thieves cannot destroy faith, hope, and love, which are the promised treasures for those who seek first the kingdom of God. We can have these treasures if we want them, because God is eager to provide.

Let us "seek first the kingdom of God." When we seek the kingdom of God, we have absolutely nothing to lose and everything to gain: new life, new hope, and new joy.

May I seek first the kingdom of God.

I will seek first the kingdom of God. I will commit myself to spiritual growth and development. I will accept the gifts of grace, faith, hope and love, as they are offered.

Prayer: *May I focus my attention on God's kingdom. May I store up the treasures of God's love.*

Am I storing up treasures of faith, hope, and love? Am I seeking first God's gifts of grace?

Taking Responsibility for Ourselves

The eye is the lamp of the body.

—Matthew 6:22

It's how we look at things that makes a difference. It's our attitude that counts, that determines whether we heal or don't heal, whether we recover from our loss, sorrow, and grief.

If we focus on darkness we will be filled with the deep shadows of depression, often refusing to take responsibility for our own lives.

If we focus on the light of God's love in Christ, our attitude will change. We will be in a much brighter condition. We will see good where once there seemed to be no goodness. We will be able to relate positively to ourselves, to others, and to God. We will know what it is to have faith, hope, and love.

What is necessary in recovery is what seems so obvious, but often is so easily forgotten: recovery depends upon how we look at our life situation, how we look at circumstances beyond our control, how we look at alternatives for dealing with everyday problems.

Each of us is responsible for ourselves, how we choose to look at life, and what we do with ourselves. It's how we look at life and death that counts; it's how we accept responsibility for what we see and do that makes the difference between recovering and not recovering.

May I accept responsibility for myself and my life.

I will choose to look at my life positively. I will choose light over darkness. I will choose life over death.

Prayer: *May I choose life over death. May I take responsibility for what I do with my life.*

Am I taking personal responsibility for my life and what I do with it? Am I choosing life over death?

Serving Only One Master

No one can serve two masters.

—Matthew 6:24

There is nothing more difficult than trying to serve two masters; nothing more disruptive and painful.

With bereavement there may come the realization we are not as centered on God as we thought we were. While this may not always be true for everyone, many feel "split" after losing a loved one.

Most serious of all is the splitting of loyalties, of trying to be loyal to opposites: loyal to the world and loyal to God, loyal to the desires of the flesh and loyal to the leading of the Spirit. Such splits cause severe problems and disrupt recovery from loss, sorrow, and grief.

There is no successful way to serve two masters. That is why Jesus makes a point of it: "No one can serve two masters." We have to be focused if we are to heal; we have to be single-minded.

We have to decide who is going to be our master.

If it is Christ we choose as master, then we will go the way of Christ, with our trust and confidence in God, and we will heal.

No one can make this decision for us. As Joshua said, "Choose for yourselves this day whom you will serve."

May I choose Christ as the master of my life.

I will serve only one master. I will serve only the Christ. I will do so in the power of the Spirit, and it shall be done.

Prayer: *May I serve only one master. May the master I serve be the Christ of God.*

Am I serving one master? Is the master I am serving the Christ of God?

Living beyond Worry

Do not worry.

—Matthew 6:25

Who doesn't know worry? Worry, the emotional and spiritual disturbance that seems to arise out of nowhere, is everywhere.

Jesus says, "Do not worry about your life, what you will eat or drink or about your body, what you will wear." But is it that simple? Haven't we told ourselves not to worry? Haven't we been told by others not to worry? And don't we continue to worry, just like everybody else?

Jesus is talking about the everyday worries most of us experience: whether we are going to get all we need of life's necessities.

We worry: "What's going to happen to me? Am I going to be taken care of? Will I have enough to last me the rest of my life? Am I going to be destitute?"

Of course, many of us worry about getting hurt again, about losing another loved one, or losing our own lives. "Don't worry," Jesus says. But obviously that's easier said than done. And yet, it's something we can learn and do by placing our trust and confidence in the Lord who is able to lead us through any and all dark valleys—even the dark valley of death and beyond.

May I turn my worries over to the Lord.

I will turn my worries over to the Lord. I will trust the Lord with my life. I will believe the Lord is waiting to heal me.

Prayer: *May I believe the Lord is waiting to heal me. May I trust the Lord with my life.*

Am I trusting the Lord with my life? Am I turning my worries over to the Lord?

Living Only Today

Do not worry about tomorrow, for tomorrow will worry about itself. Each day has enough trouble of its own.

—Matthew 6:34

Trying to live tomorrow today simply doesn't work. It can produce a lot of needless worry, with all of its attendant pain and confusion.

There is no way we can live tomorrow today. We can think about tomorrow, even make plans as to what we want to be doing, but actually, we can only live today.

By trying to live tomorrow today, we miss this moment. We miss this day.

This day will have passed us by without our even having really been here.

It is important to live life one day at a time. This includes not attempting to solve tomorrow's problems today.

When we are trying to work on the future we are not living in the present, nor are we healing.

Rather, we are putting off our recovery, trying to swim upstream.

We do what is best for ourselves when we live one day at a time.

May I not worry about tomorrow.

I will live this day to its fullest. I will work on one problem at a time. I will not worry about what is coming my way tomorrow or in the days ahead.

Prayer: *May I not worry about tomorrow. May I live this day fully and may I heal.*

Am I ready to live one day at a time? Am I willing to let tomorrow take care of itself?

Asking to Be Given

Ask and it will be given to you.

—Matthew 7:7

In our bereavement we may simply sit down, and maybe complain about how we are not able to get up and do something about our situation.

It's as though we want healing without having to pay any of the cost, without having to make any kind of an investment of ourselves in the healing process.

"You have not because you ask not," Jesus tells us. If we want something, we must not expect it to come on a silver platter.

Let us understand we must become invested, and this begins with our asking for what we want.

Healing and health do not come by wishing it to be so. We must be ready to define ourselves, to tell the Lord precisely what it is we want.

Asking is the key to the door for our recovery from loss, sorrow, and grief.

Asking is our way of becoming open to the help and healing of the Lord.

Remember: "Ask and it will be given to you."

May I ask the Lord for what I want.

I will ask the Lord for what I want. I will trust the Lord to hear when I ask. I will believe the Lord will provide what is best for me.

Prayer: *May I believe the Lord answers prayer. May I ask the Lord to help me heal.*

Do I believe the Lord answers prayer? Am I asking the Lord to help me heal?

Seeking to Find

Seek and you will find.

—Matthew 7:7

Seeking doesn't always come easy. In fact, there are times when it is too difficult to be a seeker on our own. We simply are too tired, or lonely, or sorrowful, or are out of energy, and very low on hope.

The first step into hope is believing the promise of the Lord: "I will not leave you desolate. I will come to you, and abide with you, and you with me." The second step is to seek the Lord through prayer and meditation. The third step is to wait on the Lord to lead, to guide, and to give.

But first, we must seek the Lord.

Recovery belongs to seekers. To those who seek life and recovery into faith, hope, and love.

A friend's beloved wife suddenly dies. We ask our friend, "Do you want to live?" He answers, "Of course I want to live. I have never doubted that I wanted to live. I am a seeker."

He is on his way to the recovery of his broken heart.

He knows it is true, "Seek and you will find."

He is taking responsibility for his own life and recovery.

And, most certainly, he will heal.

May I seek the Lord.

I will seek the Lord. I will enter into prayer and meditation. I will wait on the Lord to show me the way.

Prayer: *May I expect the Lord to bless me with goodness and mercy. May I seek the Lord's goodness and be ready to share it.*

Am I seeking the will of God for my life? Am I expecting the Lord to bless me?

Investing in Order to Be Healed

Knock and the door will be opened to you.

—Matthew 7:7

As with yesterday's meditation, we again are faced with *effort,* the need to put something out in order to take something in.

Jesus usually asked some effort of those he healed.

Often he expected people to tell him what they wanted him to do for them.

Sometimes he made them wait, as was the case with Mary and Martha, whose brother Lazarus died before Jesus got to him.

To get help we must ask, seek, and knock; we must expend some effort, must enter into the process of our healing.

When we do so, the doors are opened, and we begin to heal.

While much of our healing depends on our willingness to wait for the Lord to move, there also is the element of investment, the expenditure of energy.

Before the door is opened for us to heal, we must knock.

This is how we say, "Here I am, ready and eager for you to help me heal."

When we invest ourselves in the Lord, the Lord is able to invest us with the power to heal.

May I be ready to invest myself in my healing.

I will invest myself in my healing. I will ask the Lord to help me heal. I will expect the Lord to help me.

Prayer: *May I not hesitate to seek the Lord's help. May I wait on the Lord to open the doors to my healing.*

Am I asking for help? Am I expecting the Lord to answer me?

Building on Solid Foundations

The rain came down, the streams rose, and the winds blew and beat against that house; yet it did not fall.

—Matthew 7:25

Jesus is talking about the life of a human being based on faith in God.

No matter what befalls that life, there will be no total collapse, regardless how savage the force set against it.

But sometimes it doesn't seem that way, especially when we are in the pits of our sorrow and our anxiety is high, and we are confused about ourselves and how to deal with so many painful problems.

However, if we build the house of our life on the foundation rock of God's promise to be our faithful Lord, we can be assured we are not going to crack up or fall apart and blow away.

To believe God's promise never to leave or forsake us is to build our lives upon the rock that cannot be shaken.

Let us remember God is faithful.

Let us remember God will never leave or forsake us.

God always is ready to help us along the way.

God never refuses to bless us.

Such are the solid foundations of God's promises upon which we are invited to build our lives.

May I build my life on God's solid foundation.

I will rest my life in the Word and promises of God. I will trust the Lord to hold me secure in love and care. I will not be afraid of what is to come.

Prayer: *May I not be afraid of what is to come. May I be secure in God's Word and promises.*

Am I building my life on the firm foundation of God's Word and promises? Am I trusting the Lord with my life?

Trusting the Healer

I will go and heal him.

—Matthew 8:7

A powerful military man comes to Jesus, asking for help. He wants Jesus to heal his servant. Jesus agrees to do so. The servant is healed.

So it is with our pain and sorrow. We too can be healed, but first we must ask for healing, just as we said two days ago.

Asking is the signal, given to the Lord, that not only do we want to be healed, but we also are ready to enter into the healing process—to do whatever is necessary to recover from loss, sorrow, and grief.

Once we are determined to be healed, Jesus enters in, and Jesus begins to heal us.

While we will not know, in advance, how the healing will take place, or how long it will be until the process is completed, we can rest assured that sooner or later our sorrow will be replaced by joy.

Jesus says, "I will come and heal you."

But for this to happen we must want him to help us, just as we have been saying in our meditations.

The mighty military man, from another nation and religion, asked a poor carpenter's son to heal his servant. That was the beginning we must also make.

May I trust the Lord to come and heal me.

I will ask Jesus to help me. I will trust the Lord to hear me. I will believe the Lord is going to heal me.

Prayer: *May I ask Jesus to help me. May I trust the Lord to restore my soul.*

Am I asking Jesus to help me heal? Am I trusting the Lord to restore my soul?

Trusting the Lord to Know

The Son of Man has no place to lay his head.

—Matthew 8:20

Jesus knows our condition much better than we.

Jesus knows what it feels like to be "out in the cold" with no place to lay his head, with no place of his own.

In times of loss, sorrow, and grief, it is natural to look for some place to lay our heads, so to speak; it is natural to look for shelter.

There are those days when there seems to be no sheltered places to find rest for our souls.

There is a vacancy, an emptiness, a sense of having nowhere to go, no place of our own.

These are times to remember the Lord endures our pain and carries our sorrows.

The Lord is with us in our suffering to lead us through.

"I know where you are, how you feel," Jesus is saying.

"Remember that I have been there. I have had nowhere to lay my head."

Jesus knows where we are.

Jesus understands.

Jesus cares.

May I trust the Lord to know where I am.

I will believe the Lord knows where I am. I will trust the Lord to understand how I feel. I will turn to the Lord for consolation and hope.

Prayer: *May I turn to the Lord for consolation and hope. May I believe the Lord always knows me.*

Do I believe the Lord knows me? Am I turning to the Lord for consolation and hope?

Believing the Lord to Save

Why are you so afraid?

—Matthew 8:26

It was a mighty storm. The boat was filling with water and about to sink. Jesus was peacefully sleeping when his disciples awakened him with their cries for help. Jesus asked, "Why are you so afraid?"

Jesus knew *what* they were afraid of. They were afraid of dying. He also knew *why* they were afraid. They were afraid because they hadn't yet committed their lives completely to him, into his care and keeping. Until such a commitment is made, we are all afraid.

Of course, we are not yet spiritually perfected. Our faith is still too shallow. There still are too many ifs, and buts, and maybes, too many seeming dangers and chances for us to be destroyed.

However, there also is the alternative to fear.

"Perfect love drives out fear," the Bible tells us.

When we allow ourselves to be filled with the love of Christ, when our trust in the master is strong, fear subsides.

Let us turn our lives over to the care and keeping of Jesus, trusting him completely.

May I believe the Lord saves.

I will believe the Lord saves. I will trust the Lord to be with me. I will turn my fears over to the Lord.

Prayer: *May I trust the Lord to take care of me. May I not be afraid.*

Am I trusting the Lord to take care of me? Am I turning my fears over to the Lord?

Accepting the Healing

Get up, take your mat and go home.

—Matthew 9:6

They brought the paralyzed man to Jesus and laid him before the Lord.

For years there had been the sorrow of hopelessness, no way out.

Then there came this carpenter. It was reported that he had special powers, that he could heal and even bring people back to life.

Somewhere, in this man from Nazareth, there was a promise for a better day for a paralyzed man.

And it wouldn't be the healing alone that would bring hope.

Rather, it would also be that someone really cared, that someone actually would reach out to touch.

That someone was willing to help.

In our loss, sorrow, and grief we also must know that we are cared for and loved.

Jesus also is saying to us, "Get up, take your bed of sorrow, and walk."

Jesus knows us in our distress.

Jesus cares about us in our pain.

Jesus heals us of our loss, sorrow, and grief.

May I accept the healing of the Lord.

I will turn to the Lord for help. I will wait for the Lord to touch me. I will accept the healing of the Lord.

Prayer: *May I turn to the Lord for help, for healing. May I accept the healing of the Lord.*

Am I turning to the Lord for help and healing? Am I accepting the healing of the Lord?

Being Ready to Follow Jesus

Follow me.

—Matthew 9:9

Jesus has two favorite words: *follow me.* And for those who do, life begins to change.

We begin to take risks.

Excitement for life and living begins to grow.

Love of self, of others, and of God increases.

Self-image improves.

But, in times of distress it is not as easy to be a follower of Jesus.

It is much easier to simply lie down and try to forget about our painful loss, or to run and hide, to quit, to give up.

But following Jesus is not a call to quit, to lie down, to give up, to turn over and go to sleep.

Following Jesus means we become ready to enter into the struggles of life, including the pain of our sorrow.

Following Jesus means we enter a new dimension for life and living, where there still is pain, but also healing.

"Follow me" is not a command we must follow, or else be destroyed; "follow me" is an invitation to new life, new hope, and new joy.

May I be ready to follow Jesus wherever he leads me.

I will follow Jesus. I will go with him wherever he leads me. I will do what Jesus asks me to do.

Prayer: *May I be ready to follow Jesus. May I do what the Lord asks of me.*

Am I a follower of Jesus? Am I doing what Jesus asks of me?

Celebrating His Presence

How can the guests of the bridegroom mourn as long as he is with them?

—Matthew 9:15

There is a time when joy comes unexpectedly.

We find ourselves feeling better, even without realizing what is happening.

It may be that the hardest part of our bereavement is coming to an end. We are taking off our clothes of mourning.

A deeper sense of the presence of Christ has grown and taken root.

We have become more conscious of our eternal relationship with God and others.

We have come to know that as Christ lives, so also we will be alive forever—together with our loved ones.

It is as though we are guests celebrating at a wedding feast.

We have reason for joy because the Lord is eternally with us, and we are eternally with the Lord.

May I be filled with joy in the presence of the Lord.

I will not feel guilty about feeling better. I will rejoice in the eternal presence of Christ in my life. I will not cling to my sorrow.

Prayer: *May I not cling to my sorrow. May I experience the joy of my Lord's presence.*

Am I ready to be joyful? Am I ready to celebrate the presence of Christ in my life?

Becoming a New Creation in Christ

No one sews a patch of unshrunk cloth on an old garment.
—Matthew 9:16

If we try to patch a hole in an old piece of clothing with new cloth that wasn't pre-shrunk, and then wash the garment, the new cloth will shrink, tearing the old garment in the process, making the hole larger.

If we try to hold onto the old, try to keep things as they used to be before our loved one passed on, the wounds will only get bigger.

There comes a time when we must give up the idea of patching: after the wounds have been thoroughly washed, after we have honestly dealt with the pain of our loss.

The time comes for wounds to be healed, rather than patched by wishful thinking.

Christ offers us new life with new possibilities for growth and development.

Christ says, "Behold I am making everything new."

This is not patchwork, make-believe, or wishful thinking.

This is new life, new hope, and new joy inspired by God's love.

We don't have to try to bring back what is over and done and gone.

May I be a new creation in Christ.

I will not try to bring back what is gone. I will not try to patch what has been torn. I will trust God to make me a new creation in Christ.

Prayer: *May I become a new creature in Christ. May I not try to bring back what is gone.*

Am I trying to bring back what is gone? Am I becoming a new creature, with new life in Christ?

Entering Our Healing

Take heart . . . your faith has healed you.

—Matthew 9:22

Healing and hope are for those who seek. There is nothing that can really be done to lift us until we want to be helped, as was the case with the woman who insisted on touching the edge of Jesus' cloak in a valiant effort to gain healing.

To be helped she had to believe healing was possible, and that the Lord had power to deliver her from her infirmity.

She took heart in the presence of the Lord and was determined to do something about her condition. Her immediate goal was to make contact with Jesus.

How shall we take heart? Must we not also believe our sorrow can be turned into joy? Must we not be convinced a power greater than ourselves is able to do for us what we cannot do for ourselves? And must we not also believe life is eternal, that death is swallowed up in victory?

What is it that gives us a new outlook on life and death? Is it not the assurance Jesus gives new life to all who seek it?

And is there not new life and hope for us when we go to the Lord with our deepest burdens, praying only for his will and the power to carry it out?

May I enter into my healing.

I will enter into my healing. I will go to the Lord in prayer. I will pray to be able to know and do God's will.

Prayer: *May I trust God's will is to heal me. May I enter into my healing.*

Do I believe Christ has the power to restore my life? Am I entering into my healing?

Believing Christ Is Able

Do you believe that I am able to do this?

—Matthew 9:28

We must become involved in our deliverance from loss, sorrow, and grief.

But the question is whether we believe Jesus has the power to heal our broken spirits, our sorrowful hearts, whether Jesus is able to restore us to life.

The blind man asks for healing and the question Jesus asks has to do with his readiness to be helped: "Do you believe that I am able to do this?"

What if the man had said, "I'm not all that sure." Or, "I don't really think so but I can't lose for trying." Or even, "You show me first and then I'll decide whether I'll believe in you."

To *believe* means to have trust and confidence, to be persuaded of something being true. The question is whether we have trust and confidence in Christ's power to help us see new life, hope, and joy.

Christ must wait for us to answer the question, "Do you believe that I can bring healing to your troubled soul?" It is an answer that each of us must give for ourselves.

May I believe Christ is able to heal my brokenness.

I will believe Christ is able to heal my wounded spirit. I will trust the Lord to lift me up. I will gratefully accept the healing of the Lord.

Prayer: *May I go to Christ with my deepest needs. May I trust the Lord to do what is best for me.*

Am I believing the power of Christ to heal? Am I trusting the Lord to do what is best for me?

Traveling Lightly

Do not take along any gold or silver.

—Matthew 10:9

The disciples were going on their first missionary journey and the Lord told them to take no provisions, not even a change of clothing, and no money.

They were to trust God, which is the first step toward bonding with the Lord. We are like those first disciples. We too are being asked to extend our confessions of faith into life and living, day by day, with trust in God's care and keeping.

We are being asked to lay aside our fears of what is to come.

We are being asked to go with the Lord into the unknown, believing we will not be left or forsaken.

We are being asked to lay aside our concerns about security, about what is going to happen to us when there is recession or depression, or sickness and death.

We are being asked to go on a journey of faith, absolutely believing and trusting the Lord, who will be with us every step of the way.

We are being asked to lay aside all that is not useful to our spiritual growth, and our recovery from loss, sorrow, and grief.

May I leave behind what no longer is useful.

I will listen to the voice of my Lord. I will do what I am asked to do. I will lay aside whatever is necessary, in order to recover and live.

Prayer: *May I believe God. May I do what Christ asks of me.*

Am I willing to do what Christ asks of me? Am I willing to leave behind what no longer is useful for my recovery and healing?

Seeing What Is Hidden

There is nothing concealed that will not be disclosed, or hidden that will not be made known.

—Matthew 10:26

Somewhere in the midst of our sorrows and grief is the deep desire to find answers to the questions: "Who am I? What am I doing here? What's happening to me? Where am I going?"

With these questions there can be the sensation that we don't really know very much about anything, that we actually are in the dark, or at least are knowing only in part.

At such times we may feel alone and isolated, as though we are the only ones who can't understand the mysteries of God. Of course, this is not true. No one knows it all.

We are born into mysteries and called to live within them: mysteries about ourselves, others, God, and the universe. Also, there are mysteries about life and death and eternity.

The promise is that one day we will see and know. One day the mysteries will be unfolded before us, including the questions that are now being answered, little by little.

Now we know in part, but one day we shall know completely, as we are completely known by God.

May I be given to know the mysteries of God.

I will believe God is leading me to see the mysteries of life and death. I will trust God to help me see more clearly. I will let God lead me from darkness into light.

Prayer: *May I permit God to lead me through darkness into light. May I trust God to show me the mysteries of life and death.*

Am I trusting God to show me the mysteries of life and death? Am I permitting the Lord to lead me through darkness into the light?

Being Important to God

Don't be afraid; you are worth more than many sparrows.
—Matthew 10:31

Someone once said, with a deep sense of awe and gratitude, "It is such a privilege to be a human being."

At the time he said this, he was ill with terminal cancer, and in pain.

We all need a sense of privilege, of value, of self-worth, and the conviction we are involved in something worthwhile.

Otherwise life is not only difficult but seemingly useless.

There is nothing more difficult than trying to live out our lives when we feel worthless.

Jesus wanted to convince his hearers they were of great value to God. Not simply as a nation. Not just as an organized religion, or as pious practitioners of the faith. But simply as human beings, beloved of God.

Jesus wants us to know we are worthwhile to God, even when we don't feel important to ourselves or anyone else.

May I believe I am important to God.

I will take another look at myself. I will believe I am a person of value, regardless of the condition in which I find myself. I will be kind to myself.

Prayer: *May I see and believe I am important to God. May I treat myself with respect and kindness.*

Do I believe I am important to God? Am I treating myself with respect and kindness?

Losing and Finding Life

Whoever finds his life will lose it, and whoever loses his life for my sake will find it.

—Matthew 10:39

Jesus is saying that if we try to hang onto our lives, like a leech, we are bound to lose. If we do everything only for ourselves, with no thought of others and their good, we lose. But if we give our lives in the service of God, we win.

By losing our lives in service we gain new life.

Understanding this principle of unconditional giving is important for our recovery from loss, sorrow, and grief.

By opening our clenched fists, we win.

By giving we gain our own life and affirm the purpose for which we were born.

By giving we find fulfillment as the emptiness of our souls is filled with God.

A widow specialized in having people in for dinner. At the time of this writing, she is 88 years young, and her God-given gift is cooking.

Every week she feeds lonely people, and says, "I could sit here and cry, but by feeding people I find joy. My kitchen is my altar." This is part of her recovery program from loss, sorrow, and grief.

May I lose my life in service.

I will serve God. I will be of service to others. I will lose my life in service and find my new life in God.

Prayer: *May I lose my life in the service of God. May I find my life in the service of God.*

Am I losing my life in the service of God? Am I finding my life in serving others?

Seeing the Healing Hand of God at Work

The blind receive sight, the lame walk.

—Matthew 11:5

All of us have a need to see, hear, and believe. But often during times of bereavement, it is difficult even to look, much less to see and believe.

Our grief can loom so large there is no room for seeing, hearing, or believing the work of God in the world or our lives.

Nevertheless, we need to know God is alive and at work, that God cares, that God is able to do what we cannot do for ourselves—to know and believe there is healing.

In prison, John the Baptist needed reassurance. "Are you [Jesus] the one who was to come, or should we expect someone else?"

The answer given to John was simple: "See what is being done. The blind receive their sight and the lame walk, and good news is preached to the poor."

With that assurance, John could go to his death satisfied.

We too can know and believe because of the works of God in the world and in our own lives. If we look closely, we can see the handprint of the Almighty all around and within us—the print of love and power and healing.

May I see the healing hand of God at work.

I will look for the healing hand of God in the world. I will look for the healing hand of God in my own life. I will see and I will believe God.

Prayer: *May I look for the healing hand of God at work in my life. May I see the work of God and believe in my own healing.*

Am I seeing the hand of God at work in the world? Am I seeing the healing hand of God at work in my own life?

Hearing the Good News

And the good news is preached to the poor.

—Matthew 11:5

What possibly can be good news when everything has gone so badly for us? When there is so much pain, loss, sorrow, and grief in this beaten world? Where people are so cruel to each other, and where death eats us up?

The good news is that God is active in our world, that the Lord comes to us precisely where we are, assuring us we are not forgotten or forsaken.

While this may not seem the way things are, nevertheless it is true. The good news is God cares for us, the Lord is looking out for us, the Lord loves us.

In our loss, sorrow, and grief we are the "poor" who need the good news preached to us. The good news of deliverance from sin and death and loneliness, from loss, sorrow, and grief.

How else would we come to know the love of the Lord unless someone called us to attention?

May I believe the good news of God's love given to me.

I will tune myself into the goodness of God. I will see and hear the good news of the gospel. I will believe God loves me.

Prayer: *May I hear the good news of the gospel. May I believe God loves me.*

Do I hear the good news of the gospel? Do I believe God loves me?

Going to the Lord for Help

Come to me, all you who are weary and burdened, and I will give you rest.

—Matthew 11:28

There are many moments when we feel the burdens of life weighing down heavily upon us, when everything seems like "too much."

With sorrow and grief often come feelings of being put upon, of being given too much to bear, of not being able to go on with any measure of hope and joy.

It is during such times that the promise of our Lord becomes so important to hear: "Come to me, all you who are weary and burdened, and I will give you rest."

Christ offers the invitation to do something positive with our lives:

to come to him just the way we are,
to share our burdens with him and others in prayer,
to lay our burdens at his feet,
to accept solace, comfort, hope, and strength to go on,
to be his own, to live under him in his kingdom, to serve him.

May I go to the Lord with my burdens.

I will go to the Lord with all my burdens, one by one. I will share my burdens with the Lord in detail. I will ask the Lord to help me carry my burdens.

Prayer: *May I bring my burdens to the Lord. May I be given strength to carry them.*

Am I taking my burdens to the Lord? Am I receiving strength to carry them?

Finding Rest for Our Souls

Take my yoke upon you and learn from me, for I am gentle and humble in heart, and you will find rest for your souls.
—Matthew 11:29

"Rest for our souls." How beautiful the thought.

No more crippling anxiety. No more needless fear, anger, guilt, shame, restlessness, and resentment. But is this true?

Can we actually find rest for our souls by going to the Lord with our burdens?

The experience of God's people says this is true; when we yoke ourselves to Jesus our souls find rest. Release from sorrow and grief, like many other human maladies, can be best found by binding ourselves to Jesus.

Jesus offers to help us carry our burdens, and, if need be, to carry us. But we have to trust the Lord with our lives, believing Christ will do for us what we cannot do for ourselves.

By yoking ourselves to Jesus we become bonded to him in friendship and love. We receive new faith, new hope, new love, and new joy.

This bonding with Christ is the "mystical union" in which we find ourselves doing things we never believed possible: seeing the glory and possibilities for newness of life.

May I go to Christ and find rest for my soul.

I will bind myself to Christ. I will ask the Lord to help me. I will find rest for my soul.

Prayer: *May I bind myself to Christ. May I find rest for my soul.*

Am I binding myself to Christ? Am I finding rest for my soul?

Knowing and Connecting

The knowledge of the secrets of the kingdom of heaven has been given to you.

—Matthew 13:11

As we go through our bereavement and the process of recovery, there is opportunity to grow emotionally and spiritually.

However, in the early stages of our loss, sorrow, and grief, this is not easy to see.

But Jesus assures us, just as he assured his disciples, that we are going to know the secrets of the kingdom of heaven—even in the midst of our sorrows.

The most important secret we are given to know is that we are not alone, that the Lord is with us, that we have nothing to fear, that everything is working together for good.

We all need to know the secret of being connected. This secret is in our relationship to Christ.

Once we are connected to Christ we are connected to ourselves, to others, to God.

Christ is the first secret of the kingdom of heaven, and Christ is the secret of our recovery from sorrow and grief.

The secret of Christ opens us to many other secrets of love, joy, and peace.

May I come to know the secret of Christ in my life.

I will seek to know the secrets of the kingdom of heaven. I will seek to know Christ more intimately. I will be closely connected to Christ.

Prayer: *May I become more deeply connected to Christ. May I know the secrets of the kingdom of heaven.*

Am I seeking the secrets of the kingdom of heaven? Am I being more securely connected to Christ?

Seeing, Hearing, and Believing

Blessed are your eyes because they see, and your ears because they hear.

—Matthew 13:16

Recovery from bereavement includes seeing and hearing new things, beginning with spiritual things.

The disciples were blessed because they were seeing spiritual reality. What they were destined to see would come through a terrifying experience: seeing their Lord nailed to a cross, seeing their dreams for the future dying right before them.

They were blessed for having been with Jesus, even though they really didn't understand what he was talking about, but they would live long enough to find out.

They were blessed because their life with the Lord changed the course of their lives, moving them out of fear into love.

They were blessed because they had the words of the Lord to remember, as well as other experiences such as a fish fry on the beach with their Lord after the resurrection.

They were blessed because they saw, they heard, they believed Christ.

Because of Christ they were able to put aside what had been, in order to move on to what was yet to come, with the blessed assurance that the Lord was with them all the way.

May I see, hear, and believe Christ.

I will look to Christ to bless me. I will listen for Christ to speak to me. I will trust Christ to give me new life and hope.

Prayer: *May I turn to Christ to see and hear. May I be blessed with the presence of the Lord.*

Am I turning to Christ to see and hear God's promises? Am I being blessed by the presence of Christ in my life?

Sowing the Good Seed of God's Word

The kingdom of heaven is like a man who sowed good seed in his field.

—Matthew 13:24

When our souls are at rest in God we experience the fruits of the kingdom of heaven.

By what we choose to do with our lives—the investments we make of ourselves in the life and teachings of our Lord—we begin to experience new hope, joy, love, and serenity.

It is like a farmer who, deciding to plant a field, makes certain the seed is pure, and that there are no weed seeds, or as few as possible. There is concentration, attentiveness, determination, dedication, and faith that once the seed is planted there will be a bountiful harvest.

This also holds true for our recovery from bereavement. There is an investment to be made, with deep respect for the "field" of our hearts and lives, with deep respect for the "seed" of God's Word and promises.

Planting the good seeds of faith, hope, and love is our privilege and joy. The more we are ready to invest ourselves in the sharing of God's Word with others, the sooner we experience freedom from loss, sorrow, and grief.

May I plant the good seeds of faith, hope, and love.

I will take responsibility for my life and what I do with it. I will plant the good seed of God's Word. I will look forward to a harvest of serenity, peace, and joy.

Prayer: *May I sow the good seed of God's Word. May I see the harvest of faith, hope, and love.*

Am I sowing the good seed of God's Word? Am I expecting an abundant harvest of faith, hope, and love?

Starting Small

The kingdom of heaven is like a mustard seed.

—Matthew 13:31

The Lord starts with the smallest of the small in order to bring about the growth of the human spirit, the spirit able to accept and celebrate the creation.

Just as the mustard bush is able to accept nesting birds, or the womb of a mother is able to accept the tiny fertilized egg, bringing to life a human being, so also are we able to accept and celebrate the gifts of God.

As we pursue our program of recovery there comes the time when things begin to change for the better, even though we don't notice the change right away; change is slow at first, like the little mustard seed growing into a mighty bush.

We don't realize, right away, that anything different is happening, that we actually are recovering and growing.

Nevertheless, as we go on living the Word and promises of God, we begin to change. We begin to lighten up.

Life becomes less burdensome. We are more able to enjoy ourselves, enjoy others, and enjoy God.

The little mustard seed of faith starts to grow, becoming a blessing to others. That's the process of spiritual growth into recovery.

May my faith grow from small to large.

I will trust the slow process of life and growth. I will believe God works from small to large. I pray the Lord will help me grow and serve.

Prayer: *May I trust God to help my faith to grow. May I be able to serve God's purpose for my life.*

Am I trusting God to help me grow? Am I ready to serve God's purpose for my life, to love and to give?

Being Raised Up Slowly

The kingdom of heaven is like yeast.

—Matthew 13:33

From what some say, the kingdom of heaven comes like a revolution, or like lightning striking fast and hard, jolting us awake. And it is in this way one would hope to recover from loss, sorrow, and grief—all of a sudden.

All of a sudden, we wish, the pain would be gone.

But as we discover, that is not how recovery works.

Recovery is like yeast. Slowly it gives rise to faith, hope, and joy. Little by little, working from within, having been thoroughly mixed and kneaded together with everyday experiences, recovery grows in us.

Each of us, in a sense, is like a loaf of unbaked bread, a hunk of dough. Yeast, which is the Word of God in Christ, is at work inside. At first we can't see anything happening, even though the yeast is active.

It can be helpful to remember this thought about yeast because that's how God works recovery in us. That's how our recovery takes place—like yeast raising dough, little by little.

May I see how God is working to heal.

I will not try to push things along too fast. I will not try to rush my recovery. I will believe God is at work in my life, and that eventually I will heal.

Prayer: *May I believe God is at work in my life. May I wait on the Lord to bring about my recovery.*

Do I believe God is at work in my life? Am I waiting patiently for my recovery into faith, hope, love, and joy?

Seeking the Treasures of God

The kingdom of heaven is like treasure hidden in a field. When a man found it, he hid it again, and then in his joy went and sold all he had and bought that field.

—Matthew 13:44

A treasure is not a treasure unless someone wants it and is going after it.

It is like this for us in the living of our lives day by day.

We need to believe there is something of value, something that will be helpful for our recovery and growth.

Once we believe there is this hidden treasure, and that we can actually have it, things begin to change for the better.

No longer are we listless.

No longer do we feel helpless, alone, forsaken.

There are new experiences to be had, new life and new growth. And we are optimistic about ourselves because our faith in God is growing.

Hope begins to dawn, and we are becoming excited about the living of our lives.

This is called the treasure of recovery from loss, sorrow, and grief. It is the open door to the promise, "Behold, I am making everything new."

May I seek the treasures of God.

I will believe there are treasures waiting for me. I will believe God wants me to seek the treasure chests of faith, hope, and love. I will ask God to lead me.

Prayer: *May I seek God's treasured gifts of faith, hope, and love. May I believe these treasures are mine to have.*

Am I seeking the treasures of God? Am I believing I can have the gifts of faith, hope, and love?

Making a Total Investment

The kingdom of heaven is like a merchant looking for fine pearls. When he found one of great value, he went away and sold everything he had and bought it.

—Matthew 13:45-46

We have a simple story for today. So simple we might miss its meaning.

The story is about a pearl merchant. All his life he has been buying and selling pearls.

Perhaps he has experienced some tedium because pearls look alike, even though every one is different.

Perhaps he was asking himself whether this was all there is to life, doing what he had been doing for so long.

Perhaps he wondered where his life was headed, and was asking himself the question, "Is this all there is to my life?"

Sound familiar?

But then, one day he spots a pearl, the likes of which he had never seen before. Something happens inside of the pearl merchant. His spirit is stirring. He feels a new enthusiasm, new determination. He must have that pearl, at any price. Even at the cost of all his other pearls put together.

May I invest myself totally.

I will invest myself totally. I will trust God to show me the way into renewed faith, hope, and love. I will pursue the pearl of great price.

Prayer: *May I see my recovery as the pearl of great price. May I hold nothing back in my search for new life, new hope, and new joy.*

Am I seeking the best that can be for me and my life? Am I making a total investment in my program for recovery?

Being Satisfied

They all ate and were satisfied.

—Matthew 14:20

There were 5000 hungry people eagerly following the Lord that day. People who had lost sight of themselves, people going after the buried treasure and the pearl of great price, going after Jesus and leaving all else behind.

Then came the end of the day. There seemed to be nothing to eat. Except, as we are told in another account, there was one lad who had five loaves of bread and two fish, which he offered.

He offered all he had.

What happened after that we have no way of knowing. But suddenly, or so it seems, there was more food to eat than anyone needed.

Did others reach under their garments, where food was carried in those days? Did they see the fearless giving of the little boy and decide they could also share what they had with others?

Did they come to understand that to give is to live and that to live is to give?

We don't know what was gained that day. But we are told that they all ate and were satisfied.

And that's what sharing can do. It can satisfy the longing of the human heart to share and be shared.

May I be ready to share myself with others.

I will be ready to share myself with others. I will give with no holding back. I will be satisfied.

Prayer: *May I give of myself. May I hold nothing back.*

Am I ready to give of myself to others? Am I holding anything back?

Receiving the Keys to the Kingdom

I will give you the keys of the kingdom of heaven.
—Matthew 16:19

The title of our meditations for recovery is *Living the Promises of God.* One of the bigger promises of our Lord is the scripture for today: the keys of the kingdom of heaven.

What can this mean for us as we move on with our recovery from loss, sorrow, and grief?

It can mean that the treasures of God's grace are ours to have: faith, hope, and love.

The treasures of patience, kindness, and forgiveness.

The treasures of gratitude, with thanksgiving, and joy.

These are keys that open us to the mysteries of God, that lift us out of the pits of our sorrow and give us new life.

Jesus promises the keys of victory.

Life over death.

Joy beyond sorrow.

Hope rather than despair.

These promises are bound not only on earth, but also in heaven.

May I gladly accept the keys of the kingdom.

I will believe the promises of God. I will believe the keys of the kingdom are being offered to me. I will believe all of God's gracious gifts are mine to have.

Prayer: *May I see the keys of the kingdom of God. May I gratefully receive what God offers.*

Do I see the keys of the kingdom of God in my recovery? Do I see, for myself, new life, new hope, and new joy?

Losing and Gaining

Whoever wants to save his life will lose it, but whoever loses his life for me will find it.

—Matthew 16:25

Because we are human, we want to live. Sometimes, when we have been deeply hurt, we want to cling.

For instance, when we lose a loved one, we may want to hang tightly on to them.

However, the time comes when we must let go, if we are to recover from loss, sorrow, and grief. We have to stop trying to save our lives.

We must release ourselves from what once was, and stop clinging to what is gone.

We must make deep investments of ourselves, pointing our energies in new directions.

When we lose ourselves in God, things begin to change for the better.

No longer do we have to cling to what is gone; no longer do we have to live in the dark shadows of life.

Now we are able to walk in the light of God's love.

Having given up everything of ourselves to the Lord, we gain all that can ever be gained: new faith, new hope, new life.

May I be willing to lose in order to gain.

I will let go of what is gone. I will invest myself in what can be. I will lose myself in Christ, and find new life.

Prayer: *May I lose my life in Christ. May I find new life in Christ.*

Am I losing my life in Christ? Am I finding new life in Christ?

Becoming Like Little Children

Unless you change and become like little children, you will never enter the kingdom of heaven.

—Matthew 18:3

Jesus is not asking us to be childish.

On the contrary, Jesus never could tolerate too much childishness, especially when it was demonstrated in his disciples when they wanted everything to go their own self-centered ways.

What Jesus desires of us is our readiness to believe what he teaches, and to do it.

Innocently.

Trustingly.

Enthusiastically.

In their raw and unhampered state children are believers. They are simple believers in God, with a readiness to trust God and an eagerness to commit themselves to God.

When we become as little children, in this respect, we are able to recover from loss, sorrow, and grief.

With innocence.

With trust.

And even, with enthusiasm.

May I be a trusting child of God.

I will place my trust and confidence in Christ Jesus my Lord. I will believe the Lord is with me every step of the way. I will fear no evil.

Prayer: *May I trust Christ Jesus with my life. May I fear no evil.*

Am I willing to be a child of the Lord? Am I willing to trust the Lord with my life?

Living in the Community of Christ

Where two or three come together in my name, there am I with them.

—Matthew 18:20

We were not created to go it alone.

In our loss, sorrow, and grief we need the support of Christ's community.

Somehow, we must be certain to take care of ourselves in this regard; to take it upon ourselves, as personal responsibility, to find a healing community.

Seeking the presence of Christ in others, in community, is important for recovery from loss, sorrow, and grief.

It is in God's people that we are going to find the presence of Christ as we are gathered in his name, to do his will.

It is important to find such a service community and to become part of it.

It is by entering into the presence of Christ that we gain needed strength and hope.

The presence and power of Christ is found where people are gathered who are dedicated to the Lord, and are intent about their service to God.

May I find new life in the community of Christ.

I will seek the community of believers. I will be a part of the community of Christ. I will not try to go it alone.

Prayer: *May I open myself to the community of Christ. May I find my healing in fellowship with others.*

Am I finding the presence of Christ in community? Am I being healed by the fellowship of others in Christ?

Believing All Things Are Possible

With God all things are possible.

—Matthew 19:26

When we started on our pathway to recovery from loss, sorrow, and grief, there may have seemed to be no way through the darkness.

It may have seemed as though there would be no end to the pain, no beginning of joy.

How could we ever feel better again?

How could the heaviness be lifted?

How could we ever make our way through the deep valleys that lie ahead?

The answer is simple: "With God all things are possible."

With God's help we are able to recover our lives and go on—not just with resignation, but with confidence and with faith, hope, and love.

This is the miracle of recovery: the impossible becomes possible. That which couldn't heal is being healed because, "with God, all things are possible."

May I give thanks because all things are possible.

I will give thanks to the Lord. I will rejoice in the gifts that have been given to me. I will bless the Lord with all of my heart, mind, and soul.

Prayer: *May I always give thanks to the Lord. May I bless the Lord with my life given to the Lord.*

Am I ready to bless the name of the Lord? Am I ready to give thanks to the Lord for my recovery?

Serving with Joy and Gladness

Whoever wants to become great among you must be your servant.

—Matthew 20:26

Recovery results in new attitudes and new ways of life, new ways for solving problems—for finding the gifts of faith, hope, and love.

Recovery from loss, sorrow, and grief doesn't leave us the same as we once were. Our outlook is refreshingly different.

Recovery brings us to an understanding that the only meaningful and genuinely rewarding life is that of service; we serve as we have been served by God's love.

As Jesus took the basin and the towel, having removed his clothing to wash his disciples' feet, so also are we invited to wash one another through acts of service.

The Lord himself is our example, showing us what it means to be the servant of others.

As we follow Christ, we continue in our recovery with joy and gladness.

Recovery is serving the Lord.

May I serve the Lord with joy and gladness.

I will serve the Lord with joy and gladness. I will give myself completely to the Lord. I will go where I am led and do what I am given to do.

Prayer: *May I serve as I am being served by the Lord. May I give myself with no holding back.*

Am I serving the Lord with joy and gladness? Am I giving myself completely to the Lord?

Watching and Praying

Watch and pray.

—Matthew 26:41

Sometimes the road to recovery is longer than expected. We discover that we are never really completely through with it.

The sorrow pops up from time to time even though we have been released from its bindings.

We are still quite vulnerable, always in danger of slipping and falling back into the dark valleys.

"Watch and pray so that you will not fall into temptation."

Simply stated this means, "Stay very close to the Lord."

Each day we fall away and each day we must be reborn.

That is why Jesus urges us to watch and pray—to keep us from falling away and to remind us to stay close to him.

Therefore, before we go to sleep, let us give thanks to the Lord. When we rise from sleep, let us give thanks to the Lord.

Let us believe and live the promises of God. Let us watch and pray and give thanks to God.

May I watch and pray—living the promises of God.

I will believe the promises of God. I will live the promises of God. I will be watchful and I will pray.

Prayer: *May I believe and live the promises of God. May I always be in an attitude of watchfulness and prayer.*

Am I believing and living the promises of God? Am I being watchful in prayer?

Paul F. Keller is a pastor, writer, and film director from Edina, Minnesota. His award-winning films include *The Supper, The Church in the World,* and *The Sound of the Cricket.* Since 1963, Pastor Keller's major work has been in the ministry of consolation, dealing with grief and loss.